THE PSYCHOLOGY OF THE LANGUAGE LEARNER

INDIVIDUAL DIFFERENCES IN SECOND LANGUAGE ACQUISITION

Second Language Acquisition Research
Theoretical and Methodological Issues
Susan M. Gass, Jacquelyn Schachter, and Alison Mackey, Editors

THE PSYCHOLOGY OF THE LANGUAGE LEARNER

INDIVIDUAL DIFFERENCES IN SECOND LANGUAGE ACQUISITION

Zoltán Dörnyei

University of Nottingham

Routledge
Taylor & Francis Group
New York   London

Routledge is an imprint of the
Taylor & Francis Group, an informa business

First Published by Lawrence Erlbaum Associates, Inc., Publishers
10 Industrial Avenue
Mahwah, New Jersey 07430

Transferred to digital printing 2010 by Routledge

Routledge
Taylor and Francis Group
711 Third Avenue
New York, NY 10017

Routledge
Taylor and Francis Group
2 Park Square
Milton Park, Abingdon
Oxon OX14 4RN

Cover design by Kathryn Houghtaling Lacey

**CIP information for this volume can be obtained by contacting the
Library of Congress**

Includes bibliographical references and index.

ISBN 0-8058-4729-4 (alk. paper)

You will go out in joy
and be led forth in peace;
the mountains and hills
will burst into song before you,
and all the trees of the field
will clap their hands.
Instead of the thornbush will grow the pine tree,
and instead of briers the myrtle will grow.

(Isaiah, 53: 12-13)

CONTENTS

Preface

The study of language learner characteristics, or *individual differences* (IDs), has a long tradition in second language studies and nobody would question that factors such as language aptitude, motivation, or learning styles are important contributors to success in mastering a foreign language. Accordingly, the existing literature on individual difference variables is extensive. Curiously, however, there are very few book-length summaries of the topic—in fact, there is only one single-authored monograph on language learning IDs, Peter Skehan's (1989) seminal title on *Individual Differences in Second Language Learning*. Since the publication of that book a great deal of research has been conducted in the field to explore the language learner, and an updated overview has been due for some time. In response to this need, the last five years have seen the publication of no fewer than four anthologies on learner issues (although not all from an ID perspective), edited by Breen (2001), Cook (2002), Cornwell and Robinson (2000), and Robinson (2002). These volumes are all of high quality, with chapters written by some of the best known experts in the field. So what justifies the writing of the current book? Let me mention three reasons:

- An authored book can offer certain useful features that anthologies, by definition, cannot: A unified voice and style, an integrated text, and a more even coverage of the domain without duplications or gaps.

- Anthologies are, by definition, selective: They focus on key issues and often ignore smaller but nevertheless important subareas that do not warrant a whole chapter. This is certainly true in our case, as none of the four works mentioned above address, for example, 'learner beliefs,' or 'learning styles,' let alone lesser known variables such as 'creativity'. So far such topics have been discussed primarily in journal articles and, to a lesser extent, in thematic monographs targeting only the specific ID variable in question.

- In this book I would like to extend the traditional boundaries of individual differences and include some important learner variables—most notably various personality traits—that are not normally discussed in this context in the L2 literature.

Having said that, *The Psychology of the Language Learner: Individual Differences in Second Language Acquisition* intends to be a standard ID book, following the tradition of L2 scholars—particularly that of Peter Skehan and Peter Robinson—working in the individual differences paradigm. I have learned a great deal from the work of the two Peters, for which I am grateful. The following friends and colleagues have given me valuable feedback on various parts of the manuscript: Andrew Cohen, Peter MacIntyre, Kim Noels, Rebecca Oxford, Peter Robinson, and Ema Ushioda; I really appreciate their helpful suggestions and comments and I hope they find that the final manuscript addresses many of the points raised. I would also like to express my sincere thanks to Sue Gass, the series editor, and Cathleen Petrce, my editor at Lawrence Erlbaum Associates. Their initial encouragement and their ongoing support and friendship have been invaluable!

—*Zoltán Dörnyei*

1

Introduction: Definition, Brief History, and Taxonomy of Individual Differences

Why do individuals differ so much in second language attainment success? After all, every healthy human being in an intact social environment masters a first language to a degree of fluency that, in other skill domains, would be recognized as elite or near elite levels...
(Segalowitz, 1997, p. 85)

Ever since the early days of its existence, the field of psychology has been trying to achieve two different and somewhat contradictory objectives: to understand the *general principles* of the human mind and to explore the *uniqueness* of the individual mind. The latter direction has formed an independent subdiscipline within the field that has traditionally been termed *differential psychology* but recently more frequently referred to as *individual difference research*. As the term suggests, *individual differences* (IDs) are characteristics or traits in respect of which individuals may be shown to differ from each other. Admittedly, for many psychologists such differences constitute mere distractions to their work: How much easier it would be to formulate valid conclusions and generalizations about the human species if everybody was alike! Research results would then apply to everyone and, based on these findings, we would be able to design effective therapy or intervention that would suit all. Thus, in this ideal world "rules and regulations could be developed to cover all situations, and there would be no unknowns" (Breslin, 1994, p. 224). Alas, although the distinctness that each of us displays may be seen by some as a nuisance, it is still there—and the world may be a better place for it. One of the most important ways in which the social sciences differ from the natural sciences, in fact, stems from the existence of individual differences. The molecules of a cell, if treated identically, will respond identically, whereas human behavior—even that of identical twins—may vary significantly in response to a certain stimulus.

To reiterate, although variability is a central feature of the human species, many researchers find individual differences detrimental to social sciences and this also applies to the domain of educational studies. As Alexander and Murphy (1999) summarized, a dominant trend in educational psychology has been to characterize the teachers and students who populate classrooms as 'learning communities' and to think in terms of the collective more than the individual. Within this orientation, the authors argue, a focus on differences between individual students may be cast as counterproductive to efforts to build communities that work together for the educational good. This is to a certain extent true: The main reason, for example, for applying a group dynamics-based perspective in educational situations is the conviction that the learner group as a social unit can and does override certain individual differences, an assumption I fully subscribe to with my 'group dynamics hat' on (e.g., Dörnyei & Murphey, 2003).

The tension between the individual and the collective also appears in language studies. We can well imagine that second language acquisition (SLA) researchers may become rather irritated with IDs when these prevent the neat formulation of species-wide themes concerning, say, how humans acquire a particular language aspect over time: IDs tend to bring in a *'Yes but...'* factor because there will always be people to whom some findings do not apply. One exception to this variability in language acquisition is often thought to be the process of first language (L1) acquisition, because this always (or almost always) leads to native-level proficiency in the language. But, contrary to common belief, research had demonstrated (cf. Bates, Dale, & Thal, 1995; Shore, 1995) that IDs are active even in this domain, resulting in different learning styles and rates, as well as subsequent strengths and weaknesses in the ultimate attainment of our mother tongue. The outcome of the acquisition of an L2 is significantly more diverse than that of an L1, ranging from zero to native-like proficiency, and a great deal (but not all) of this outcome variance is attributable to the impact of IDs.

The discussion so far may have given the impression that I consider IDs rather unpleasant features whose only function is to annoy us. Far from it. Along with many researchers, I believe that IDs are fascinating and their study can be immensely exciting. Furthermore, they are also very important from a practical point of view: IDs have been found to be the most consistent predictors of L2 learning success, yielding multiple correlations with language attainment in instructed settings within the range of 0.50 and above (cf. Dörnyei & Skehan, 2003; Sawyer & Ranta, 2001). No other phenomena investigated within SLA have come even close to this level of impact.

So what exactly are these controversial constructs? How can we define them? How many of them are there? And what do we know about their role? This book has been written to answer these questions according to the state of the art of our current knowledge. Although the following chapters will present a thorough overview of past research, my primary purpose for writing this book has not been to provide a book-length literature review but rather to offer conceptual clarification. Most of the ID variables are associated with a complex and rather diverse body of research and theorizing within the field of psychology, and the greatest problem in using these variables in L2 studies has been, in my view, the lack of sufficient theoretical coherence. Accordingly, my key concern in each chapter will be to define the concepts in question and to operationalize them in measurable terms, which is also why the text is accompanied by the descriptions of the most important assessment instruments.

My second objective in writing this book has been to show that IDs are related to some of the core issues in applied linguistics and that they can be meaningfully linked to the most important processes underlying SLA. This link has not been explored sufficiently yet and in a review of the field Segalowitz (1997) was right to conclude that although the L2 literature does identify some of the key phenomena concerning the role of IDs in L2 acquisition, very little is said about the actual processes and mechanisms that are responsible for causing the differential learning impact. However, research since 2000 has made considerable advances into this direction and there is now a sound theoretical basis for establishing meaningful links between ID research and SLA.

Looking beyond L2 learning, I also believe that the study of IDs concerns some of the basic questions of our human existence in general; after all, we are talking about personality, motivation, abilities, and the like—we would be hard pressed to identify another set of psychological factors of similar significance. And, to go even further, IDs are not limited to the human species, but occur throughout the animal scale. As Anastasi (1994) states, investigations of animal behavior, from unicellular organisms to anthropoid apes, reveal wide individual differences in learning, motivation, emotionality, and other measurable traits. As she pointed out,

> So large are these differences that the distributions of individual performance overlap even when widely separated species are compared. When tested with the same learning problem, for example, the brightest rat in a given sample may excel the dullest monkey. (p. 419)

DEFINITION

IDs are seemingly easy to define: They concern anything that marks a person as a distinct and unique human being. While this may appear by and large true—particularly if we adopt a broad conception of IDs—we need to set some restrictions to avoid regarding, for example, someone's tendency to wear a brightly colored T-shirt or a bow tie as an ID. Therefore, all scientific definitions of IDs assume the relevance of *stability:* Differential psychology emphasizes individual variation from person to person only to the extent that those individualizing features exhibit continuity over time (De Raad, 2000). Yet, even with this restriction the kind and number of ways an individual can be different is extensive, due to the innumerable interactions between heredity and environment that occur throughout one's life span. Although the discussion of the nature or nurture debate—that is, whether individual differences are due to heredity or environmental influences—is outside the scope of this book, I tend to agree with Anastasi's (1994) conclusion that the inherited genetic information sets broad limits to one's development and within these limits, what individuals actually become depends on their environment.

So, can the term *individual differences* be further narrowed? It can and it has been: The majority of the books and articles dealing with the subject tend to cover fewer than a dozen ID factors. This is because the actual practice of differential psychology does not focus on mere idiosyncrasies, even when these are stable ones, but rather on broader dimensions that are (a) applicable to everyone and (b) that discriminate among people (Snow, Corno, & Jackson, 1996). As Michael Eysenck (1994, p. 1) summarized it very clearly,

> Although human beings differ from each other in numerous ways, some of those ways are clearly of more significance to psychology than others. Foot size and eye color are presumably of little or no relevance determinants of behavior (although foot size may matter to professional footballers!), whereas personality appears to play a major role in influencing our behavior.

Thus, ID constructs refer to dimensions of enduring personal characteristics that are assumed to apply to everybody and on which people differ by degree. Or, in other words, they concern stable and systematic deviations from a normative blueprint. We should note that these descriptions reflect well the basic dilemma for the scientific study of human differences, namely how to conceive of general laws or categories for describing human individuality that at the same time do justice to the full array of human uniqueness (Kolb, 1984). Placing ID research in a historical context is a useful first step in exploring this dilemma.

BRIEF HISTORY OF INDIVIDUAL DIFFERENCE RESEARCH

The origins of ID research go back to the end of the 19th century: Charles Darwin's cousin, Sir Frances Galton (1822-1911), is usually credited with being the first to investigate individual differences scientifically, and Galton's empirical and methodological research, which also involved developing appropriate statistical techniques for data analysis, is also seen as the genesis of quantitative psychology in general. Following Galton, ID research was firmly and irreversibly put on the research agenda at the turn of the century by the work of French psychologist Alfred Binet (1857-1911). He became interested in individual differences partly as a result of his observations of the different ways his daughters solved problems, and his 1895 article co-authored by Victor Henri on "individual psychology" was the first systematic description of the aims, scope, and methods of the topic. The real impetus to further research was given by the construction of the first intelligence test by Binet and his colleague, Theodore Simon, and ever since the publication of this instrument in 1905 it has been intelligence research and measurement theory that have driven the study of individual differences forward.

The Binet-Simon intelligence scale was devised to separate slow and fast learners in the French school system, and adaptations were soon prepared for use in Germany and Britain. The popularity of intelligence testing spread quickly as the potential use of intelligence measures for selection and recruitment procedures was recognized. In the first half of the 20th century several other ability tests were developed and employed, and significant advances were made in statistics to provide analytical techniques to process and evaluate the test scores, making up what is commonly referred to as the *classical testing theory*. This theory was then applied to the design of tests of personality, attitudes, specific cognitive aptitudes, and other psychological constructs.

The first listing of virtually all differential characteristics was constructed by Gordon Allport and Henry Odbert in 1936: They collected 17,953 descriptive words from an English dictionary and argued that each of these potentially suggested an individual-difference variable. During the subsequent decades this extensive, and frankly unmanageable, list has been condensed by others to the key variables that are discussed currently under the ID rubric (for further details, see chapt. 2 on identifying a parsim-onious set of personality traits). The field rapidly gained momentum and by the 1950s it had generated enough empirical research on cognitive, affective, and psychomotor characteristics for Anne Anastasi to prepare her seminal summary of *Differential Psychology* in 1958. With ongoing developments in the study of personality, motivation, and various cognitive abilities, ID research is still a powerful area within psychology, having its own society, the *International Society for the Study of Individual Differences*, and dozens of academic journals targeting either individual differences in general (e.g., *Personality and Individual Differences*) or some specific ID factor (e.g., *Intelligence*). The importance of IDs has also been widely recognized in educational contexts and a great deal of research has been conducted in educational psychology on how to adapt instruction to the strengths, weaknesses, and preferences of the learners.

INDIVIDUAL DIFFERENCES IN SECOND LANGUAGE STUDIES

It has been long observed that there is a particularly wide variation among language learners in terms of their ultimate success in mastering an L2 and therefore the study of IDs, especially that of *language aptitude* and *language learning motivation*, has been a featured research area in L2 studies since the 1960s (for past reviews, see e.g., Breen, 2001; Cohen & Dörnyei, 2002; Cornwell & Robinson, 2000; Dörnyei & Skehan, 2003; Ehrman, 1996; Ellis, 2004; McGroarty, 2001; Oxford, 1999c; Oxford & Ehrman, 1993; Sawyer & Ranta, 2001; Robinson, 2002; Segalowitz, 1997; Skehan, 1989, 1991, 1998). In the 1970s the momentum of ID studies was further augmented by influential research on the *good language learner* (for a retrospective review, see MacIntyre & Noels, 1994; for a new perspective, see Norton & Toohey, 2001). The results of this line of investigation indicated in a fairly consistent manner that besies a high degree of language aptitude and motivation there were other learner factors that helped students to excel, in particular the students' own active and creative participation in the learning process through the application of individualised learning techniques. Thus, *language learning strategies* were included into the inventory of important learner characteristics, and Peter Skehan's (1989) seminal book on the subject, *Individual Differences in Second Language Learning*, and his follow-up overview paper under the same title (Skehan, 1991), also added *learning styles* to the 'canonical' list of IDs in language learning.

Thus, IDs have been researched extensively in L2 studies, making the area one of the most thoroughly studied psychological aspect of SLA. As already mentioned, these studies have typically found IDs to be consistent predictors of L2 learning success, and yet in an overview of ID research Sawyer and Ranta (2001) correctly pointed out that the L2-related ID literature has remained relatively uninfluential within the broader field of SLA. This curious situation of isolation, I believe, largely stems from the fact that the original product-oriented conception of the two key ID factors, aptitude and motivation, was incompatible with the inherently process-oriented stance of SLA. We will come back to this issue in the subsequent chapters in detail, but as a preliminary let me note that recent developments in both aptitude and motivation research have successfully broken out of this isolated position by offering a closer and more organic integration with other areas of investigation into how languages are acquired.

TAXONOMY OF INDIVIDUAL DIFFERENCES AND THE
STRUCTURE OF THIS BOOK

What are the most important individual differences and how will they be discussed in this book? In the narrowest sense, individual differences in psychology have been equated with *personality* and *intelligence* (see e.g., Birch & Hayward, 1994; Eysenck, 1994; Snow et al., 1996), but usually the term is interpreted more broadly. The International Society for the Study of Individual Differences lists temperament, intelligence, attitudes, and abilities as the main focus areas, whereas in his recent overview of the field, Cooper (2002) talks about four main branches of IDs, abilities, personality, mood, and motivation. Topics of interest for the journal *Individual Differences Research* involve a particularly broad range, covering all areas of "personality, interests and values, spirituality, affective disposition, coping style, relationship style, self and identity, the individual in groups and interpersonal contexts, attitudes and perceptions, cognitive functioning, health and lifestyle, assessment, and individual differences related physiological, organizational, and education topics." Finally, in the recently published *Encyclopedia of Psychology*, sponsored by the American Psychological Association, De Raad (2000) offered a similarly broad specification, with possible characteristics including "attitudes, values, ideologies, interests, emotions, capacities, skills, socio-economic status, gender, height, and so forth" (p. 41), and as Revelle (2000) described in the same encyclopedia, research on individual differences ranges "from analyses of genetic code to the study of sexual, social, ethnic, and cultural differences and includes research on cognitive abilities, interpersonal styles, and emotional reactivity" (p. 249).

Thus, the concept of 'individual differences' is rather loose, containing certain core variables and many optional ones. It seems clear that for a book addressing individual differences from an educational perspective one needs to select *personality, ability/aptitude,* and *motivation* to start with as these are invariably seen as principal learner variables. Accordingly, each of these attributes will be addressed in a separate chapter (chaps. 2 through 4) and the discussion of personality will also cover related concepts such as *temperament* and *mood*. In the L2 field, as we have seen, two further factors have traditionally been treated as key IDs, *learning styles* and *language learning strategies*. I will follow this tradition (chaps. 5 and 6), although the chapter on 'learning strategies' will shift the focus from the actual learning techniques applied by the students—that is, 'learning strategies' proper—to the learners' *self-regulatory capacity* that underlies their strategy use. Finally, chapter 7 carries the vague title of Other Learner Characteristics to allow me to describe five ID variables that for one reason or another have not been discussed in the previous chapters and do not warrant a chapter of their own: *anxiety, self-esteem, creativity, willingness to communicate* (WTC), and *learner beliefs.*

Let me conclude this introductory chapter by mentioning three issues that I originally wanted to cover but decided to exclude in the end. First and foremost are the learners' age and gender. Both variables have been shown to play a significant role in affecting language learning success and there is a considerable amount of literature on them. The problem with these two basic demographic variables is, however, that they affect every aspect of the SLA process, including virtually all the other ID variables, and therefore their discussion would have been rather different from the rest of the material in the book, both in terms of length and coherence. For this reason I believe that both topics would warrant a book-size summary, and the fact that no such volume has been written yet indicates the enormity of the task. Interestingly, Ellis's (2004) recent review of ID factors also excluded 'age' from the variables considered on similar grounds (and gender is not mentioned in his summary at all).

Similarly to Skehan's 1989 book, I also planned a chapter on *ID research methodology.* The reason why I eventually decided against this is not the lack of relevance of the topic. To the contrary: I believe that ID research is inextricably linked to psychometrics and research methods, with the issue of *questionnaire design* being at the forefront (cf. Dörnyei, 2003c). However, because I am going to discuss specific assessment principles and techniques throughout the chapters in an ongoing manner, the material that would have remained for a separate methodology chapter would have mainly concerned quantitative data analysis and statistics. And because the range of statistical procedures used in ID research covers most of the standard statistical repertoire, I felt that such a discussion has been much better done in the numerous available handbooks and manuals on statistics. Let me highlight here just one interesting publication of this type: Few people in the L2 field know that Robert Gardner, one of the leading researchers in the area of L2 motivation (which is my own main specialization field), is also an international expert on statistics and has published a recent book entitled *Psychological Statistics Using SPSS for Windows* (Gardner, 2001b).

Finally, let me state that I have made a number of strong claims in this book which might generate controversy and which even some of my friends whose opinion I value will disagree with. Although I did my best to support these claims with arguments, I fully accept that there may be angles that I have not considered. Therefore, I sincerely welcome any future discussion of the issues raised in the following chapters—my hope is that this process will result in a fuller understanding of the role of IDs in second language acquisition (and also that friendships will remain).

2

Personality, Temperament, and Mood

Without any doubt, personality is the most individual characteristic of a human being and therefore it is appropriate to start the summary of individual differences with a description of the various personality factors. Having said that, the chapter on personality was not the first in my original plan of this book for two main reasons: From an educational perspective, the role and impact of personality factors are of less importance than those of some other ID variables such as aptitude and motivation and the amount of research targeting personality in L2 studies has been minimal compared to the study of most other ID variables discussed in this book. Yet, in the end the personality chapter moved forward because, as Pervin and John (2001, p. 3) put it, "Personality is the part of the field of psychology that most considers people in their entirety as individuals and as complex beings." Let us therefore start our exploration of ID factors with this most general aspect of individual differences.

The study of personality is one of the main themes in psychology and the subdiscipline specialized in this area is called—not surprisingly—*personality psychology*. This very active field has its roots in classic psychoanalytic theory at the beginning of the 20th century and its history bears the marks of all the major psychological paradigms, from the behaviorist and humanist to the social-cognitive. In addition, we also find in the literature numerous isolated personality measures of varying levels of breadth, often with no linkage to any specific personality theory. Thus, the taxonomical and theoretical complexity of the domain cannot be done justice in a single chapter such as this, as a small library could be filled with publications pertaining to the topic. Therefore, instead of attempting to provide a comprehensive summary, I first focus on conceptual and definitional issues and then describe the 'big picture' by outlining the main trends in contemporary personality psychology. Finally, I narrow the focus down to the relationship between personality and learning and especially language learning.

DEFINITIONS

What is personality? The Collins Cobuild Dictionary defines *personality* as one's "whole character and nature." This is not a bad summary; however, De Raad (2000) points out that in scientific use the term 'character,' which also involves a certain moral aspect, has gone out of fashion and has become replaced by the more neutral term 'personality,' representing the complex of all the attributes that characterize a unique individual. According to Pervin and John's (2001) standard definition, personality represents those characteristics of the person that "account for consistent patterns of feeling, thinking, and behaving" (p. 4). Such a broad view obviously allows for a wide range of approaches but the emphasis in all of these approaches has been on 'consistent patterns:' Personal experience suggests that that there is a certain constancy about the way in which an individual behaves, regardless of the actual situation. Indeed, every language contains a wide array of adjectives to describe these patterns, ranging from *aggressive* to *kind* or from *lazy* to *sociable*, and there seems to be a fair deal of agreement among people about such categorizations—this suggests that these adjectives represent underlying personality traits. Personality theories, then, attempt to identify these traits and organize them into broad personality dimensions.

The first main issue that emerges when we examine 'personality' is the recognition that different scholars use the term rather differently, to cover different breadths of human nature. As a first step, therefore, it is useful to distinguish 'temperament' and 'mood' from 'personality.' Although there are no unequivocal definitions, *temperament* is typically used to refer to individual differences that are heavily rooted in the biological substrate of behavior and that are highly heritable (Snow et al., 1996), the kind of characteristics whose traces we can already detect in early childhood. Ehrman, Leaver, and Oxford (2003, p. 314) describe them as "biological differences in life and learning." Thus, temperament and personality are seen as broadly overlapping domains, with temperament providing the primarily biological basis for the developing personality (Hogan, Harkness, & Lubinski, 2000). Leaver, Ehrman, & Shekhtman (in press) describe that the Classic Greek temperamental taxonomy proposed over 2,000 years ago by Hippocrates and Galen is still seen as one of the most valid and stable models in many countries today. The model describes four personality types: *phlegmatic* (unflappable and slow to take action), *sanguine* (easily but not strongly excited and having short-lived interests), *choleric* (impetuous and impulsive, often ambitious and perfectionist), and *melancholic* (inclined to reflection).

In contrast to the very stable and enduring construct of 'temperament,' a 'mood' refers to a highly volatile, changing state that is still not completely random. Instead, it represents "familiar surges of emotions" (Cooper, 2002, p. 262) that we experience often (although not necessarily) in response to life events. This, however, raises a question: If moods are 'states' rather than 'traits,' why are they mentioned in this book? After all, ID variables have been conceptualized as enduring personal characteristics that are stable and systematic deviations from a normative blueprint. Mood states obviously do not fall into this category, as the whole point about distinguishing between 'states' (highly volatile, frequently changing features) from 'traits' (stable and constant properties) is to highlight the different degree of transience of the disposition in question. While this is true, mood states have a place among ID variables because individuals differ consistently in the mood states they seem to adopt, display, or submit to in given types of situations. That is, as Snow et al. (1996) explain, they are emotional states that "seem to have become more general and frequent response tendencies—that is, traits" (p. 256). According to Matthews, Davies, and Westerman (2000), there exist only three separate dimensions of mood states: *energy–fatigue*, *tension–relaxation*, and *pleasure–displeasure*. However, at present little is known about how moods become long-lasting or pervasive, or how they change as situations change, even though this would be highly relevant knowledge for educational purposes, because, as Matthews et al. summarize, there is a definite relationship between mood and performance: On the one hand, moods can interfere with task processing and can impair performance; on the other hand, moods can also energize and mobilize processing.

Because of insufficient research findings in the literature and the space limitations of this book, the rest of the chapter does not elaborate on temperament and moods any further but focuses on factors associated with personality proper.

DIFFERENT APPROACHES TO THE STUDY OF PERSONALITY

Personality is such a crucial aspect of psychology that every main branch of psychological research has attempted to contribute to the existing knowledge in this area. Thus, the scope of theorizing can be as broad as the differences among the various paradigms in psychology. This is why the field of personality is "filled with issues that divide scientists along sharply defined lines and lead to alternative, competing schools of thought" (Pervin & John, 2001, p. 25). These competing schools and paradigms have, in turn, identified a plethora of personality factors that sometimes differ only in label while referring nearly to the same thing, or—which can be more confusing—have the same label while measuring different things. In this rather chaotic 'Tower of Babel' (Funder, 2001) it has been a most welcome development in the past 15 years that a new consensus has emerged in personality psychology with regard to the main dimensions of human personality. As a result, current research in the field is dominated by only two taxonomies focusing on personality traits, Eysenck's three-component construct (e.g., Eysenck & Eysenck, 1985) and the 'Big Five' model (e.g., Goldberg, 1992, 1993; McCrae & Costa, 2003). Furthermore, the two models overlap considerably: Eysenck's model identifies three principal personality dimensions, contrasting (1) *extraversion* with *introversion*, (2) *neuroticism* and *emotionality* with *emotional stability*, and (3) *psychoticism* and *toughmindedness* with *tender-mindedness*. The Big Five construct retains Eysenck's first two dimensions, but replaces psychoticism with three additional dimensions of *conscientiousness, agreeableness,* and *openness to experience.* A wide variety of empirical studies have tested these models and found that they provide a good representation of the central features of personality. At present the Big Five construct in particular is gaining momentum to the extent that it seems almost ubiquitous in the current literature (Funder, 2001). I give a detailed description of the Big Five construct in a separate section below, but let me address some more general issues first.

To start with, although the leading role of the Big Five model in research publications is undeniable, we should note that there is more to personality psychology than the Big Five trait paradigm. Psychoanalytic theories are still active areas and insightful contributions are also made by research in the behaviorist, social-cognitive, and humanistic vein. Therefore, one challenge for the field is to integrate the rather disparate approaches. A second important issue, which is related to second language studies more directly, concerns the impact of *situational factors* on the variation of personality and behavior. Because this issue is also relevant to some other ID variables (most notably motivation), let us look at it more closely.

Although personality psychology has, by intention, concentrated on stable and distinctive personality properties since its beginnings, it has become increasingly clear that by assuming absolute cross-situational consistency of most traits we can understand only part of the picture because there is evidence for cross-situational variability. As Pervin and John (2001) summarized, "To a certain extent people are the same regardless of context, and to a certain extent they also are different depending on the context" (p. 290). Thus, a broader picture of personality requires complementing static trait-centered theories describing the structure of personality with more dynamic models that describe the situated processes associated with personality in specific contexts. The fact that the latter processes exist are well-known even for non-specialists, evidenced by sayings such as *"this brought out the best/worst of me…"* and there has been a significant amount of research examining these processes, for example in the psychoanalytic paradigm. What is needed in future research is an integration of the two, seemingly conflicting, perspectives into a unifying framework. Although this is a definite challenge, it is not an impossible task because, as Mischel (1999) argues, "dispositions and processing dynamics are two complementary facets of the same phenomena and the same unitary personality system" (p. 56).

Finally, before we examine the Big Five model in more detail, let me briefly mention a third challenge for the study of personality. Along with several other scholars, Cooper (2002) emphasizes that our job is not finished by arriving at a personality structure model that most researchers would accept (such as the Big Five model): Merely establishing the structure of personality is only the first step in any scientific study of individual differences, and the logical subsequent step is to investigate the *development* of personality. It is evident that the potential determinants of an adult's personality include both environmental factors related to the nature of the home in which the person was raised as a child, and biological factors related to hereditary factors associated with the genetic make-up. Here again, however, we find an unfortunate separation of research directions between scholars studying these aspects, highlighting the need for future integration. In conclusion, although the study of human personality has generated a great amount of knowledge, personality psychology has still a long way to go before a comprehensive account of the interrelationship of all the relevant facets and factors can be achieved. Therefore, it is likely to remain an active and developing field in psychology for the foreseeable future.

The 'Big Five' Model

Research that intends to apply personality factors as independent, background variables requires a fairly straightforward and parsimonious system that still captures a considerable proportion of the variance. The *Big Five model* offers exactly this, which explains the overwhelming current popularity of the theory. Furthermore, the five proposed dimensions of the theory make common sense even to non-specialists, which is partly due to the genesis of the construct. The original and quite ingenious idea behind the theory goes back to research conducted in the 1930s and 1940s by Allport, Odbert, and Cattell (for more details, see Cooper, 2002): These scholars assumed that if there was a certain consistency about how people behaved, then this must be reflected in *adjectives* in the language people used to characterize each other. Collecting all the possible such adjectives in a given language would, therefore, provide a comprehensive list of personality factors, and by submitting these adjectives to factor analysis we might distill a smaller number of underlying personality dimensions or traits. As De Raad (2000) summarized in the *Encyclopedia of Psychology*, it took several decades before this psycholexical approach produced the Big Five as a solid framework, and the main researchers who were responsible for the final breakthrough were Lewis Goldberg, Robert McCrae, and Paul Costa (e.g., Goldberg, 1992,

1993; McCrae & Costa, 2003). Costa and McCrae have also developed an assessment instrument, the 'NEO-PI,' that operationalizes the model in a psychometrically appropriate manner (cf. Table 2.1).

Let us examine the five main components of the Big Five construct (the initials of which enable the acronym OCEAN). As described in Table 2.1, all the five dimensions are rather broad, comprising several important facets, which are usually referred to as *primary traits*. Because the model originated in adjectives, an effective way of describing the main dimensions is listing some key adjectives they are associated with at the high and the low end.

- *Openness to experience:* High scorers are imaginative, curious, flexible, creative, moved by art, novelty seeking, original, and untraditional; low scorers are conservative, conventional, down-to-earth, unartistic, and practical.

- *Conscientiousness:* High scorers are systematic, meticulous, efficient, organized, reliable, responsible, hard-working, persevering, and self-disciplined; low scorers are unreliable, aimless, careless, disorganized, late, lazy, negligent, and weak-willed.

- *Extraversion–introversion:* High scorers are sociable, gregarious, active, assertive, passionate, and talkative; low scorers are passive, quiet, reserved, withdrawn, sober, aloof, and restrained.

- *Agreeableness:* High scorers are friendly, good-natured, likeable, kind, forgiving, trusting, cooperative, modest, and generous; low scorers are cold, cynical, rude, unpleasant, critical, antagonistic, suspicious, vengeful, irritable, and uncooperative.

- *Neuroticism–Emotional stability:* High scorers are worrying, anxious, insecure, depressed, self-conscious, moody, emotional, and unstable; low scorers are calm, relaxed, unemotional, hardy, comfortable, content, even tempered, and self-satisfied.

These adjectives have been selected because they are the most commonly cited ones in the various descriptions of the Big Five model, including Costa and McCrae's (1992) manual of the 'NEO-PI' described above (cf. Table 2.1). When we look at the list it becomes evident that some of the scales are rather 'skewed' in terms of their content, with one end of the scale being clearly more positive than the other (in the Conscientiousness and Agreeableness scales, for example, nobody would want to score low).

Table 2.1. A description of Costa and McCrae's (1992) 'NEO-PI' (Revised version)

The NEO-PI-R is a self-report paper and pencil questionnaire, covering the five main domains of the Big Five model, each represented by six lower level facets (i.e., a total of 30). These facets are, in turn, represented by 8 items each, resulting in a total of 240 items.

Dimensions and facets	Description and sample items (in italics)
Neuroticism	This scale covers emotional adjustment and stability at one extreme, and maladjustment and neuroticism at the other.
• Anxiety	• *I am easily frightened.*
• Angry Hostility	• *I often get angry at the way people treat me.*
• Depression	• *Sometimes I feel completely worthless.*
• Self-Consciousness	• *At times I had been so ashamed I just wanted to hide.*
• Impulsiveness	• *I have trouble resisting my cravings.*
• Vulnerability	• *When I'm under a great deal stress, sometimes I feel like I'm going to pieces.*
Extraversion	This scale reflects extraversion at one extreme and introversion at the other.
• Warmth	• *I really like most people I meet.*
• Gregariousness	• *I like to have a lot of people around me.*
• Assertiveness	• *I am dominant, forceful, and assertive.*
• Activity	• *I usually seem to be in a hurry.*
• Excitement-Seeking	• *I like to be where the action is.*
• Positive Emotions	• *Sometimes I bubble with happiness.*

Openness to Experience	This scale taps an openness to new experiences, thoughts, and processes at one end, and a rejection of such at the other end.
• Fantasy • Aesthetics • Feelings • Actions • Ideas • Values	• *I have an active fantasy life.* • *I am intrigued by the patterns I find in art and nature.* • *How I feel about things is important to me.* • *I often try new and foreign foods.* • *I have a lot of intellectual curiosity.* • *I consider myself broad-minded and tolerant of other peoples' lifestyles.*
Agreeableness	This scale represents a type of 'easy-going' at one end and 'hard-headed' at the other end
• Trust • Straightforwardness • Altruism • Compliance • Modesty • Tender-Mindedness	• *I believe that most people are basically well-intentioned.* • *I would hate to be thought of as a hypocrite.* • *I try to be courteous to everyone I meet.* • *I hesitate to express my anger even when it's justified.* • *I tried to be humble.* • *We can never do too much for the poor and elderly.*
Conscientiousness	This scale reflects a complex trait sometimes called 'Will to Achieve' or 'Character,' reflecting a high desire at one end and a lower desire at the other.
• Competence • Order • Dutifulnes • Achievement Striving • Self-Discipline • Deliberation	• *I pride myself on my sound judgment.* • *I never seem to be able to get organized.* (Reversed score) • *When I make a commitment, I can always be counted on to follow through.* • *I've worked hard to accomplish my goals.* • *I am a productive person who always gets the job done.* • *I always consider the consequences before I take action.*

The crucial question about the validity of the Big Five construct is whether the five dimensions subsume all there is to say about personality. Funder's (2001) answer was 'almost certainly no.' As he argued, whereas almost any personality construct can be mapped onto the Big Five, we cannot derive every personality construct from the combinations of the Big Five. "This lack of comprehensiveness becomes a problem when researchers, seduced by convenience and seeming consensus, act as if they can obtain a complete portrait of personality by grabbing five quick ratings" (p. 201). We should note, however, that by accepting this conclusion we are closing a historical circle: First there was an amplitude of mixed, often narrowly defined traits; then some broad secondary dimensions, or 'supertraits,' were identified; and now these broad dimensions may be found lacking. No wonder that Matthews (1999) concludes that "Deciding whether to work with broader or narrower traits is a perennial problem for personality psychology" (p. 268).

Myers-Briggs Type Indicator (MBTI)

Humans have for thousands of years been characterized according to some basic types, not only by ordinary people but also by scholars. Eventually, the various, relatively simple typologies proposed in the literature were invariably rejected as too simplistic, except for one, Carl Jung's theory of three bipolar types: *extraversion–introversion*, *sensing–intuiting*, and *thinking–feeling* (for a detailed description of Jungian personality models from an L2 perspective, see Leaver et al., in press). The survival of this typology is due to the combination of a number of reasons: First, it appears to tap into some basic truths about the structure of personality; second, besides Freud, Jung was the other great 20th century psychologist who has become a 'cult figure' even among non-specialists; and last but not least, Jung's theory of psychological types forms the basis of a highly successful personality type inventory, the *'Myers-Briggs Type Indicator'* (MBTI), constructed by a daughter-and-mother team, Isabel Myers and Katharine Briggs (1976),[1] who also added a fourth dichotomy to Jung's taxonomy: *judging–perceiving*. In contemporary practice, when researchers refer to the MBTI they sometimes do not mention Jung's underlying theory, indicating that the inventory has developed an identity of its own, which is understandable in the light of the

---

[1]The fascinating life story of Isabel Briggs Myers, a woman on the peripheries of academia and entirely devoted to the development of the MBTI, can be found at the Web site of the *Center for Applications of Psychological Type* (http://www.capt.org), the official promoter of the MBTI, originally founded by Myers.

fact that this is the most widely employed personality test in the world, with more than 2 million copies in 16 languages used each year by individuals and organizations.

The use of the term *indicator* in the title of the MBTI, instead of the more common 'test' or 'inventory,' is not a mere stylistic issue. It is related to the fact that the dimensions of the MBTI do not refer to traditional scales ranging from positive to negative (e.g., like those in the NEO-P). Rather, they indicate various aspects of one's psychological set-up and, depending on their combinations, every type can have positive or negative effects in a specific life domain. This value-neutral approach is very similar to what we find with learning styles (see chapt. 5), where scholars also emphasize that the various style dimensions carry no value judgment and that an individual can be successful in every style position, only in a different way. In fact, partly because of this similarity, the MBTI has often been used in L2 studies as a *learning style* measure. This is justifiable insomuch as, as Ehrman (1996) explains, the MBTI personality dimensions have cognitive style correlates; for this reason Ehrman calls these factors 'personality styles.' We should note, however, that within the domain of psychology the MBTI is considered a personality type inventory.

The four dichotomies targeted by the MBTI are as follows (for more details, see Leaver et al., in press):

- *Extraversion–Introversion,* referring to where people prefer to focus their attention and get their energy from: the *outer world* of people and activity or their *inner world* of ideas and experiences. This facet is also part of the Big Five model and has already been described there (see also chapt. 5, for further details).

- *Sensing–Intuition,* referring to how people perceive the world and gather information. 'Sensing' concerns what is real and actual as experienced through one or more of the five senses; a sensing person therefore is empirically inclined and tends to be interested in the observable physical world with all its rich details (Ehrman, 1996). In contrast, a person on the 'intuitive' end of the continuum does not rely on the process of sensing and is less interested in the factual details; instead, he/she relies on the process of intuition, preferring the abstract and imaginative to the concrete, and tends to focus on the patterns and meanings in the data.

- *Thinking–Feeling,* referring to how people prefer to arrive at conclusions and make decisions. 'Thinking' types follow rational principles while trying to reduce the impact of any subjective, emotional factors; they make decisions impersonally on the basis of logical consequences. 'Feeling' types, on the other hand, are guided by concern for others and for social values; they strive for harmony and show compassion; they are slow to voice criticism even if it is due but are quick to show appreciation; thus, they 'think with their hearts' (Ehrman, 1996).

- *Judging–Perceiving,* referring to how people prefer to deal with the outer world and take action. Judging types favor a planned and orderly way, seeking closure and finality, whereas people on the perceiving end of the scale like flexibility and spontaneity and therefore like to keep their options open. They often resist efforts of others to impose order on their lives (Ehrman, 1996).

The MBTI requires people to make forced choices and decide on one pole of each of the four preferences. The permutation of the preferences yields sixteen possible combinations called "types", usually marked by the four initial letters of the preferences (because two components start with an 'I,' 'intuition' is marked with the letter 'N'); for example, Myers' own type preference was Introversion–Intuition–Feeling–Perceiving (INFP). This is the level where the instrument and the underlying personality type theory come into its own: The 16 MBTI types have been found to be remarkably valid because, as Ehrman (1996) explained, the combinations are more than the sum of the parts: They outline real, recognizable character types and thus the inventory has proved to be useful in a wide variety of contexts, from counseling to making personnel decisions in industry. Leaver et al. (in press) argue that none of these sixteen possible types can be considered better per se than any of the others although they add that there are likely to be environments that provide a better fit for some types than for others.

PERSONALITY AND LEARNING

Whereas no one would doubt that personality variables and types are important factors in determining our behavior in general, from an educational perspective the real question is to what extent these dispositions affect learning. The rest of the chapter addresses this issue, first from a general perspective and then narrowing down the focus to SLA.

Several studies have attempted to identify the personality correlates of academic achievement (for recent reviews and studies, see Chamorro-Premuzic & Furnham, 2003a, 2003b; Farsides & Woodfield, 2003; Lounsbury, Sundstrom, Loveland, & Gibson, 2003). Although the emerging overall picture is rather mixed, if not bleak, some patterns did seem to emerge over the years. Within the Big Five paradigm, if we look at the component structure in Table 2.1 it is clear that the two dimensions that are intuitively most closely related to learning are Openness to Experience and Conscientiousness. There is some evidence for these positive associations, and especially Conscientiousness has produced consistent results, both in school and college contexts. Extraversion, on the other hand, has been found to have a negative relationship with academic success due to the introverts' greater ability to consolidate learning, lower distractibility, and better study habits. Similarly, Neuroticism has also displayed a negative relation with learning achievement due to the anxiety factor that it subsumes. However, even in the studies that do report a significant association between personality and learning measures, this relationship rarely explains more than about 15% of the variance in academic performance (for an exception, see Chamorro-Premuzic & Furnham, 2003b, which reports a prediction rate of almost 30%).

Furthermore, the moderate but significant results reported in the literature can be counterbalanced by many studies which failed to obtain any significant correlations between personality and learning measures. And even when meaningful personality–achievement correlations were found in one setting, they often could not be replicated in another. Because of this less-than-straightforward picture it is to some extent up to the various scholars' own beliefs how they interpret the big picture. To me it seems that Aiken's (1999) general conclusion about personality–behavior relations is fairly accurate: "Despite the large number of hypotheses concerning personality that have been generated over the years, on one test of their validity—the ability to make accurate behavioral predictions—they have not fared very well" (p. 169). So what is the reason for these at best inconclusive, and certainly counter-intuitive, results? At least four main points can be mentioned:

(1) *Interaction with situation-specific variables.* There is some evidence that personality factors interact with various variables inherent to the social context of the learning situation, which prevents generalized linear associations (such as correlations) from reaching overall significance. Skehan (1989), for example, reported on a study by Wankowski that related extraversion–introversion to age, and found that this personality trait affected achievement differently before and after puberty in the investigated sample: Below puberty extraverts had an advantage over introverts and after puberty it was the other way round. Wankowski explained the shift with the different learning environments students were exposed to, as a result of which the nature of the 'achieving personality' changed. This makes sense: it is not difficult to think of certain types of learning situations in which an outgoing and sociable person would excel and some other contexts which would favor his/her more quiet and sober counterparts. Perhaps it is for this reason that Naiman, Fröhlich, Stern, and Todesco's (1978) study on the good language learner listed both extraversion and introversion as a positive attribute. In the same vein, Matthews et al. (2000) argued that the nature of the actual tasks students engage in imposes a personality bias. For example, extraverts tend to perform well under conditions of high stimulation or arousal, which

means that some difficult tasks might provide the optimum level of arousal for them, whereas introverts in the same task might be overaroused, which impairs their performance. The issue of individual sensitivity to specific educational situations which 'afford' specific learning opportunities will be further discussed in chapter 3 when describing Peter Robinson's work on aptitude-treatment interactions.

Farsides and Woodfield (2003) also believed that the personality–learning relation is to a great extent the function of contextual features. In their view, students relatively high on Openness to Experience should thrive in educational settings that promote and rewarding critical and original thought, but not in settings that emphasize the acquisition of received wisdom. Their study also produced an unexpected result, namely the Agreeableness correlated significantly with long-term academic achievement as expressed by course grades. A closer analysis revealed that this influence was entirely mediated by situational factors: The particular course which the study focused on had a strong seminar component and it was found that Agreeable students went to seminars more often than did less Agreeable students; this more intensive participation in this course element, in turn, was rewarded by improved final course grades. The authors therefore concluded that students relatively high on Agreeableness should thrive when instruction and assessment occur within social interaction, while those lower in Agreeableness should fare better in educational settings where students are less socially interdependent (or are even negatively interdependent).

(2) *Need for less simplistic models.* Although it is clear from the above that the relationship between personality factors and learning achievement is often not direct and linear but rather indirect, mediated by various modifying variables, the typical research design reported in the literature is still correlational, testing for simple personality trait–learning outcome relationships. Aiken (1999) points out that this way we are unlikely to achieve more accurate behavioral predictions because

> For the most part, what we have in psychology, and in the psychology of personality in particular, is a collection of interrelated assertions concerning human behavior, cognitions, and feelings, but far less than a systematic structure from which unerring predictions and explanations can be made. (p. 169)

Investigating second language learning, MacIntyre and Charos's (1996) results provided support for the need for more complex theoretical constructs: The researchers found that global personality traits were implicated in the learning process primarily via their influence on language-related attitudes, anxiety, perceived competence, and motivation, rather than through their direct impact on learning outcomes. In fact, Lalonde and Gardner (1984) also found that although personality traits did not appear to correlate with language measures, "there were many meaningful relations with measures of attitudes and motivation" (p. 230). An example of a more complex model that includes a featured personality component in the L2 field is the Willingness to Communicate (WTC) construct by MacIntyre, Clément, Dörnyei, and Noels (1998), in which personality forms an important part of the basic layer of the construct, with four further layers of variables conceptualized between personality traits and communicative behavior (see chapt. 7, for more details).

(3) *Supertraits or primary traits.* As we have seen above, the Big Five construct consists of five main dimensions, or 'supertraits,' and 30 facets, or 'primary traits.' Although the rationale for clustering the primary traits into supertraits was that the facets in one dimension were interrelated, when it comes to their relationship with academic success we find differences among the interrelated primary traits in terms of their impact on learning. This difference obviously reduces the supertraits' predictive capacity, but the alternative, that is, to examine the personality–learning relation at the primary trait level, would in effect mean giving up the Big Five construct with all its merits. Yet, in the light of the limited success in using the Big Five dimensions for explaining academic success, Chamorro-Premuzic and Furnham (2003b) proposed to examine the primary traits because people with identical superfactor scores may have very different primary trait factor scores. In their study, they did indeed find that several primary traits associated with the supertraits Neuroticism, Extraversion, and Conscientiousness were differentially correlated with academic performance. Matthews et al. (2000) also highlighted the fact that some of the strongest links between personality and performance had been obtained at the primary trait level (notably between anxiety and performance).

(4) *Methodological issues.* The inconclusive results in the literature are also partly due to various methodological limitations or inconsistencies. Different studies, for example, have used different criteria for academic success, ranging from exam marks, grade point average, and final degree results to situated course-specific evaluations such as course grades. In addition, as Farsides and Woodfield (2003) pointed out, different studies have permitted considerably different time lapses between the collection of predictor and criterion data, with a range of a few weeks to several years. A further potential source of insignificant results is that many of the studies employed convenience samples (the most typical being psychology majors at the university of the researchers) and in such pre-selected samples the variance in ID variables can be so restricted that it may in some (but not all) cases prevent correlation-based coefficients from reaching statistical significance. We

must recognize at this stage that these methodological problems are just as relevant in the field of L2 studies.

In conclusion, most specialists in the field would agree that past research has not done justice to the assumed relation between personality variables and learning outcomes: As mentioned earlier, even carefully executed studies rarely manage to explain more than about 15% of the variance in academic success. This relatively low percentage, however, may not be so surprising if we consider the following: Personality traits can in many ways be compared to the ingredients of a cooking recipe and it is a known fact that a good cook can usually prepare a delicious meal of almost any ingredients by knowing how to combine them. In a similar vein, one can argue that we should not expect many strong linear relationships (expressed, e.g., by correlations) between individual personality traits and achievement, because successful learners can combine their personality features to best effect by utilizing their specific strengths and compensating for their possible weaknesses (Brown, 2000). Thus, my personal feeling is that the conclusion often found in the literature that personality is not sufficiently related to academic achievement to be of real significance in educational settings is misleading: Ability and motivation—the two ID variables that have been found to be responsible for most of the variance in students' academic performance—simply do not explain the whole picture, since personality factors act as powerful modifying variables. I believe that future research with more elaborate theoretical constructs and research designs is likely to document personality effects better.

PERSONALITY AND LANGUAGE LEARNING AND USE

Let us now narrow down our focus to the examination of the personality correlates of language learning and use. In a review written in 1990, Adrian Furnham concluded that there had been comparatively little programmatic research on the relationship between personality and first language, and ten years later Dewaele and Furnham (2000) confirmed that this situation had not changed. Furnham explained this partly by a lack of any real interest in the personality-language interface on the part of either psychologists or linguists, which is coupled with a difference in the typical level of analysis applied in the two fields. Personality psychologists, according to Dewaele and Furnham (1999), intend to explain linguistic behavior at a global level (e.g., by looking at verbosity) without going into a detailed micro-analysis (e.g., looking at discourse markers), as is usually done by linguists. Interestingly, we find exactly the same situation in motivation research (cf. chapt. 4), with social psychologists taking a macroperspective of the general motivational orientations that characterize whole communities, and applied linguists pursuing a more situated micro-analysis, also taking into account process-oriented and contextual factors.

In addition to such conceptual differences, Furnham (1990) drew attention to certain methodological issues that have also played a role in the paucity of relevant interdisciplinary research. The main methodological difficulty, according to Furnham, is the bewildering array of ways to measure both personality and speech, with the possible methods tapping slightly different aspects. The complexity of selecting the best measurement approach and instruments has clearly served as a deterrent both for linguists and psychologists, and so did the fact that the various combinations of the selected measures often produced mixed results, making the interpretation of the findings difficult.

The most researched personality aspect in language studies has been the extraversion–introversion dimension. This is understandable, since this trait is fundamental to a number of personality theories, from the MBTI typology to Eysenck's model and the Big Five construct. Furthermore, as Furnham (1990) pointed out, it is relatively easy to produce a reliable measure of this trait and there are also several obvious commonsense relationships between extraversion and language use. Indeed, research has found that extraverts are more talkative and use fewer pauses that introverts, while the latter tend to use more formal speech with more careful grammatical constructions. We will come back to the extraversion–language relationship when discussing the second language correlates of this personality trait.

As discussed in the introductory chapter, individual differences are seen as more salient in second language acquisition and use than in our native language, since we find considerably more variability in the learning outcomes and language use characteristics of L2 learners than their L1 counterparts. Accordingly, we can find a fair amount of research focusing on the interrelationships of personality and L2 learning/use, and the rest of this chapter is devoted to the review of this body of research. We can divide past research into four main groups: (a) early studies, (b) the study of extraversion and introversion, (c) research using the MBTI, and (d) other investigations.

Early Studies

It has been a longstanding observation in applied linguistics that some people are simply more gifted language learners than others, which naturally led researchers to test whether this giftedness was related to personality features. Accordingly, the 'good language learner' studies (e.g., Rubin 1975; Naiman et al., 1978; Stern, 1975; for a review, see MacIntyre & Noels,

1994) attempted to relate personality factors such as extraversion, willingness to take risks, lack of inhibition, and self-esteem to successful language learning. The assumption that the good language learner had a unique personality set-up was also shared by language teachers: According to a questionnaire survey by Lalonde, Lee, and Gardner (1987), more than 83% of the teachers rated the good language learner to have prominent personality features and 11 traits were found to yield consensual agreement. These were: meticulous, persevering, sociable, independent, inquisitive, involved, organized, active, flexible, assertive, and imaginative. The first four of these traits were also represented in the profile obtained by Naiman et al.'s (1978) study using open-ended questions. Examining French immersion programs, Swain and Burnaby's (1976) also found that parents considered certain personality traits important qualities for success, but out of the four such factors identified—happy, cheerful, talkative, and having a tendency toward perfectionism—only the last one, perfectionist tendencies, correlated significantly with L2 performance.

Extraversion and Introversion

Similarly to first language studies, the personality dimension that has attracted the most attention in the L2 field has been extraversion–introversion, particularly because the MBTI, which has been frequently employed in L2 studies (see below), also contains a featured extraversion–introversion facet. Yet, the emerging picture about the role of extraversion–introversion has been rather negative, with scholars either concluding that the relationship between this trait and learning was insignificant or mixed. Dewaele and Furnham (1999) have explained that the bad reputation of the extraversion variable in the L2 field is the result of not distinguishing properly between written and oral language criteria, as exemplified by the influential study by Naiman et al. (1978) just mentioned, which only examined criterion measures from written language and found no significant relationships between these and extraversion. However, Dewaele and Furnham have argued that in the studies where extraversion scores are correlated with linguistic variables extracted from complex verbal tasks (i.e., conversations), a clear pattern emerges: Extraverts are found to be more fluent than introverts both in L1 and L2 and particularly in formal situations or in environments characterized by interpersonal stress. As the authors explain, introverts can suffer from increased pressure because the arousal level exceeds their optimal level, which in turn inhibits the automaticity of speech production. They slide back to controlled serial processing, rather than automatic parallel processing, which overloads their working memory. As a consequence, their speech slows down, they hesitate more often, they tend to make more errors, and they are unable to produce utterances of great length (cf. also Dewaele & Furnham, 2000). Thus, it is, in effect, the lack of sufficient short-term memory capacity that causes the introverts' breakdown in fluency. A further, related insight into the superior fluency of extraverts has been provided by a recent study by Dewaele (2004), in which he found that extraverted L2 speakers tended to use colloquial words freely whereas introverts tended to avoid them.

Being disadvantaged at L2 communication would, of course, mean that introverts can benefit less from learning opportunities and speaking practice that require participation in communicative tasks and situations. For this reason, Skehan (1989) proposed that within the field of second language learning we should be able to observe a more prominent positive effect of extraversion than in other learning domains, where—as we have seen—introverts have usually been found to have an advantage. On the other hand, Skehan also pointed out that SLA involves many learning tasks and processes which go beyond learning-by-doing or talking-to-learn, and these aspects of learning would seem to relate more easily to the introvert. That is, with regard to L2 learning, both extraversion and introversion may have positive features, depending on the particular task in question. This ambiguous situation might explain why earlier studies in the literature have produced rather equivocal or insignificant findings (cf. Kiany, 1997, and the review in it).

The use of the MBTI

The MBTI is currently the most often used personality type inventory in the world and this is also true of the L2 field. In applied linguistic studies MBTI scores are usually reported as 'learning style' rather than personality measures (e.g., Bailey, Onwuegbuzie, & Daley, 2000). Although Ehrman's (1996) argument that certain personality constructs have considerable learning implications is certainly valid, and several psychological publications emphasize the link between psychological type and learning style (e.g., Lawrence, 1997), I feel that to maintain conceptual clarity it is better to refer to the MBTI factors, similarly to Ehrman, as 'personality dimensions with cognitive style correlates' rather than learning styles.

Empirical studies using the MBTI have produced—not unlike other studies looking at the relationship between personality traits and learning (see previous discussion)—mostly weak or mixed results. For example, in a study examining English majors in Indonesia, Carrell, Prince, and Astika (1996) concluded:

> As in similar studies, we did not find many direct, simple relationships between learning styles and language performance measures. Although

there were some correlations between extraversion/introversion and the vocabulary tests, and between judging/perceiving with the grammar tests, by and large there were few direct relationships between learners' type preferences and their language performance. (p. 95)

In a study of 855 Foreign Service Institute students, Ehrman and Oxford (1995; Ehrman, 1994) obtained similar results. Although they did find some statistically significant differences between various MBTI types, most of the results were rather weak. Having seen the theoretical problems concerning any direct personality–achievement link, these findings are not surprising (in fact, the opposite would be more unexpected).

An important point about personality types in the L2 field has been highlighted by Moody (1998). The researcher administered the MBTI to a large sample of college students at an American university and found that language majors as a group considerably differed from students of science, engineering, and business in their personality characteristics. The fact, the author warned, that language specialists displayed unique type preferences might foreshadow the danger that language teachers and text writers may unconsciously design programs for students of their own type, which may structure the system so that some other students will be at a disadvantage. This issue, in fact, is quite similar to the teacher–student learning style mismatch to be discussed at the end of chapter 5.

Other Studies

Several studies not mentioned before have incorporated certain personality variables in their research design (e.g., Brown, Robson, & Rosenkjar, 2001; Dewaele, 2002; Ely, 1986; Griffiths, 1991; Lalonde & Gardner, 1984; Verhoeven & Vermeer, 2002; Wakamoto, 2000), without any consistent picture emerging. For example, Lalonde and Gardner conducted an ambitious study to relate a series of personality traits to measures of attitudes, motivation, language aptitude, and second language achievement. However, the researchers admitted that "Because of the past research, it was expected that few of the personality measures would correlate highly with indices of second language achievement" (p. 225). They were correct in their assumption, as they found a general lack of relationship between personality variables and objective measures of French achievement or self-ratings of French proficiency.

Of the studies listed above, Verhoeven and Vermeer's (2002) investigation deserves special attention, as, to my knowledge, this study has been the first to use the Big Five personality construct in L2 research. The purpose of the investigation was to examine the communicative competence of young teenage language learners in the Netherlands in relation to their personality characteristics (and also to compare these learners with a native-speaking sample). Following Bachman and Palmer's (1996) taxonomy, communicative competence was operationalized in terms of three main constituents: *organizational competence* (measured by standardized discrete-point tests of vocabulary, grammar, and reading), *strategic competence* (measured by two rating scale for teachers to judge the children's planning of communicative behavior and monitoring communication), and *pragmatic competence* (measured by student performance on eight different role-play tasks). It was found that only Openness to Experience correlated substantially with the linguistic abilities of the children across all the three competencies (with a mean correlation of 0.43). Extraversion was associated only with strategic competence, but the highly significant correlation ($r = 0.51$) between the two variables was very much in line with the theoretical considerations reported in the section on extraversion–introversion above. Conscientiousness had a moderate correlation with organizational competence ($r = 0.28$), whereas the other two facets of the Big Five model (Agreeableness and Neuroticism) were unrelated to L2 communicative competence. These findings are interesting in themselves and they also indicate that if scholars include in their research paradigm a more elaborate conception of L2 proficiency than a global L2 proficiency measure, stronger and more meaningful relationships can be identified.

CONCLUSION

Although the adjectives 'weak,' 'mixed,' 'equivocal,' and 'insignificant' have been rather frequent in this chapter when talking about empirical results concerning the relationship between personality and learning, the overall picture does not appear so bleak for a number of reasons: First, personality psychology appears to have reached a growing consensus in the conceptualization of the main dimensions of human personality, which makes the use of personality factors as independent variables in research studies easier and more reliable for non-psychologists. The application of the Big Five model in L2 studies is likely to shed new light on the relationship between personality and language learning, particularly if elaborate language measures are employed as criterion variables.

Second, past research has provided sufficient evidence that personality factors are heavily implicated in the learning process in general and in SLA in particular. I argued that one reason for not obtaining strong and consistent results has been the wide variation in the research methodologies applied in terms of learning targets, achievement measures, types of treatment, etc. across studies. A second reason is that many researchers may not have asked the right questions when trying to test personality–achievement contingencies. Although there does not seem to be a powerful direct link between personality traits and holistic learning outcomes (as measured, for example, by proficiency test scores), if we conceptualize 'learning' in a more situated and process-oriented manner, personality variables can shed light on several subprocesses. One possible area of research in this vein is looking at the personality correlates of the choice and use of learning strategies (or self-regulation in general; cf. chapt. 6) (e.g., Ehrman & Oxford, 1995; Wakamoto, 2000).

Third and related to the above point, the available data suggests that examining the *combined effect* or *interrelationship* of personality traits and other ID variables may also yield meaningful insights. Even if personality factors do not directly determine the degree of an individual's academic success, they certainly shape the way people respond to their learning environment. It is quite likely that people of different personality types pursue differential behavioral patterns, which will have an impact on their participation in a range of learning tasks, from classroom activities to real-life practices of intercultural communication. Thus, personality traits can be seen as potent modifying variables and in this sense they are similar to learning styles in their function.

In summary, I believe that Dewaele and Furnham (1999) were right when they concluded that "the success of recent studies in exploring the relationship between personality and oral language should help the important and hitherto neglected interface between applied linguistics and personality psychology" (p. 537), particularly, because the emerging results are likely to have important theoretical and applied implications for both groups of scholars. Therefore, I sincerely hope that future research designs in L2 studies will increasingly include personality traits as independent variables.

3

Language Aptitude

The concept of *language aptitude* is related to the broader concept of *human abilities*, covering a variety of cognitively-based learner differences. We have seen in the Introduction of this book that the study of individual differences in ability has been one of the most established areas in psychology, and as Cooper (2002) pointed out, it is certainly one of the most applicable notions for a variety of domains, from educational to occupational and industrial contexts. According to Cooper's overview, ability testing stretches back 4000 years to when the Chinese used a form of ability test to select candidates for their civil service, and indeed, the accurate identification of who will be able to benefit from a particular course of education, or which job applicants are likely to perform best if appointed, are still seen as areas that have important financial and personal benefits.

In a recent review of intelligence research, Sternberg (2002) reported research findings which indicate that ability tests predict roughly 25% of individual-difference variation in school performance, which is, if we take into account the great number of other factors that are likely to influence school achievement, an impressive proportion, the highest amongst all the ID variables and indeed amongst all the known factors that modify school performance. When we look at the real world rather than educational contexts only, intelligence scores, according to Sternberg, still account for about 10% of the variation in success on average. In the domain of L2 learning, aptitude has traditionally been seen as a key factor and, for example, in a large-scale survey of individual differences, Ehrman and Oxford (1995) found that aptitude measures were the ID variables most strongly correlated with L2 proficiency. Interestingly, in their sample language aptitude scores explained exactly the same amount of variance that Sternberg reported for the educational domain in general: 25%. Thus, aptitude is a strong predictor of academic success, which warrants a closer look at what components this notion subsumes, how it is measured, and what its role is in the SLA process.

BASIC CONCEPTUAL ISSUES

Let us start our discussion with some basic conceptual issues. This is necessary because the terms *ability*, *aptitude*, and *intelligence* are commonly used in everyday parlance and therefore it is all too easy to mix up their popular meaning with their scientific definition. The general term *(human) mental ability* is typically used in psychology to refer to a variety of human traits that are involved in thinking, reasoning, processing information, and acquiring new knowledge. In other words, mental abilities reflect cognitive processes and skills. When describing such processes and skills, experts and non-specialists alike use several terms, most notably 'ability,' 'aptitude,' and 'intelligence.' How do these differ from each other?

Although some scholars distinguish between ability and aptitude, in typical practice the two are used synonymously. Furthermore, in educational contexts such as second language learning, ability is often used to mean 'learning ability,' that is, the individual's potential for acquiring new knowledge or skill. Thus, 'language aptitude' means exactly the same as 'language ability' and is typically meant to denote 'language learning ability.' What about intelligence? Intelligence is yet another synonym for 'ability' but when it is used on its own (i.e., not in a phrase such as 'spatial intelligence' or 'verbal intelligence') it usually has a broader meaning, referring to a general sort of aptitude that is not limited to a specific performance area but is transferable to many sorts of performance. This general usage is explained by the fact that scores on all subtests of abilities measured by intelligence tests are positively intercorrelated, which makes it possible to compute a single higher-order factor, usually labeled as *'g,'* that describes the commonalities of the various abilities. The famous/infamous IQ coefficient is intended to assess this general *g* factor.

'Intelligence' in the scientific sense is not a unitary construct and several theories have been proposed in the past to describe the hierarchical organization of the many constituent abilities identified. Describing these theories would go beyond the scope of this book but to illustrate the kinds of constructs we can find in the literature let me briefly mention a few famous taxonomies. In the 1920s, Spearman described intelligence as a combination of a general factor (*g*), which is available to an individual to the same degree for all intellectual acts, as well as several specific factors which vary in strength from one act to another. Ten years later Thurstone distinguished seven primary mental abilities: verbal comprehension, word fluency, number facility, spatial visualization, associative memory, perceptual speed, and reasoning. In the 1960s, Guilford's famous structure-of-intellect model contained an elaborate structure made up of as many as 150 different factors. At about the same time, Cattell's influential theory divided up general intelligence into *fluid intelligence* and *crystallized intelligence*. Fluid intelligence is the ability to adapt to novel situations, as manifested in performance on tests of reasoning ability about sequences of abstract shapes or manually assembling larger objects from groups of novel shapes. Crystallized intelligence consists of knowledge and skills acquired by experience and education, and is specific to certain fields and domains, such as knowledge of history or mathematical skills. Currently Gardner's (1983) 'multiple intelligence' model and Sternberg's 'successful intelligence' construct attract particular attention (the latter will be further discussed in a separate section).

This brief description illustrates well two important points about aptitude: (a) There is no universally accepted theory or definition of intelligence and neither is there a canonical list of 'real' mental abilities. (b) The multicomponential nature of mental abilities implies, by definition, that we can expect some variation within individuals with regard to their specific abilities; that is, for example, someone with a superior verbal ability may be relatively weak at reasoning tasks.

Ability and Language Learning

As we have seen above, the term *intelligence* is often used to denote the 'ability to learn' and in fact, the first ever intelligence test, the 1905 Binet-Simon Intelligence Scale, was originally developed to identify pupils who could not benefit from regular instruction in school classrooms because of their limited mental ability. Ever since these early days, intelligence has been closely associated with learning success, and therefore it was only a question of time that attempts were made to conceptualize the specific ability to learn a foreign language. This ability has been referred to under a variety of names, ranging from 'language aptitude' and a special 'propensity' or 'talent' for learning an L2 to more colloquial terms such as a 'flair' or 'knack' for languages. Indeed, language aptitude is one of those psychological concepts that are readily recognizable for researchers and laypeople alike, and nobody would question that the innate ability to learn another language, as a child or as an adult, varies significantly from individual to individual. Yet, when we give the concept a closer scrutiny, it also becomes clear that what lies behind the popular surface meaning is rather ambiguous: Even language teaching experts would find it difficult to define what exactly this 'language flair' involves and, similarly to their colleagues in mainstream psychology, scholars specializing in language aptitude research display considerable diversity in the conceptualization of the construct.

The crux of the problem is that, strictly speaking, there is no such thing as 'language aptitude.' Instead, we have a number of cognitive factors making up a composite measure that can be referred to as the learner's overall capacity to master a foreign language. In other words, foreign language aptitude is not a unitary factor but rather a complex of "basic abilities that are essential to facilitate foreign language learning" (Carroll & Sapon, 1959, p. 14); thus, the concept concerns a variety of cognitively-based learner differences. While this definition has been adequate for several decades, recent research into specific cognitive skills and capacities related to learning, such as 'working memory' or 'phonological coding/decoding,' makes it questionable as to whether it is still useful to use the umbrella-term of 'language aptitude.' However, because standard measures of language aptitude remain relatively good indicators of learning success across a wide range of situational parameters, the concept is still widely used in the general sense, making it similar to the generic term of 'intelligence.'

LANGUAGE APTITUDE RESEARCH: FROM THE BEGINNINGS TO THE 1990S

Language aptitude testing was originally motivated by exactly the same reasons as the testing of intelligence, namely to identify hopelessly untalented students in state schools. In an article describing the beginning of language aptitude testing, Spolsky (1995) explains that in the 1920s and 1930s the U.S. school curriculum allocated such little time to the study of foreign languages that language learning failure became all too common. With articles written about the 'deplorable mortality in foreign language classes,' the educational authorities commissioned the design of so-called 'prognosis tests' to help to identify prospective 'causalities.' Between 1925 and 1930, three such prognosis tests were prepared and these were then used for many years. These tests did not have any firm theoretical foundation but their design was based on two main approaches that every language aptitude test has followed ever since: Spolsky labels these approaches *analytical* and *synthetic* The former involves constructing tasks that tap specific cognitive abilities that are assumed to play a significant role in language learning; these tasks are in the students' first language and usually concern some aspect of verbal intelligence. In contrast, the synthetic approach involves devising mini learning tasks that the students have to carry out as part of the test-taking process, and based on their achievement in learning certain aspects of an artificial language or a rare existing L2, generalizations are made about the learners' likely performance in a real language learning program.

Thus, the ultimate goal of the first test design period of the 1920/1930s was, in effect, to increase the cost-effectiveness of language education and it was exactly the same thinking 30 years later, in the 1950s and 1960s in the U.S., that led to the second wave of aptitude test development, which we can call the 'golden period' of scientific language aptitude testing (Rees, 2000).

This period was heralded by two systematic test development programs by John Carroll and Stanley Sapon on the one hand and by Paul Pimsleur on the other. Two commercial aptitude batteries for the use with adolescents and adults stem from this early work: the *Modern Language Aptitude Test* (MLAT; Carroll & Sapon, 1959), and the *Pimsleur Language Aptitude Battery* (PLAB; Pimsleur, 1966). There are other aptitude tests available (see later) but these two have been by far the most widely used and referred to. Let us examine them in more detail.

The Modern Language Aptitude Test (MLAT), the Pimsleur Language Aptitude Battery (PLAB), and the Underlying Theoretical Constructs

Ever since the MLAT and the PLAB were introduced, language aptitude has been equated in most research studies with the scores of one of these (or some other, similar) tests and the tacit understanding in the L2 research community has been that language aptitude is what language aptitude tests measure. Although such a pragmatic test-based definition might appear rather unscientific, the fact is that the study of cognitive abilities has often been characterized in the past by such an atheoretical and assessment-based approach in psychology. Rather than adhering to an explicit theory of intelligence, the 1905 Simon-Binet intelligence test, for example, was also constructed following a trial-and-error process of selecting a set of tasks that would effectively discriminate between a group of very bright and a group of rather slow school kids, and Carroll and Sapon (1959) followed a similar 'hands-on' psychometric approach when they developed the first scientific language aptitude test, the MLAT. In the authors' words:

> The Modern Language Aptitude Test is the outcome of a five-year research study conducted during the years 1953-1958 at Harvard University. In the course of this study, many varieties of verbal tests were devised and tried out; the present test is comprised of a group of relatively uncorrelated sub-tests which more or less consistently showed good validity and made unique contributions to the prediction of success in foreign languages. The experimental tests were administered to about five thousand persons. (p. 3)

Note that Carroll and Sapon did not even mention any theoretical work in this account; instead, what they highlighted was the trying out of a great number of intuitively appealing task types that were expected to tell good and bad language learners apart (i.e., in which good learners were significantly more successful than their slow counterparts) and then selecting the tasks that worked best in this respect. Thus, during this process, Carroll and

Sapon followed a simple, and in psychology well established, three-step recipe for test design: (1) Based on some external criterion, select a group of people with high levels of the attribute under investigation and a second group with low levels. (2) Ask them to do a variety of tasks related to the attribute in question. (3) Choose the tasks that separate the two groups best without the different tasks correlating too highly with each other, as high correlations would indicate that the tasks do not provide unique information but only duplicate the others.

Tables 3.1 and 3.2 provide a description of Carroll and Sapon's (1959) MLAT and Pimsleur's (1966) PLAB, the latter battery also constructed following a similar approach. A comparison of the two instruments illustrates well the weakness of the atheoretical, assessment-driven approach: Although some of the tasks in the two batteries are similar and obviously tap into the same underlying construct (e.g., MLAT's 'Phonetic Script' and PLAB's 'Sound-Symbol Association'), there are also considerable differences, with the PLAB placing greater emphasis on auditory factors and less on memory than the MLAT. Furthermore, the PLAB also contains two items that clearly stand out: 'Grade Point Average' and 'Interest in Foreign Language Learning.' No-one would claim that a student's achievement in, say, history is part of their language aptitude, or that motivation—measured by the interest item—is a cognitive ability that would qualify to be a component of the aptitude complex. Yet, based on the 'include-if-it-helps-to-discriminate-good-and-bad-students' principle, these sub-sections cannot be easily excluded because empirical data concerning past academic achievement and motivation tend to be strong predictors of language learning success. In fact, Pimsleur (1966, p. 14) stated explicitly that because motivation "proved to be significantly related to foreign language learning," its inclusion did contribute to the predictive capacity of the instrument. Furthermore, an analysis of the validity studies reported in the PLAB manual reveals that for certain high school samples (in schools C and D), the grade point average subtest was not only the best predictor of the achievement criterion but it was also a better predictor than the total PLAB score (Rees, 2000). In a study conducted in the 1980s, Curral and Kirk (1986) also found that the overall Grade Point Average was "the best single predictor of performance in foreign language courses" (p. 110).

Table 3.1. The Modern Language Aptitude Test (MLAT)

The MLAT is a paper-and-pencil test battery, composed of five parts. Its administration takes about 60-70 minutes. The standardization of the administration is insured by the use of recorded material that includes the instructions and the phonetic material for certain parts (Parts 1 and 2). The five constituent sections are as follows:

1. **Number Learning:** Subjects hear some numbers in a new language (only numbers 1-4, 10-40 and 100-400), and are provided with some auditory practice to learn them. Then they must translate 15 numbers between 1 and 400 into English.

2. **Phonetic Script:** First students hear a set of short nonsense words while they follow their printed phonetic script, which is presented in fairly simple and regular symbols. Then they hear one word at a time and must choose from four printed alternatives. The whole task includes 30 sets of four words each.

3. **Spelling Clues:** This part looks like a vocabulary test in that subjects must choose, from five alternatives, the word which is nearest in meaning to a test word, thus the results depend on vocabulary knowledge in one's first language. A unique feature of the task is that the test word is not spelled normally but phonetically. There is a total of 50 test words.

   E.g., ernst

A. shelter	D. slanted	E. impatient
B. sincere	E. free	

4. **Words in Sentences:** This test measures 'grammatical sensitivity.' First subjects are presented with a key sentence in which a word or phrase is underlined. In the sentence (or sentences) following the key sentence, five alternative words or phrases are underlined. Subjects must select the one that performs the same function as the underlined word in the key sentence. There are altogether 45 key sentences.

   E.g., Mary is cutting the <u>APPLE.</u>

   <u>My brother John</u> is beating <u>his dog with a big stick.</u>
     A   B   C D   E

5. **Paired Associates:** In this test students have a total of four minutes to memorize 24 Kurdish/English word pairs. Retention is tested by means of a multiple choice test in which subjects must choose the proper equivalent for each Kurdish word from five English alternatives. All the distracters are selected from the 24 English words contained in the original list, which makes the test more difficult.

Table 3.2. The Pimsleur Language Aptitude Battery (PLAB)

The PLAB is a paper-and-pencil test battery, composed of six parts. Its administration takes about 60 minutes. The standardization of the administration is insured by the use of recorded material that includes the instructions and the phonetic material for certain parts (Parts 5 and 6). The six sections are as follows:

1. *Grade Point Average:* Students have to report the grades they last received in English, history, mathematics, and science.

2. *Interest in Foreign Language Learning:* On a five-point scale, students are to indicate their degree of interest in studying a modern foreign language.

3. *Vocabulary:* The individual's word-power in English is measured in a multiple choice format. 24 fairly difficult adjectives are listed, followed by four words each for the student to choose the synonym from.

    E.g., prolonged
    >   A. *prompt*   C. *difficult*
    >   B. *decreased*   D. *extended*

4. *Language Analysis:* Subjects are presented with a list of words and phrases in a fictitious language, and their English equivalents. From these they must deduce how to say other things, and select the correct answer from alternatives provided. There are 15 English phrases to be 'translated' into the fictitious language, each followed by alternative 'translations' to choose from.

    E.g., The list below contains words from a foreign language and the English equivalents of these words.

    > **Gade** .... *father, a father*
    > **Shi** .... *horse, a horse*
    > **Gade shir le** .... *Father sees a horse.*
    > **Gade shir la** .... *Father sees a horse.*
    > **be** .... *carries*

    Using the above list, figure out how to say each of the statements below. As soon as you decide how to say a statement, look at the four answers given beneath it and choose the one which agrees with yours.

    > **A horse carried Father**
    >
    >   A. *gade shir be*   B. *gade shir ba*
    >   C. *shi gader be*   D. *shi gader ba*

• 5. *Sound Discrimination:* Subjects are taught, by means of a tape re-

> cording, three similar sounding words in a foreign language. Then they hear 30 sentences spoken in the language and must indicate which of the three words each sentence contains.
>
> - *6. Sound–Symbol Association:* Subjects hear a two- or three-syllable nonsense word and must indicate which of four printed alternatives it is.

These observations are good illustrations of the fact that if properly conducted, the trial-and-error method can produce instruments with adequate psychometric capacities, yet these outcomes are somewhat *ad hoc* with two separate attempts in our case resulting in two rather different instruments that also contain certain theoretically questionable elements. The other side of the coin is, however, that reliable instruments that *appear* to tap into some psychological construct can subsequently be used to define the content and the boundaries of the construct in question. This has been, for example, the dominant route in intelligence research: By submitting various intelligence test scores to complex multivariate statistical analyses, researchers were able to specify a number of underlying cognitive abilities (cf. Carroll 1993), and this is exactly the route that Carroll (1973, 1981) and Pimsleur (1966) took to distil the constituents of the theoretical construct of language aptitude.

According to Carroll (1981), language aptitude comprises four constituent abilities:

1. *Phonetic coding ability,* which is considered the most important component and is defined as "an ability to identify distinct sounds, to form associations between these sounds and symbols representing them, and to retain these associations" (p. 105). Carroll (1973) argued that the student's main problem is not so much that of discriminating sounds, as it is that of identifying sounds or string of sounds as unique entities and storing them in long-term memory. This ability therefore involves the coding, assimilation, and remembering of phonetic material.

2. *Grammatical sensitivity,* which is "the ability to recognize the grammatical functions of words (or other linguistic entities) in sentence structures" (Carroll, 1981, p. 105), or in other words, "the individual's ability to demonstrate his awareness of the syntactical patterning of sentences in a language and of the grammatical functions of individual elements in a sentence" (Carroll, 1973, p. 7). Although this ability does not require any knowledge of grammatical terminology, it implies an awareness of grammatical relationships.

3. *Rote learning ability,* which is the "ability to learn associations between sounds and meaning rapidly and efficiently, and to retain these associa-

tions" (Carroll, 1981, p. 105). It refers to the capacity to remember large amounts of foreign language materials.

4. *Inductive language learning ability*, which is "the ability to infer or in-duce the rules governing a set of language materials, given samples of language materials that permit such inferences" (Carroll, 1981, p. 105), or in other words, the ability to "identify patterns of correspondences and relationships involving either meaning or grammatical form" (Car-roll, 1973, p. 8) from the primary language data.

Pimsleur (1966) conceptualized the 'aptitude for learning a modern lan-guage' in terms of three factors:

1. *Verbal intelligence*, that is, "the knowledge of words and the ability to reason analytically in using verbal materials" (p. 14).

2. *Motivation*, whose problematic position within the aptitude complex has already been mentioned briefly.

3. *Auditory ability*, which is "the ability to receive and process information through the ear" (p. 14).

This taxonomy shares some common features with Carroll's aptitude construct: Pimsleur's 'verbal intelligence' component is similar to 'gram-matical sensitivity' and the 'inductive language learning ability,' whereas 'auditory ability' bears a resemblance to the 'phonetic coding ability.' There are, however, some basic differences between the two constructs. First, be-cause the PLAB does not include any memory component, this is completely missing from Pimsleur's theoretical conceptualization. Second, although it was Carroll who identified the 'inductive learning ability' component, the MLAT only measures it indirectly whereas the PLAB specifically targets this component. Third, Pimsleur conceived language learning ability in a broader sense than did Carroll by including motivation as one of the con-stituents. This is not in line with the generally accepted view that aptitude and motivation are two independent factors (e.g., Gardner & MacIntyre, 1992). In a comparison of Carroll and Pimsleur's work, Skehan (1989) sug-gested that the differences observed between the two scholars' approaches reflected "Carroll's background in psychology and learning ... and Pim-sleur's greater involvement in linguistics" (p. 29).

    In the 1980s Skehan (1986, 1989) conducted an ambitious research pro-ject to shed further light on Carroll's aptitude construct and as a result ar-gued that it was more appropriate to view aptitude as consisting of only three components rather than four: *auditory ability*, *linguistic ability*, and *memory ability*. Auditory ability is essentially the same as Carroll's phonetic coding ability, and memory ability corresponds to rote learning ability. The main difference lies in proposing a new component, linguistic ability, which draws together Carroll's grammatical sensitivity and inductive language learning ability. This is justifiable, in Skehan's view, partly by the fact that the evidence distinguishing the two factors is not extensive and partly by the theoretical observation that Carroll's two components appear to differ mainly in their degree of emphasis rather than in their nature (Skehan 1989, 1998).

Post-Carroll Aptitude Research

The creation of the MLAT and the PLAB was followed by further test construction work, resulting, for example, in the York Language Aptitude Test (Green, 1975), the Defense Language Aptitude Battery (Petersen & Al-Haik, 1976), the Aptitude Test for Studies in Modern Languages (Trost & Bickel, 1981), the German Aptitude Test (Miller & Phillips, 1982), and VORD (Parry & Child, 1990), but there is a general agreement in the literature that the new batteries did not demonstrate superiority over the MLAT (cf. Sawyer & Ranta, 2001; Sparks & Ganschow, 2001). Indeed, even some of the authors of the new tests themselves 'conceded defeat;' for example, after administering the Defense Language Aptitude Battery to over 1,000 subjects, Petersen and Al-Haik found that although the new test was designed to discriminate better among higher aptitude students in order to compensate for the plateau effect of MLAT (cf. Kiss & Nikolov, in press), the observed increase in the predictive validity of the instrument was only marginal. Parry and Child fared even worse: In an ambitious study comparing various aptitude batteries to their newly developed VORD, which focuses primarily on the grammatical analysis of a linguistic system similar to the grammar of Turkish, they found that the MLAT was "the best overall instrument for predicting language-learning success" (p. 52). Thus, in spite of the efforts to develop instruments for various situational and learner types, the results repeatedly pointed to the adequacy of a "one-test-fits-all" practice (Pardee, 1998, p. 11)

Between the initial instrument-developing efforts and the 1990s we also find a steady though not very strong flow of research studies (e.g., Curral & Kirk, 1986; Curtin, Avner & Smith, 1983; Eisenstein, 1980; Neufeld, 1978, 1979; Nizegorodcew, 1980; Schneiderman & Wesche, 1986; Skehan, 1986, 1989; Wesche 1981; Wesche, Edwards & Wells, 1982; Zeidner, 1986), but we can largely agree with the summary that Carroll made in 1990 when looking back on the 30-year history of the MLAT:

> Since 1959, the publication date of the MLAT, there has been considerable research that throws light on the components of foreign language

aptitude and that provides information that might be useful in revising this and other batteries of foreign language aptitude tests. For the most part, this research has not suggested any major change in the components of foreign language aptitude that have been recognized from the start. (p. 14)

Why did such an important predictor of L2 learning success receive such limited attention? The reasons, according to Skehan (2002), were three-fold: Language aptitude had been perceived as (a) undemocratic with respect to learners, (b) out-of-date conceptually, and (c) of little practical explanatory value. As he argued, determining a learner's fixed endowment of language learning capacity was seen to work against the learner-centered principles of modern language education, particularly because aptitude had come to be associated with certain outmoded methodologies such as the audiolingual method. The general feeling in the profession was that although aptitude might be predictive for the context of structured input and practice-oriented activities, it was less relevant to the communication-based, meaningful language use that characterized the new emerging language teaching paradigm, communicative language teaching (we will come back to this issue in a separate section below). Furthermore, several theoreticians of the time (e.g., Bialystok & Fröhlich, 1978; Gardner, 1985; Krashen, 1981) relegated aptitude effects only to classroom *learning* in contrast to the more naturalistic engagement of language *acquisitional* processes, which were seen as superior.

The past 15 years brought a marked shift in the research community's attitudes toward language aptitude. The 1990s started with the publication of an ambitious anthology entitled *'Language Aptitude Reconsidered,'* edited by Thomas Parry and Charles Stansfield (1990), with contributions including Carroll (1990), Parry and Child (1990), and Lett and O'Mara (1990), and as if this volume had given the field some fresh momentum, there followed a renewed interest in the concept throughout the decade and especially during the past few years (e.g., Child, 1998; Dörnyei & Skehan, 2003; Ehrman, 1996; Grigorenko, Sternberg & Ehrman, 2000; Harley & Hart, 1997, 2002; Kiss & Nikolov, in press; Kurahachi, 1994; Miyake & Friedman, 1998; McLaughlin, 1995; Ranta, 2002; Rees, 2000; Robinson, 1995, 1997, 2001, 2002a; 2002b; Ross, Yoshinaga & Sasaki, 2002; Sasaki, 1993a, 1993b, 1996; Sawyer & Ranta, 2001; Sick & Irie, 2000; Skehan, 1991, 1998, 2002; Sparks, Ganschow, & Patton, 1995; Sparks & Ganschow, 1991, 2001; Sparks et al., 1998; Spolsky, 1995; Sternberg, 2002; Tucker, 2000). What caused this revival? There are at least two main reasons: First, advances in cognitive psychology allowed for a more accurate representation of the various mental skills and aptitudes that made up the composite language learning ability. Second, scholars started to explore ways of linking language aptitude to a number of important issues in SLA research. The remainder of this chapter offers a summary of these developments.

TRADITIONAL ISSUES IN LANGUAGE APTITUDE RESEARCH

There have been a number of central issues in the language aptitude literature that have been raised and revisited again and again since the 1960s. In this section I address the most salient questions of this sort, whereas the following section discusses the most prominent contemporary research directions.

What Does Language Aptitude Determine?

There is a general agreement that language aptitude does *not* predict whether an individual can learn a foreign language or not. Rather, except for extremely low aptitude scores, it predicts the *rate of progress* the individual is likely to make in learning "under optimal conditions of motivation, opportunity to learn, and quality of instruction" (Carroll, 1973, p. 6). In the manual of the MLAT, Carroll and Sapon (1959) defined the predictive value of a given test score as follows:

> Knowing the individual's level of ability, we may infer the level of effort and motivation he must expend to learn successfully. A student with a somewhat low aptitude score will need to work harder in an academic language course than a student with a high aptitude test score. If the score is very low, the student may not succeed in any event. (p. 14)

L1 Versus L2 Aptitude

Is language aptitude equally related to L1 and L2 acquisition or is it specific to SLA? Although we normally speak about language aptitude in L2 contexts, it is clear that differences in language comprehension and production begin to emerge early in childhood during the mastery of our mother tongue and then affect performance in reading and writing as children progress through school (Bates et al., 1995; Shore, 1995; Sparks et al., 1998). It makes intuitive sense that such individual differences in one's native language skills are related to a learner's capacity to master a second language and some research findings support this view. In a study conducted in the 1980s, Skehan administered foreign language aptitude tests to 13 and 14-year-old children whose first language development had been investigated a decade earlier as part of Wells's Bristol Language Project (for a review, see Skehan, 1989, 1991). He found a significant positive association between the participants' first language development and their aptitude scores: There were several correlations in the order of 0.40 and above between first language measures of developing syntax (e.g., mean morpheme length of utterance, noun phrase complexity) and language aptitude. This led Skehan to conclude that aptitude for foreign languages was, to some extent, a residue of first language learning ability. However, he also emphasized that first language influences only explain part of the variance because aptitude also reflects abilities to handle decontextualized language material.

The relationship between L1 vs. L2 aptitude has also been a central theme in Sparks and Ganschow's current 'Linguistic Coding Differences Hypothesis,' which is described in a separate section later.

Language Aptitude and Age

Does language aptitude change with age either in a positive or in a negative way? On the one hand, if language aptitude is indeed a trait, it should be relatively stable. Intelligence, for example, has been found to be remarkably stable, as evidenced in a notable study by Deary et al. (2000). These scholars managed to track down 101 individuals in Scotland who took part in an intelligence survey in 1932 at their age of 11. 66 years later they sat the same test and the correlations between the two test scores reached 0.80 (after some statistical corrections). This extraordinary result indicates that a person's intelligence is a powerful predictor of their performance on the same test even several generations later and Cooper (2002) cited further evidence showing that intelligence measured in middle childhood was a good predictor of intelligence displayed in later life. The other side of the coin, however, is that age is a central factor in an individual's language learning capacity—as evidenced by the vast amount of literature on the 'critical period hypothesis' addressing age-related changes in SLA—and therefore it is not unreasonable to assume that some of the age-related variation is mediated through aptitude changes that occur over time.

Having considered this question in some depth, Carroll and Sapon (1959) found no evidence that language aptitude changed with time and two decades later Carroll (1981) confirmed that foreign language aptitude appeared to be relatively fixed over long periods of an individual's life span. Skehan's Bristol-linked research (just discussed) also suggests stability as evidenced by the significant correlations between related measures taken more than 10 years apart. Skehan (1989) therefore concluded that some language learning abilities emerge by the age of three and a half (which was the age at which the Bristol project first measured the participants' language skills). He also pointed out, however, that it is still not clear whether these abilities are innate or were influenced by the early environment the children were exposed to in the first three years of their lives.

More recently, however, Harley and Hart (1997) have shown that the picture is not so straightforward. Investigating Grade 7 and Grade 11 immersion school children they analyzed how the predictive qualities of different aptitude components changed with age. Their findings show that different components of aptitude were implicated in the different age groups: With younger children, the stronger correlations were found with the memory components, whereas with older learners it was the language analysis subtests which had the highest explanatory power. In a follow-up study, Harley and Hart (2002) found further evidence that the nature of the aptitude–outcome relationship can change with age:

> In sum, there are several findings in this study that provide some support for the argument that analytical language ability is more closely associated with second language outcomes when intensive exposure to the language is first experienced in adolescence. This relationship appears to hold, though not as strongly, even when exposure takes place in an environment outside the second language classroom. (p. 329)

Furthermore, we should also note Grigorenko et al.'s (2000) argument that the claim that aptitude is relatively fixed is dependent on how the aptitude construct is conceptualized to start with. In their view, for example, language aptitude is partly based on expertise in certain kinds of information processing that, like any other kinds of expertise, can be developed. Thus, these scholars look at language aptitude as a form of developing expertise rather than as an entity fixed at birth.

Language Aptitude and Intelligence

One of the most persistent issues in the L2 aptitude literature has been the relationship between language aptitude and general intelligence. This is understandable: If the predictive power of language aptitude is almost entirely due to the commonalities it shares with intelligence, we would need to reconsider the importance attached to the construct, whereas if we find that aptitude exerts its influence above that of intelligence, that would confirm the validity of the concept. Of course, we should realize that the whole issue is somewhat artificial because past research has revealed that both intelligence and language aptitude are composite constructs, subsuming a number of distinct components. Therefore, it is likely that instead of a clear-cut relationship between the two higher-order factors (i.e., 'intelligence' and 'language aptitude') there is a complex pattern of interrelationships between their constituent components: Some cognitive components of general (i.e., non-language-specific) mental abilities will undoubtedly play a role in one's language learning capacity, whereas some others might be irrelevant. It all depends on how we conceptualize the two constructs and what learning situation we are considering (the situational dependence of language aptitude will be discussed in detail later).

In reality, of course, when scholars talk about the relationship of language aptitude and intelligence, what they mean is the relationship between language aptitude test scores and intelligence test scores. Looking at the intelligence–language aptitude interaction from this perspective does make more sense, because it is indeed an interesting question to decide whether one's L2 learning capacity is better measured/predicted by a non-language-specific intelligence test or by a specially designed instrument focusing on language-related tasks. However, the fact that both intelligence and language aptitude batteries consist of several relatively independent subsections makes even this issue look somewhat arbitrary, because language aptitude tests usually contain certain subsections that are standard parts of intelligence tests as well, the most obvious example being that both the MLAT and the PLAB include an L1 vocabulary test, which is a central component of the measurement of intelligence in general (cf. Ehrman, 1998). Thus, we can assume that because both intelligence and language aptitude are composite constructs that involve a range of cognitive factors some of which, but not all, clearly overlap, we can expect considerable but not perfect correlation between the two higher-order factors. As the following overview of some of the past research findings will show, this has indeed been the case.

In the manual of the MLAT, Carroll and Sapon (1959) reported correlations ranging from 0.34 to 0.52 between the MLAT and various intelligence batteries. They concluded that although IQ was a correlate of foreign language success, its impact on it was smaller than on many other types of school courses:

> Most of the commonly employed intelligence tests measure a number of abilities simultaneously—verbal ability, reasoning ability, memory ability, and others. While a few of these abilities may be relevant to foreign language success, most are not and their net effect is to depress the correlation of intelligence with foreign language success. (p. 22)

Research conducted by Gardner (1985) and Skehan (1986) also confirmed the partial separation and partial relatedness of intelligence and language aptitude. Gardner and Lambert (1972) for example reported a median correlation of 0.43 between IQ and aptitude measures and Skehan (1989) quoted very similar results, a correlation of 0.44, from his earlier research. In contrast, Robinson (2002a) reported a considerably weaker relationship: In his study the correlation between scores on the Wechsler Adult Intelligence

Scale and the Language Aptitude Battery for the Japanese (Sasaki, 1996) was only 0.17, which did not even reach significance. We should also note Sasaki's (1991, 1996) results after comparing the scores of a number of intelligence and aptitude tests: She found that although a first-order factor analysis of the aptitude and intelligence scores revealed some separation between the two areas, a second-order factor analysis suggested that one common factor could account for the variance in the intelligence measures and some of the aptitude variables. Sasaki's findings echo those by Wesche et al. (1982), who compared the MLAT and Thurstone and Thurstone's Primary Mental Abilities Test.

In sum, the complex of general intelligence and the complex of language aptitude share definite commonalities but do not coincide completely. The more precisely we identify the various independent components of language aptitude, the more clearly we can establish which cognitive components have direct, indirect, zero, or even negative bearing on one's language learning capacity. Thus, I am in agreement with Sawyer and Ranta's (2001) conclusion that "treating L2 aptitude in a monolithic way obscures the nature of the relationship between general cognitive abilities and specific linguistic ones" (p. 329).

Language Aptitude, Teaching Methods, and Learning Situations

Earlier in this chapter I mentioned briefly that one reason for the decreased interest in language aptitude research in the 1970s and 1980s was the fact that the concept had come to be associated with certain outmoded methodologies such as the audiolingual method. Scholars and practitioners appeared to agree that language aptitude was less relevant to communicative language teaching, an approach that advocated meaningful language use and participatory communicative experience as the main means of language attainment, and aptitude effects were even less salient when language learning took place outside the classroom environment as part of the more naturalistic language acquisitional processes. For example, as Ehrman (1998) describes, the MLAT has become less used in the language courses offered by the Foreign Service Institute and other US agencies because "it had become the subject of some controversy" (p. 31) due, at least partly, to the just mentioned reasons. Therefore, the fundamental question is this: Are different learning methods, or types of exposure to learning input, associated with different kinds of language aptitude? In other words, how situated is the concept of language aptitude?

The answer to these questions is twofold. On the one hand, the available research evidence points to the conclusion that language aptitude has a robust effect that is not restricted to specific teaching methodologies and learning situations. Having observed the changing perception of language aptitude information in the Foreign Service Institute, Ehrman and Oxford (1995) launched a research project to test whether the reservations were justified. They found that despite the communicative changes in teaching methodology, the MLAT "continues to correlate with overall learning success at more or less the same levels as it did in the heyday of audiolingual training" (p. 76). These results confirm Carroll and Sapon's (1959) original proposal that the MLAT addresses learning abilities that are independent of methodology. In their review of language aptitude research, Sawyer and Ranta (2001) also conclude that the predictive value of the aptitude measures is maintained in a variety of settings and it is usually found to be relevant to L2 learning in both implicit and explicit conditions.

On the other hand, Peter Robinson has recently initiated an important line of research focusing on the microanalysis of the interrelationship between cognitive factors and situated SLA processes, and his results indicate that different types of learning processes are best enhanced by certain combinations of aptitude factors. This work is described in a separate section later. In addition, Sternberg's (2002) conception of aptitude, based on his theory of 'successful intelligence,' also assumes a strong situational and methodological dependency, which suggests that this issue is still far from being settled.

The Purpose of Language Aptitude Testing

There are a variety of reasons for which aptitude test scores can be used:

- *Research:* An unambiguous area of employing aptitude tests is in research studies in which scholars want to control for or further investigate cognitive ability factors.

- *Selection:* The most obvious application of a language aptitude test is in selection procedures and, indeed, most of the tests described earlier have been used as selection devices in different contexts. The Defense Language Aptitude Battery (Petersen & Al-Haik, 1976), for example, was developed and employed for the purpose of the selection of army personnel for intensive language training programs. By doing so it was hoped that the costs of the training and the amount of time it took could be reduced and hopeless language learners could be screened out.

- *Allocating resources:* By streaming language learners according to their aptitude scores, program administrators can have a more precise understanding of the extent of extra resources that the lower-aptitude groups might need to achieve the required level of proficiency.

- *Program evaluation:* By administering aptitude tests it may be possible to compare the learners' actual achievement with the achievement one might expect on the basis of their L2 learning ability. This would allow for a more accurate evaluation of the effectiveness of language teaching programs.

- *Tailoring instruction to the learners' aptitude level:* From an educational point of view this might be the most interesting line of research. Several scholars have suggested (e.g., Ehrman, 1996; Sawyer & Ranta, 2001; Skehan, 1989, 1998) that aptitude tests can be used to identify the particular cognitive strengths and learning style preferences of groups of learners, so that this diagnostic information can be used to tailor the quality and quantity of language instruction accordingly. Let us stop here for a moment and elaborate on this issue.

The original research basis for the belief that aptitude tests can serve practical, educational purposes was provided by a seminal study by Wesche (1981), who examined how instruction could be adapted to take account of aptitude differences. Wesche investigated the French language training program of the Public Service Commission of Canada, where language aptitude tests (a combination of the subtests of the MLAT and the PLAB) had long been used for prognostic and diagnostic purposes. The program offered three different types of language instruction: (a) an *audio-visual method*, (b) an *analytical approach*, and (c) a *functional approach*. The audio-visual method was the core method used with most of the students but in the other two groups learners received alternative instruction. Those who did well on the 'Words in Sentences' and 'Spelling Clues' subtests of the MLAT were assigned to the analytical approach. Those learners, on the other hand, who had good memory and auditory abilities but achieved low scores on the tests measuring analytical abilities were assigned to the functional approach to help them overcome difficulties associated with their less developed analytic abilities.

According to Wesche (1981), learners receiving this type of differentiated instruction reported overall satisfaction with the methods assigned to them and felt more comfortable during lessons. Analytic learners matched with an analytic methodology did better than such learners matched with the audiolingual methodology, and memory-oriented learners also did better with the memory-oriented functional approach that involved learning longer chunks of unanalyzed language. This Canadian example clearly shows the usefulness of the matching procedure. Skehan (1986) also reported results suggesting the emergence of the same two learner profiles, analytic and memory-oriented, and in agreement with Wesche he argued that given the right kind of instructional input both types of learner could be successful.

NEW RESEARCH DIRECTIONS AND PERSPECTIVES

The past 15 years has brought about several novel lines of investigation within the broad area of cognitive abilities in SLA. The common theme in all these directions is that they examine the impact of various *specific* cognitive ID factors and subprocesses (such as phonological coding or working memory) in detail, going thus beyond the use of the language aptitude metaphor as an umbrella term. Perhaps the most traditional in these new approaches is the development of a new language aptitude test by Grigorenko et al. (2000) in the sense that these authors still focus on the composite aptitude concept, although they conceptualize it rather differently from the Carroll-tradition. We begin the discussion with this work.

Grigorenko, Sternberg, and Ehrman's Research on Language Aptitude

Recently, Grigorenko et al. (2000) have devised a new test of L2 learning aptitude, the Cognitive Ability for Novelty in Acquisition of Language as applied to foreign language test (CANAL-FT). In contrast to the MLAT or the PLAB, which had emerged from the tradition of psychometric test development, the CANAL-FT has been theory driven, drawing on Sternberg's triarchic theory of human intelligence (Sternberg, 2002). This theory is also called the 'theory of successful intelligence' because it concerns the cognitive abilities that are necessary for success in everyday life rather than merely in school learning situations. According to the theory, intelligence is seen as the complex of three aspects: *analytical, creative,* and *practical* metacomponents. *Analytical intelligence* is involved when the components of intelligence are applied to analyze, evaluate, judge, compare, and contrast. *Creative intelligence* is called on when having to cope with novelty and when being involved in processes of creating, inventing, and discovering. *Practical intelligence* concerns dealing with problems and issues that one is confronted with in daily life, such as on the job or in the home, involving the abilities to apply and implement knowledge. Sternberg argue that there is a common set of processes underlying these three dimensions, comprising various *metacomponents* such as planning, monitoring, and evaluating, and *performance components* that are in charge of executing the instructions of the metacomponents.

The main emphasis in the CANAL-FT is on measuring how people cope with novelty and ambiguity in their learning. This is done in a naturalistic context by gradually introducing an artificial language, and testtakers are to perform a number of mini-learning tasks. These involve five knowledge acquisition processes:

1. *Selective encoding:* Distinguishing between more and less relevant information for one's purposes.

2. *Accidental encoding:* Encoding background or secondary information and grasping the background context of the information stream.

3. *Selective comparison:* Determining the relevance of old information for current tasks to enhance learning.

4. *Selective transfer:* Applying decoded or inferred rules to new contexts and tasks.

5. *Selective combination:* Synthesizing the disparate pieces of information that have been collected via selective and accidental encoding.

These five knowledge acquisition processes are operationalized at four language levels—lexical, morphological, semantic, and syntactic—and in two modes of input and output: visual and oral. The permutations of these parameters already create a complex and rich design, but the test adds one final dimension: As the authors argue, for language learning to take place, the linguistic material must be understood and *encoded* into working memory and then *stored* in long-term memory for later *retrieval*; these aspects of encoding, storage, and retrieval can be assessed through two types of recall tasks: *immediate recall* right after learning has taken place; and *delayed recall* at some substantial time interval after learning has taken place.

Table 3.3 presents a description of Grigorenko et al.'s (2000) instrument. As can be seen, it is entirely based on the gradual and incremental learning of an artificial language; interestingly, an aptitude test developed in

Table 3.3. The Canal-FT Language Aptitude Test

The CANAL-FT comprises nine sections: Five involve immediate recall and the other four are identical to these five sections except that they are presented later and involve delayed recall (the last section does not have a delayed counterpart). A common element of the sections is that they all focus on the learning of an artificial language, Ursulu. This is presented gradually, so that initially participants have no knowledge of the language; by the end of the test, however, they have mastered enough lexical, morphological, semantic, and syntactic knowledge to cope with a small story in Ursulu. The five sections are as follows:

1. *Learning meanings of neologisms from context:* Participants are presented with 24 brief paragraphs within a 2 x 3 factorial design (type of presentation: oral or visual x density of unknown words: low, medium, or high). Understanding is tested via a multiple-choice format, where students are asked to guess which of five alternatives is most likely to correspond to the meaning of an unknown neologism inserted into the text. Two multiple-choice items are presented immediately after receipt of every passage and one item relevant to every passage is presented at least 30 minutes after receipt of the passages in order to measure storage in long-term memory.

2. *Understanding the meaning of passages:* The six test items in this part are identical in form to those in Section 1, but the assessment involves comprehension of whole passages rather than merely of lexical items. Again, half of the items are presented visually, the other half orally, and the passages differ in terms of the density of unknown words. The test differs from standard reading and oral comprehension tests in the inclusion of unknown words in the passages. Such words render these passages more like those that would be encountered in the process of learning an L2.

3. *Continuous paired-associate learning*: In this test, participants are presented with 60 paired associates (word pairs), half of them visually, half of them orally. They are required to learn the successive pairings and during this process they are tested at irregular intervals on words learned more recently as well as less recently. The test differs from a straightforward paired-associates memory test in that there are certain rules that can facilitate learning, relating some of the terms to others.

4. *Sentential inference*: Participants receive 20 sets of three to five sentences in the Ursulu language with their translations presented either visually or orally. They are then presented with a new sentence, either in English or in Ursulu, and are asked to indicate—based on inferences made from the previously presented sentence pairs—which of five mul-

tiple-choice answers best represents the translation.

5. *Learning language rules:* Participants are given some vocabulary, some grammar, and some examples of how the Ursulu language works. From this type of information they are expected to learn some of the most evident rules of the language. To measure this learning, they are presented with 12 items (lexical, semantic, morphological, and syntactic) that test their understanding of the Ursulu language.

Japan at exactly the same time, the Lunic Language Marathon, by Sick and Irie (2000), also focused on how the learners (seen as 'imaginary space travelers') master aspects of the hitherto unknown language of the planet 'Luna.' With regard to CANAL-FT, to validate the test, the authors report on a correlational study in which the convergent validity of the measurement provided by the CANAL-FT was appraised by means of its correlations with the MLAT, and its discriminant validity was assessed through the test's correlations with two established intelligence measures. The initial results were promising, indicating the viability of the CANAL theory; they also highlighted future research directions, for example the need to look into how the test scores relate to working memory measures. In general, as the authors conclude, their "work should be viewed as a foundation for further development rather than as a completed effort" (Grigorenko et al., 2000, p. 401).

Sparks and Ganschow's Linguistic Coding Differences Hypothesis

A systematic line of research by Richard Sparks, Leonore Ganschow, and their associates has focused on what they have labeled the Linguistic Coding Differences Hypothesis (LCDH). According to the hypothesis, one's capacity to learn an L2 is closely related to the individual's L1 learning skills, and L2 learning difficulties stem in part from native language difficulties (e.g., Sparks, 1995; Sparks & Ganschow, 1991, 1999, 2001; Sparks et al., 1995, 1998). The central cognitive factor the theory focused on is *'linguistic coding,'* which refers to L1 literacy skills such as phonological/orthographic processing and word recognition/decoding (i.e., single-word reading). The LCDH proposes that these abilities serve as the foundation for learning an L2, and an insufficient level of development in linguistic coding skills has a profound impact on L2 learning ability, resulting in a serious handicap. Thus, linguistic coding ability can be seen as a primary ID variable.

Sparks, Ganschow, and their colleagues have accumulated an impressive amount of evidence supporting their hypothesis and there is also some data from other research that is in accordance with their conclusions. One of the main types of LCDH studies has involved conducting comparative analyses of good and poor L2 learners in various age groups and learning situations to see whether they differed in their linguistic coding skills. As Sparks and Ganschow (2001) summarized, the findings consistently revealed that (a) successful L2 learners exhibited significantly stronger L1 literacy skills than unsuccessful learners, and they were also superior on L1 syntactic measures but not on semantic tasks; and (b) successful L2 learners had significantly stronger language aptitude (measured by the MLAT). In one study the researchers also found that L2 word recognition was one of the best predictors of English proficiency. Based on these findings Sparks and Ganschow recommend that one important way of improving language aptitude measures is to elaborate on phonological measures both in the learners' L1 and L2 by including in the instruments relevant tasks such as word recognition, pseudoword decoding, phonological memory, and phonemic awareness.

The significance of L1 literacy skills in L2 studies has also been highlighted in an important longitudinal study conducted by Dufva and Voeten (1999), investigating 160 Finnish elementary school children from the first to the third grade. The researchers examined two cognitive areas, L1 literacy acquisition and phonological memory (the latter being part of 'working memory' and is discussed next) in terms of their impact on learning English as a foreign language. The longitudinal design of their investigation allowed them to establish cause–effect relationships, which they then confirmed using structural equation modeling. Measures obtained in Grade 1 were L1 word recognition and listening comprehension; in the second grade L1 word recognition, reading comprehension, and phonological memory; and in the third grade, L2 skills. The authors found that both L1 literacy and phonological memory had positive effects on L2 learning, together explaining 58% of the variance in English proficiency. This is a remarkably high figure (corresponding to a multiple correlation of around 0.76), rarely encountered in L2 studies, and its magnitude is particularly noteworthy because the tasks measuring English proficiency covered a wide range of competencies, focusing on listening comprehension, communicative skills, and active vocabulary knowledge.

The authors have also found that it is *not* the rate of development in word recognition from first to second grade that mattered but the *ultimate level* achieved by the end of Grade 2: The faster the children's speed of word recognition was, the better they were at English. In fact, the level of development of L1 word recognition was the strongest predictor of L2 learning in the whole study. Based on these results, Dufva and Voeten (1999) concluded that native language word recognition formed the basis of learning an L2. Therefore, in agreement with Sparks and Ganschow (2001), they recommended that educators assess L1 literacy skills early on so that at-risk children can be provided with intensive literacy instruction, especially in the prerequisites of word recognition (e.g., phonological awareness), in order to enhance their learning an L2.

An additional element of Sparks and Ganschow's (1995, 1999; Sparks, Ganschow & Javorsky, 2000) overall thesis has been that affective differences between students with lower and higher levels of L2 skills (e.g., differences in anxiety) are a consequence of their differing levels of self-perceptions about their L2 learning skills. Thus, as they claimed, students with high levels of anxiety, poor language attitudes, and low motivation in the L2 classroom are likely to be those who have a history of and current difficulty with some aspect of their native language skills. This view has been strongly contested by MacIntyre (1995a, 1995b, 1999) and Horwitz (2000; for more detail, see the discussion on anxiety in chapt. 7).

Working Memory and Language Aptitude

Research into the relationship between *working memory* and SLA appears to be one of the most promising current directions in language aptitude studies, and as Miyaki and Friedman (1998, p. 339) conclude, "working memory for language may be one (if not the) central component of this language aptitude." Memory has traditionally been part of every aptitude model but with a complex domain such as memory the secret lies in the details, that is, how the construct is conceptualized. With regard to the memory component of the MLAT, even Carroll (1990) admitted that he had never been completely confident about the validity of the rote-learning subtest. And given that memory research has made enormous progress during the past two decades in cognitive psychology, we can safely conclude that this area lends itself to improvement in modern aptitude testing.

Working memory involves the "temporary storage and manipulation of information that is assumed to be necessary for a wide range of complex cognitive activities" (Baddeley, 2003, p. 189); thus, it underpins our capacity for thinking and has important specific implications for language processing. Gathercole and Thorn (1998), for example, drew attention to the possible contribution of the verbal component of working memory, the 'phonological loop,' to the learning of the sound patterns of new L2 words. Indeed, the concept of working memory appears to be an ideally suited memory construct for SLA purposes because besides its phonological short-term memory constituent it also comprises a featured 'attention' component, and the role of attention and attentional capacity has been a key research target in recent SLA research (cf. Robinson, 2003). For this reason, Ellis

(2001) emphasized that the concept deserves much more consideration than it has been thus far given in L2 studies.

In an analysis of the role of working memory within the language aptitude complex, Sawyer and Ranta (2001) agreed that working memory capacity may be the key to elaborating the concept of language aptitude and to integrating aptitude into the SLA process. They argue that the concept has several advantages over the traditional short-term memory construct, which it has replaced in the literature, because working memory is more than a passive transitional storage stage preceding long-term memory: It is a more active system, comprising an independent temporary cognitive workspace or 'computational arena' (Miyake & Friedman, 1998) with ongoing processing functions (hence the 'working' part of the term), used for sequential cognitive processes, such as the comprehension and production of language.

How is the construct of 'working memory' structured? In 1974 Baddeley and Hitch proposed that it could be divided into four subsystems (for a recent review, see Baddeley, 2003):

(1) *The phonological loop* is the specialized verbal component of working memory, concerned with the temporary storage of verbal and acoustic information. The stored material is subject to rapid decay (over approximately two seconds) but the loss of information can be offset by 'subvocal rehearsal,' which reactivates the decaying representations and which can also translate visual information into phonological form.

(2) *The visuospatial sketchpad* is the visual equivalent of the phonological loop, responsible for integrating spatial, visual, and kinesthetic information into a unified representation, which can be temporarily stored and manipulated. This system is involved, for example, in everyday reading tasks but its functioning has been less studied than that of the phonological loop. Baddeley suggests, however, that similarly to the phonological loop, the visuospatial sketchpad also has a storage and a processing component (the letter termed the 'inner scribe') which can, for example, translate verbal information into an image-based code.

(3) *The central executive* is the most important and least understood aspect of working memory, responsible for its attentional control. It constitutes the supervisory attentional system that allocates attentional resources and regulates the selection, initiation, and termination of processing routines (e.g., encoding, storing, and retrieving). Thus, it receives, coordinates, and integrates information from the subsystems of the visuospatial sketchpad and the phonological loop as well as from long-term memory to carry out complex cognitive tasks such as future planning, decision making, mathematical calculations, and reasoning. It is also involved in performing reading and comprehension, and—interestingly—

in trouble-shooting in situations in which the automatic processes run into difficulty, which links it to the use of communication strategies (cf. Dörnyei & Kormos, 1998). The central executive is of particular relevance to our discussion because the executive processes are thought to be the principal factors determining individual differences in 'working memory span' (Baddeley, 2003; Daneman & Carpenter, 1980).

(4) *The episodic buffer* has recently been added to the working memory construct to constitute a storage counterpart of the central executive, which is now seen as a purely control system without any storage capacity. The episodic buffer combines information from different sources and modalities into a single, multi-faceted code, or 'episode'—hence the 'episodic' part of the label. It is assumed to underpin the capacity for conscious awareness.

The overall capacity of working memory can be expressed in terms of the *working memory span*. This has proved to be a robust predictor of a wide range of complex cognitive skills and it is highly correlated with performance on the type of reasoning tasks that underpin standard tests of intelligence. It is measured by instruments and procedures whereby participants are typically required to combine some sort of (a) processing and (b) storage of information in a dynamic and simultaneous manner; thus, the assessment goes beyond traditional memory tests such as digit or word span measures. Table 3.4 describes one of the best-known instruments developed by Daneman and Carpenter (1980).

Miyake and Friedman (1998) emphasized that although working memory plays a central role in all forms of higher-level cognition, its role is particularly featured in language processing because both the production and the comprehension of language requires the processing of sequences of symbols over time in a linear manner. This linearity inherently necessitates a temporal storing capacity and the ability to integrate information from the stream of successive discourse. According to the current conceptualization, working memory matches these simultaneous processing and storage requirements perfectly. The authors therefore conclude that individual differences in LI working memory capacity for language are closely related not only to L2 working memory capacity and L2 language comprehension skills but also to the speed and efficiency of the acquisition of L2 knowledge.

Table 3.4. Description of Daneman and Carpenter's (1980) Reading Span Test

Participants are asked to read aloud a set of unrelated sentences and then recall the final word of each sentence in that set. The 9 to 16 word long sentences were taken from general knowledge quiz books and each ended in a different word; e.g.,

- *"You can trace the languages English and German back to the same roots."*
- *"The Supreme Court of the United States has eleven justices."*

The processing element of the test is provided by the task that after reading each sentence the participants have to decide whether it was true or false—the sentences are of moderate difficulty, with half of them being true and the other half false.

The total test contains three sets each of two, three, four, five, and six sentences and the participants are presented increasingly longer sets until they fail to recall the sentence-final words of all three sets at a particular level.

The level at which a participant is correct on two out of three sets is taken as a measure of the individual's reading span. Being correct on only one set at a particular level is given a credit of .5. Miyake and Friedman (1998) added that in some studies the reading span measure has been the total number of sentence-final words recalled from all the trials.

The test also has a listening version, which works along the same lines and which correlates well with the reading span.

Sawyer and Ranta (2001) reported a number of studies that have demonstrated a fairly strong relationship between working memory capacity and L2 proficiency, as well as between L1 and L2 working memory capacity. Their conclusion is quite positive:

> If further research confirms WM [working memory] capacity to be a stable individual difference among learners, its potential importance in SLA will be clear. Assuming that noticing is crucial to learning, and attention is required for noticing, and attention at any moment is limited by WM capacity, then there must logically be a close relationship between amount of learning and size of WM. It is also likely that WM serves as an arena in which the effects of other components of aptitude are integrated. (p. 342)

Finally, let me return to Segalowitz's (1997) synthesis of SLA, cognitive, and neuropsychological frameworks mentioned earlier. Based on his

broad review of the literature, Segalowitz highlights the paramount importance of *neurocognitive flexibility* for the successful handling of the complexity of linguistic input. As he argues, the full processing of linguistic input requires the recognition of a number of diverse aspects, ranging from
sound sequences through syntactic patterns to nonlinguistic cues, and it also
requires the coordination of one's own communicative responses in a situa-
tionally appropriate manner. Thus, Segalowitz continues, effective L2 performance entails rapid shifting of attention from one communicative dimension to another, which presupposes a "high degree of perceptual and production fluency and the requisite neurocognitive flexibility to accomplish this"
(p. 104). It seems to me that the degree of flexible attentional and resource
control that Segalowitz outlines is to a large extent the function of one's
working memory capacity, which again underlines the importance of the
concept of working memory regarding second language acquisition and use.

Robinson's Research on the Aptitude–Treatment Interaction

A central issue in ID research, and one that has emerged in aptitude research
in particular, is the question as to whether there are any optimal combinations of ID variables that are especially conducive to efficient learning. Of
course, this question would not have risen if some scholars had not assumed
that such constellations of learner traits existed; one researcher in particular,
Richard Snow, was influential in highlighting the potential importance of
such ID variable clusters, or as he called them, *aptitude complexes*. His initiative has been taken up by several of his colleagues and students (cf. Ackerman, 2003; Corno et al., 2002) because, "Although isolated traits often
have ... substantial impact on learning outcomes, it may be that combinations of traits have more predictive power than traits in isolation" (Ackerman, 2003, p. 92). Furthermore, the concept of 'aptitude complexes' can
also be combined with Cronbach's 'aptitude–treatment interaction' approach
that concerns the ways by which mental abilities interact with learning conditions, resulting in a powerful situated ID paradigm for learning. This is the
theoretical foundation that Peter Robinson (e.g., 2001, 2002d, in press) drew
on when he launched his pioneering research program on language aptitude-
treatment interaction. He conceptualized language aptitude as the sum of
lower level abilities, grouped into cognitive factors, which differentially
support learning in various learning situations/conditions.

We have already seen that the relationship between language aptitude
and learning methods/situations has traditionally been a focal issue in aptitude studies; indeed, in his review of the history of language aptitude research Spolsky (1995) pointed out that scholars claimed already in the 1930s
that language aptitude could only be defined in the context of the teaching

method that was to be used. Segalowitz (1997) approached the question from a very different perspective—the synthesis of SLA, cognitive, and neuropsychological frameworks—yet arrived at the same conclusion: "what we perceive as language learning ability is not a fixed characteristic of a person but rather a complex reflection of the whole learning situation" (p. 108). He viewed the learner as situated in a "complex, dynamic, communicative environment that imposes many different kinds of cognitive demands" (p. 107), and as he argued, "Individuals will differ in L2 mastery, therefore, as a function of how effectively their perceptual and cognitive processes can meet these demands" (p. 107).

The significance of Robinson's aptitude research lay in the fact that he has made the first attempt in the L2 field to describe concrete sets of cognitive demands that can be associated with some basic learning types/tasks, and then to identify specific aptitude complexes to match these cognitive processing conditions. He argued that this approach not only had theoretical implications but was also a fruitful directions in terms of practical relevance:

> Profiling individual differences in cognitive abilities, and matching these profiles to effective instructional options, such as types of pedagogic tasks, interventionist 'focus on form' techniques, and more broadly defined learning conditions, is a major aim of pedagogically oriented language aptitude research. (p. 113)

With regard to the specific learning types, Robinson distinguished three conditions of exposure to input—implicit, incidental, and explicit learning—and then discussed a number of *cognitive resources* (e.g., attentional or working memory capacity) and *primary abilities* (e.g., pattern recognition or processing speed) that combine to define sets of *higher-order abilities* directly involved in carrying out learning tasks (e.g., noticing the gap, or metalinguistic rule rehearsal). These second-order abilities can then be grouped into aptitude complexes that exert an optimal influence on learning in specific learning conditions, such as focus on form via recasts; incidental learning via oral or written content (by means of orally or typographically salient 'input floods'); and explicit rule learning.

This is clearly a complex, multilayered system, which needs to be elaborated on to come truly into its own. However, the framework succeeds in taking into account two crucial aspect of learning abilities, their situational dependence and their combined impact. These are indeed major advances because L2 learning aptitude is conceived here as a dynamic construct, reflecting the interrelationship of clusters of learner variables with the cognitive demands of specific L2 learning tasks and instructional techniques (Robinson, in press). Such a dynamic conceptualization also makes aptitude research more compatible with SLA research, for example in the study of input and output, language learning tasks, and different types of learning, as well as in the analysis of different instructional approaches (Robinson, 2001). Thus, Robinson has been the first scholar to create viable links between ID research and aspects of SLA, and I can only hope that his suggestions and initial framework will be taken up by other researchers in an effort to enrich our knowledge about how various cognitive skills impact on L2 acquisition and performance.

Skehan's Conception of Language Aptitude and SLA

In conclusion to our discussion of language aptitude, let us look at another line of research, by Peter Skehan, that has great potential for future developments because—similarly to Robinson's theory just outlined—it attempts to relate various aptitude components to the different phases of the SLA process. This approach, therefore, can also lead to a closer integration of the study of SLA and aptitude. Skehan (1998, 2002; Dörnyei & Skehan, 2003) argued that by taking a componential approach to analyzing aptitude we may identify certain aptitudinal constituents that are relevant not simply to formal classroom learning but also to various general aspects or stages of SLA processing. Furthermore, Skehan maintained that aptitude is also illuminating regarding the nature of cognitive abilities in general and is central to any evaluation of the relevance of Universal Grammar for L2 learning. He noted, however, that this reinterpretation of aptitude and its linkage with putative SLA processing stages and other mental constructs goes beyond the models of language aptitude which currently exist, and highlighted the lack of correspondence between the currently available aptitude sub-tests and the theoretically plausible aptitude constituents.

Table 3.5 presents Skehan's proposal of theoretical matches between stages of SLA and aptitude components. The putative aptitude constructs shown in the table are the results of Skehan's attempt to first determine whether learners would show individual variation in the various L2 processing phases and if so, whether this variation could be explained by the effects of existing language aptitude components. If the answer to the first question was yes and to the second no, Skehan proposed an additional aptitude construct. In the aptitude column in the table the components that have not as yet been explicitly addressed by existing aptitude tests are printed in italics. This is an interesting example of SLA research serving as a driving force for extending aptitude research. Some of the correspondences indicated in the table require little justification; for example, phonetic coding ability can be related to input processing; language analytic ability (grammatical sensitivity and inductive language learning) to central processing; and memory-as-retrieval to output and fluency. Skehan admits that the system described in Table 3.5 is speculative but, as he claims, his emphasis at this stage has been not so much to identify all the components of SLA and aptitude in a comprehensive manner and to establish their exact matches as to illustrate the full potential of this approach.

With some operational updating, some of the existing aptitude constructs may be serviceable starting points for this reconceptualization of aptitude; however, there are a number of areas indicated in the right-hand column of Table 3.5 which are simply unrepresented at present, and which need to be addressed at an operational level if SLA and aptitude are to come into a more satisfactory relationship. Table 3.5, in other words, also suggests a research agenda regarding areas where new aptitude sub-tests could beneficially be developed (Skehan, 2002).

Table 3.5. Skehan's proposal of SLA stages and aptitude constructs

SLA Stage	Corresponding Aptitude Constructs
Input processing strategies, such as segmentation	*Attentional control* *Working memory*
Noticing	Phonetic coding ability *Working memory*
Pattern identification	Phonetic coding ability *Working memory* Grammatical sensitivity Inductive language learning ability
Pattern restructuring and manipulation	Grammatical sensitivity Inductive language learning ability
Pattern control	*Automatization* *Integrative memory*
Pattern integration	*Chunking* *Retrieval memory*

CONCLUSION

Although the progress of language aptitude research has not always been even, we can conclude that this line of investigation, as a whole, has been a success story within L2 studies. This is partly justified by the long history and the amount of high-quality research associated with this area and partly by the active involvement of some outstanding cognitive psychologists, most notably John Carroll and Robert Sternberg, in the conceptualizing of language aptitude: These researchers have been world leaders in their broader field, and their contribution puts language aptitude research in a unique place among the study of other psychological areas in SLA.

Reviewing the past research activity in the field, it becomes clear that after the relative lull in the 1970s and 1980s, language aptitude research has recovered completely and currently it is one of the most promising areas of SLA research. There is strong evidence that there exist some robust cognitive abilities that have a pervasive influence on all aspects of L2 attainment, and contemporary language aptitude researchers appear to display sufficient psychometric know-how and psycholinguistic background to explore these abilities.

It is also clear that the area of language aptitude research is in transition and we can observe several general trends:

- Contemporary research is leaving behind the Carroll tradition and is drawing increasingly on cognitive psychology, psycholinguistics, and neurolinguistics.

- The term *language aptitude* is becoming increasingly restricted to refer to composite measures obtained by means of aptitude batteries, whereas scholars who focus on specific cognitive abilities, such as working memory, tend to avoid using the term.

- There is a move, similarly to other areas within individual difference research (e.g., motivation), to view language aptitude in a situated manner, examining the dynamic interplay between aptitude and context.

- Contextually sensitive measures of language aptitude open up brand new possibilities for integrating aptitude research into mainstream SLA studies, and they also allow researchers to link cognitive abilities to instructed SLA and classroom practice in a useful way.

There are several directions for language aptitude research that are likely to be productive in the future. One that has been pioneered by Peter Robinson in L2 studies involves the study of aptitude measures in combination with other ID variables in various trait complexes, also examining the interaction of these complexes with instructional and situational variables. The second important area is to explore further the role of working memory both in SLA and the language aptitude complex. I fully agree with Miyake and Friedman (1998) that the 'working-memory-as-language-aptitude' proposal is a promising hypothesis, particularly because, as these scholars point out, language working memory can capture the essence of all the three important components of the language aptitude construct proposed by Skehan (1989) on the basis of Carroll's conception: language analytic capacity, memory ability, and phonetic coding ability. However, we should also note Robinson's (2002a) caution that working memory capacity alone cannot be equated with aptitude for language learning; as he argued, effective aptitude complexes also subsume other cognitive abilities and therefore the undoubtedly prominent working memory processes needs to be supplemented by other ID variables in any future conceptualization. A third area that might be fruitful is to further examine the influence of cognitive skills associated with L1 learning on the capacity to master an L2, following the research efforts of Sparks, Ganschow, and their associates, as well as Dufva and Voeten. Finally, a line of investigation that has considerable future potential is Skehan's proposal to try and explicitly link certain aptitude components with specific phases of the SLA process.

4

Motivation and 'Self-Motivation'

It is appropriate that the coverage of language aptitude in chapter 3 should be followed by the discussion of the other major ID variable that has been found to significantly affect language learning success: *motivation*. It is easy to see why motivation is of great importance in SLA: It provides the primary impetus to initiate L2 learning and later the driving force to sustain the long and often tedious learning process; indeed, all the other factors involved in SLA presuppose motivation to some extent. Without sufficient motivation, even individuals with the most remarkable abilities cannot accomplish long-term goals, and neither are appropriate curricula and good teaching enough on their own to ensure student achievement. On the other hand, high motivation can make up for considerable deficiencies both in one's language aptitude and learning conditions, and Robert Sternberg (2002), one of the leading aptitude researchers of our time (whose work was briefly described in chapt. 3), goes as far as to say that:

> Much of what appears to be foreign-language learning aptitude may reflect a valuing process. In Belgium, those who learn Flemish as a first language are much more likely to learn a second and even a third language than are those who learn French as a first language. Why? Can anyone seriously believe that the difference is one of language-learning aptitude? Probably not. Rather, the difference is that of the perceived need for additional languages. There is a practical need for additional languages, and the languages are taught with this practical use in mind. (p. 19)

This argument is almost exactly the same as the one put forward by Robert Gardner and Wallace Lambert (1972) more than 30 years ago, namely that although language aptitude accounts for a considerable proportion of individual variability in language learning achievement, motivational factors can override the aptitude effect. In certain language environments, as Gardner and Lambert point out, where the social setting demands it (e.g., when the L1 is a local vernacular and the L2 is the national language), many people seem to master an L2, regardless of their aptitude differences.

Let me conclude this introductory section with a personal note: This chapter is somewhat different from the others in the sense that when discussing other ID factors I have taken on the role of the informed observer and largely restricted my contribution to a selective review of other people's work, whereas much of the material in this chapter concerns my own research. Ever since the beginning of my PhD research in the mid-1980s, which had been inspired by Gardner's seminal work, I have been actively examining the relationship of motivation and L2 attainment, and therefore my account of the topic will be inevitably subjective. My intentions in this chapter are twofold: First, I would like to outline the overall history of L2 motivation research; however, in this overview I will spend less time on the past than on the present and particularly on forward-pointing new theorizing and research. During the last few years several detailed overviews of L2 motivation research have been published representing different perspectives (e.g., Clément & Gardner, 2001; Cohen & Dörnyei, 2002; Dörnyei, 1998, 1999a, 1999b, 2000a, 2001a, 2001b, 2001c, 2003b; Dörnyei & Skehan, 2003; MacIntyre, 2002) and therefore I felt it unnecessary to simply repeat what has already been said. My second objective is to offer a new perspective on L2 motivation and reexamine some of the historical tenets in this light. The new theory that I present—the 'L2 Motivational Self System'—is broad in its scope and is compatible with the major findings of past research in the field. It does not claim to provide a comprehensive answer to all the outstanding questions—I believe that just as motivation is a dynamic, ever-changing process, its research should also evolve over time. After all, motivation concerns the fundamental question of why people think and behave as they do, and we should never assume that we know the full answer.

THREE PHASES OF L2 MOTIVATION RESEARCH

L2 motivation research has been a thriving area within L2 studies with several books and literally hundreds of articles published on the topic since the 1960s. To provide a concise overview of the field, it is useful to divide its history into three phases:

(a) *The social psychological period* (1959–1990)—characterized by the work of Gardner and his students and associates in Canada.

(b) *The cognitive-situated period* (during the 1990s)—characterized by work drawing on cognitive theories in educational psychology.

(c) *The process-oriented period* (the past five years)—characterized by an interest in motivational change, initiated by the work of Dörnyei, Ushioda, and their colleagues in Europe.

The social psychological period

The initial impetus in L2 motivation research came from social psychologists working in Canada, most notably from Wallace Lambert, Robert Gardner, and their associates. Interested in understanding the unique Canadian social situation characterized by the often confrontational coexistence of the Anglophone and Francophone communities, Gardner and Lambert (1972) viewed second languages as mediating factors between different ethnolinguistic communities and thus regarded the motivation to learn the language of the other community as a primary force responsible for enhancing or hindering intercultural communication and affiliation. These researchers adopted a social psychological approach that was based on the main tenet that "students' attitudes toward the specific language group are bound to influence how successful they will be in incorporating aspects of that language" (Gardner, 1985, p. 6). This seemingly obvious recognition had major implications both for theory and classroom practice. From a theoretical point of view, it meant that the study of L2 motivation required the supplementation of traditional motivation research—which used to focus entirely on the individual—with social psychological insights and methods concerning the relationship between the L1 and L2 communities. This integration of individualistic and social psychology in the study of the antecedents of human behavior was radically new in the 1960s and was almost three decades ahead of its time: It was only in the 1990s that motivational psychologists started to show an active interest in the social context of motivation (for reviews of social motivation, see Dörnyei, 1999b, 2001c).

From an educational point of view, Gardner and Lambert's (1972) claim indicated that unlike several other school subjects, a foreign language is not a socioculturally neutral field but is affected by a range of sociocultural factors such as language attitudes, cultural stereotypes, and even geopolitical considerations. This social argument has been accepted by researchers all over the world, regardless of the actual learning situation they were working in; for example, referring to European classroom learning contexts, Marion Williams (1994) expressed thoughts that were similar to the Canadian assertion:

> There is no question that learning a foreign language is different to learning other subjects. This is mainly because of the social nature of

such a venture. Language, after all, belongs to a person's whole social being: it is part of one's identity, and is used to convey this identity to other people. The learning of a foreign language involves far more than simply learning skills, or a system of rules, or a grammar; it involves an alteration in self-image, the adoption of new social and cultural behaviors and ways of being, and therefore has a significant impact on the social nature of the learner. (p. 77)

This distinction between foreign languages and other school subjects is a very important one, and it explains partly, for example, why the theory of L2 learning and teaching has never managed to fully integrate into the broader domain of educational studies.

Gardner's motivation theory and motivation test

Robert Gardner's motivation theory has often been described in the past and therefore here I highlight three main aspects only: Gardner's *theory of second language acquisition*, his conceptualization of *integrative motivation*, and a *test battery* that he developed with his associates and which allows for the scientific measurement of a wide range of motivational factors.

Gardner's theory of second language acquisition, the Socio-Educational Model of Second Language Acquisition, is not an elaborate model but a schematic outline of how motivation is related to other ID variables and language achievement (see Gardner, 2001, for the most recent version of the model). The model posits that language achievement is influenced by integrative motivation, language aptitude, as well as a number of other factors.

Integrative motivation is a detailed, empirically based construct that is made up of three main constituents, each of which is further broken down to subcomponents (see Fig. 4.1, for a schematic representation):

- *Integrativeness*, which subsumes integrative orientation, interest in foreign languages, and attitudes toward the L2 community, reflecting the "individual's willingness and interest in social interaction with members of other groups" (Gardner & MacIntyre, 1993a, p. 159).

- *Attitudes toward the learning situation*, which comprises attitudes toward the language teacher and the L2 course.

- *Motivation*, that is, effort, desire, and attitude toward learning.

I argued a decade ago (Dörnyei, 1994b) that the interpretation of this model has been hindered by two sources of terminological difficulty: First, the term *integrative* appears in it three times at three different levels of abstraction (integrative orientation, integrativeness, and integrative motive/

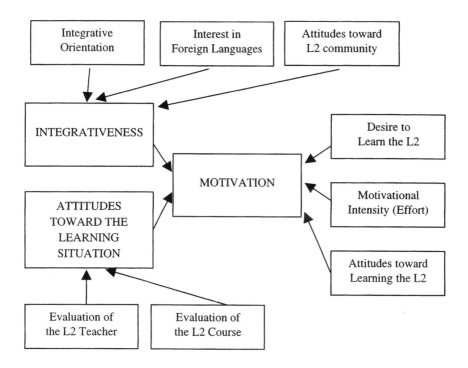

FIG. 4.1. Schematic Representation of Gardner's (1985) Conceptualization
of the Integrative Motive.

motivation), which has led to misunderstandings. The second area which causes confusion in some researchers is that within the overall construct of 'Integrative Motivation' there is a subcomponent labeled 'Motivation'. This makes it difficult to decide what is meant when Gardner talks about 'motivation' in his writings: L2 motivation in general? Integrative motivation? Or the specific 'Motivation' subcomponent of the integrative motive?

Gardner's theory has been highly acclaimed among L2 researchers and practitioners but it is fair to say that the popular interpretation has been rather different from the actual theory because L2 scholars tended to pay attention only to two prominent motivational components:

1. *An interpersonal/affective dimension*, which is usually called either *integrative orientation* or *integrative motivation.* This notion is indeed in accordance with Gardner's motivational thinking and later in this chap-

ter I analyze in detail what this component might cover and how it can be reconceptualized to fit into more recent L2 motivational theories.

2. *A practical/utilitarian dimension*, associated with the concrete benefits that language proficiency might bring about (e.g., career opportunities, increased salary). Interestingly, this dimension, which has been referred to as the *instrumental orientation/motivation*, is not part of Gardner's core theory. Although the concept of instrumental orientation does derive from Gardner's writings, in actual terms it only appears in his motivation test battery without any real theoretical clarification.

The misrepresentation of Gardner's theory as the sum of integrative and instrumental motivation has been pervasive, as evidenced even today by the many manuscripts submitted to international journals which start out by conceptualizing motivation purely (and poorly) along the instrumental–integrative dichotomy. Of course, from a human point of view this simplified misrepresentation is easy to explain in a situation where an academic field—applied linguistics—that has traditionally drawn on linguistic and educational expertise tries to incorporate such a complex psychological variable as motivation.

Recently, Gardner (2000, 2001) addressed the question of how to conceptualize Instrumental Motivation within his overall theoretical framework. He stated, "there can be other supports for motivation not directly associated with integrative motivation. Thus, there may be instrumental factors contributing to motivation, and we could label this combination of instrumental factors and Motivation as Instrumental Motivation" (Gardner, 2001, p. 7). In other words, Gardner proposes that the 'Motivation' subcomponent of the Integrative Motive can be combined with instrumentality (instead of integrativeness) to form Instrumental Motivation. This is in line with the conception that the 'Motivation' subcomponent concerns a central motivational engine that needs to be ignited by some specific learning goal such as instrumental or integrative orientation. However, integrative motivation in Gardner's model was also associated with a third major constituent, 'Attitudes toward the learning situation,' and it is not clear whether this, too, can be linked to instrumental motivation if the dominant learning goal is instrumental.

The Attitude/Motivation Test Battery (AMTB; reprinted in the Appendix of Gardner, 1985) is a multicomponential motivation questionnaire made up of over 130 items (see Table 4.1, for a list of the constituent scales with sample items), which has been shown to have good psychometric properties, including construct and predictive validity (see Gardner & MacIntyre, 1993b). It operationalizes all the main constituents of Gardner's theory of the integrative motive and it also includes the additional components of *lan-*

guage anxiety (L2 class anxiety and L2 use anxiety), *parental encouragement*, and *instrumental orientation*.

Gardner's theory was the dominant motivation model in the L2 field for more than three decades, and the AMTB as well as the advanced statistical data processing techniques that Gardner introduced set high research standards in the area. However, in retrospect, we can see that the theory has remained relatively unmodified over time: Gardner's famous 1979 summary already contained all the major elements and this lack of development contrasts with the dramatic changes that took place in mainstream motivation research in the 1980s following the 'cognitive revolution' in psychology (see next). As a consequence, by the beginning of the 1990s, there was a growing conceptual gap between motivational thinking in the second language field and in educational psychology and the time was ripe for a new phase in L2 motivation research. This does not mean, however, that Gardner's theory became marginalized—as we will see, all the main subsequent models drew on the social psychological construct extensively, and Gardner's model also persevered because of the "pervasive use of the battery of tests (Attitude/Motivation Test Battery) developed to measure it" (Jacques, 2001, p. 186).

The AMTB is a useful self-report instrument and it has been adapted for many learning contexts all over the world. Its design followed the psychometric principles governing questionnaire theory and it is a scientific assessment tool both in terms of its presentation and its content. Having said that, let me raise two issues here concerning the content validity of the test. First, as described in (Dörnyei, 1994b), three of the subscales defining the 'Motivation' subcomponent ('Desire to learn the L2,' 'Motivational intensity,' and 'Attitudes toward learning the L2') overlap at the item level, which may explain the high intercorrelations between these scales. The second issue is of a theoretical nature: In operationalizing the 'Motivation' subcomponent, Gardner included items that are related to motivated behavior, asking, for example, about the extent of volunteering answers in class. Such behaviors, however, are associated with the *consequences* of being motivated in the *motivation* →*behavior* →*outcome* chain. To illustrate this, the sample item for 'Motivational intensity' cited in Table 4.1 does not target the unobservable mental phenomenon of motivation but rather asks students to report on the amount of effort they put into doing their homework. In other studies such items are usually seen as behavioral criterion measures and researchers compute correlations between them and the learners' motiva-

Table 4.1. The constituent scales of Gardner's (1985) 'Attitude/ Motivation Test Battery'

- *Attitudes toward French Canadians* (10 Likert scale items)
  E.g., "French Canadians add a distinctive flavor to the Canadian culture."
- *Interest in foreign languages* (10 Likert scale items)
  E.g., "I would really like to learn a lot of foreign languages."
- *Attitudes toward European French people* (10 Likert scale items)
  E.g., "I have always admired the European French people."
- *Attitudes toward learning French* (10 Likert scale items)
  E.g., "I really enjoy learning French."
- *Integrative orientation* (4 Likert scale items)
  E.g., "Studying French can be important for me because it will allow me to meet and converse with more and varied people."
- *Instrumental orientation* (4 Likert scale items)
  E.g., "Studying French can be important for me only because I'll need it for my future career."
- *French class anxiety* (5 Likert scale items)
  E.g., "It embarrasses me to volunteer answers in our French class."
- *Parental encouragement* (10 Likert scale items)
  E.g., "My parents really encourage me to study French."
- *Motivational intensity* (10 multiple choice items)
  E.g., "When it comes to French homework, I:
  (a) Put some effort into it, but not as much as I could.
  (b) Work very carefully, making sure I understand everything.
  (c) Just skim over it."
- *Desire to learn French* (10 multiple choice items)
  E.g., "If there were a French Club in my school, I would:
  (a) Attend meetings once in awhile.
  (b) Be most interested in joining.
  (c) Definitely not join."
- *Orientation index* (1 multiple choice item)
  E.g., "I am studying French because:
  (a) I think it will some day be useful in getting a good job.
  (b) I think it will help me to better understand French people and way of life.
  (c) It will allow me to meet and converse with more and varied people.
  (d) A knowledge of two languages will make me a better-educated person."

- *Evaluation of the French teacher* (25 semantic differential scale items)
  E.g., "efficient ___:___:___:___:___:___:___ inefficient"
- *Evaluation of the French course* (25 semantic differential scale items)
  E.g., "enjoyable ___:___:___:___:___:___:___ unenjoyable"

tion (cf. e.g., the motivation–effort correlations in Dörnyei & Clément, 2001). Thus, the AMTB assesses both motivation and motivated behavior; this increases the instrument's predictive validity with regard to learning outcomes (e.g., course grades) because in the *motivation →behavior →outcome* chain the battery covers the combined effect of the first two elements, but the downside of this measurement gain is that from a theoretical point of view it is not easy to decide the exact nature of the underlying learner trait that the instrument targets.

Clément's Theory of Linguistic Self-Confidence

The Canadian social psychological strand also subsumes a second important research tradition, the empirical and theoretical work conducted by Richard Clément and his colleagues to examine the interrelationship between social contextual variables (including ethnolinguistic vitality), attitudinal/motivational factors, self-confidence, language identity, and L2 acquisition/ acculturation processes (for reviews, see Clément & Gardner, 2001; Dörnyei, 1999, 2001). From a motivational perspective, the most important factor studied by Clément and his associates is *self-confidence*, which in general refers to the belief that a person has the ability to produce results, accomplish goals, or perform tasks competently. It was first introduced in the L2 literature by Clément, Gardner, and Smythe (1977) to describe a powerful mediating process in multi-ethnic settings that affects a person's motivation to learn and use the language of the other speech community.

Clément and his associates provided evidence (cf. Clément, 1980; Clément & Kruidenier, 1985) that in contexts where different language communities live together, linguistic self-confidence—derived from the quality and quantity of the *contact* between the members of the L1 and L2 communities—is a major motivational factor in learning the other community's language, and determines the learners' future desire for intercultural communication and the extent of identification with the L2 group. Thus, linguistic self-confidence in Clément's view is primarily a socially defined construct (in contrast to the cognitive nature of *self-efficacy* in the motivational psychological literature), although self-confidence also has a cognitive component, the 'perceived L2 proficiency.' Clément, Dörnyei, and Noels (1994) extended the applicability of the self-confidence construct by showing that it is also a significant motivational subsystem in foreign language learning situations in which there is little direct contact with members of the L2 community but considerable indirect contact with the L2 culture through the media (e.g., as is the case with world languages such as English).

The Cognitive–Situated Period

Although the starting point of the *cognitive–situated period* in motivation research is often seen as Graham Crookes and Richard Schmidt's (1991) influential article on 'reopening the motivation research agenda,' the need for a change was 'in the air' at the turn of the 1980s and 1990s and several other publications from around the same time voiced a similar view (e.g., Brown, 1990; Julkunen, 1989; Skehan, 1989, 1991). The cognitive-situated period was characterized by the intertwining influence of two broad trends:

(a) The desire to catch up with advances in motivational psychology and to extend our understanding of L2 motivation by importing some of the most influential concepts of the 1980s. These concepts were almost entirely cognitive in nature, which reflected the effect of the ongoing cognitive revolution in psychology. Motivational psychologists representing a cognitive perspective argued convincingly that how one thinks about one's abilities, possibilities, potentials, limitations, and past performance, as well as various aspects of the tasks to achieve or goals to attain (e.g., values, benefits, difficulties) is a crucial aspect of motivation.

(b) The desire to narrow down the macroperspective of L2 motivation (i.e., the broad view focusing on the motivational disposition of whole communities, typically taken by the proponents of the social psychological approach) to a more fine-tuned and situated analysis of motivation as it operates in actual learning situations (such as language classrooms), characterized by a microperspective.

Accordingly, a growing amount of research examined the motivational impact of the main components of the classroom learning situation, such as the teacher, the curriculum, and the learner group (cf. Dörnyei. 1994a; Williams & Burden, 1997). This did not mean, however, that researchers rejected the findings of the previous period; it was generally accepted that Gardner and his associates' macroperspective was useful to characterize and compare the motivational patterns of whole learning communities and then to draw inferences about important issues such as intercultural communication and affiliation, language contact, multiculturalism, and language globalization. However, if we also want to understand the motivational features of actual language classrooms, these broad factors have little explanatory power and need to be supplemented with motives associated with the learners' immediate learning situation. This emerging situated approach was summarized by McGroarty (2001) as follows:

> Existing research on L2 motivation, like much research in educational psychology, has begun to rediscover the multiple and mutually influential connections between individuals and their many social contexts, contexts that can play a facilitative, neutral, or inhibitory role with respect to further learning, including L2 learning. (p. 86)

This process of linking motivation to contextual factors was fruitful: Researchers have repeatedly found that variables related to the language course explained a significant portion of the variance in the students' motivation, indicating that "classroom L2 learning motivation is not a static construct as often measured in a quantitative manner, but a compound and relative phenomenon situated in various resources and tools in a dynamic classroom context" (Kimura, 2003, p. 78). To illustrate the significance of situation-specific factors, let me describe briefly two interesting studies. Analyzing unsuccessful Hungarian language learners, Nikolov (2001) found that although her participants typically shared positive attitudes toward knowing foreign languages (and thus they would have been traditionally labeled as being integratively motivated), the main reasons for their lack of success in the L2 concerned their perceptions of the classroom practices they had been exposed to. As she summarized, "The most problematic areas relate to classroom methodology in general, and assessment, focus on form, and rote-learning in particular" (p. 149). Thus, for these learners situation-specific motives overrode the positive attitudes toward the L2. We may add that it is highly likely that the negative perceptions were also related to some sort of unfavorable aptitude-treatment interaction (Robinson, in press) as described in the previous chapter.

Examining a strikingly different language learning context, Israeli students learning modern spoken Arabic, Donitsa-Schmidt, Inbar, and Shohamy (2004) and Inbar, Donitsa-Schmidt, and Shohamy (2001) found that the best predictor of the intention to continue studying Arabic was the quality of the teaching program. This was, as McGroarty (2001) pointed out in a review, a remarkable finding because it showed that even when relations between language groups are marked by tension and lack of unanimity at the level of policy, L2 learners are sensitive to the quality of language instruction and the learning experience. Thus, in this case situation-specific motives overrode a generally negative language attitudinal disposition. Inbar et al. (2001) also compared the L2 attitudes of learners who were studying and who were not studying Arabic at the time they were surveyed, with each group further divided into two subgroups depending on whether the learning vs. not-learning situation was a result of their own choice or the policy or provision of the school that they attended. The researchers found an interesting pattern: Students who studied Arabic displayed higher motivation in all the dimensions measured than those who did not, and there were few differences between those who chose versus those who were assigned to study/not to study the language. Thus, the authors concluded that it was studying the language and not the 'choice vs. assigned condition' that affected students' motivation, implying that being actively engaged in learning a foreign language in a school enhanced language attitudes and motivation. This was further confirmed by Dörnyei and Csizér's (2002) national survey in Hungary, in which we also found a consistent difference between active learners and non-learners of an L2 in terms of their attitudinal/motivational dispositions, with active learners always having more positive attitudes.

The intertwining influences of situating L2 motivation and adopting new cognitive variables in the motivational paradigms were well illustrated by two featured research areas that appeared in the L2 motivation field in the 1990s: the investigation of *self-determination theory* in L2 learning and the analysis of *language attributions*. Let us look at these areas and then examine the most situated research direction in the field, the study of *task motivation*.

Self-Determination Theory

Self-determination theory (Deci & Ryan, 1985, 2002), which focuses on various types of *intrinsic* and *extrinsic motives*, has been one of the most influential approaches in motivational psychology, and several attempts have been made in the L2 field to incorporate certain elements of the theory to explain L2 motivation. Douglas Brown (1990, 1994) was one of the main proponents of emphasizing the importance of intrinsic motivation in the L2 classroom, arguing that traditional school settings cultivate extrinsic motivation, which, over the long haul, "focuses students too exclusively on the material or monetary rewards of an education rather than instilling an appreciation for creativity and for satisfying some of the more basic drives for knowledge and exploration" (Brown, 1994, p. 40).

In the 1990s, Kim Noels came in contact with two leading international experts of self-determination theory, Luc Pelletier and Robert Vallerand, and this association inspired her to conduct empirical research into the L2 applications of the theory; over the following years Noels and her associates added several further studies to the initial project, resulting in a systematic research program (McIntosh & Noels, 2004; Noels, 2001a, 2001b; Noels, Clément & Pelletier, 1999, 2001, Noels, Pelletier, Clément & Vallerand,

2000). In line with the general thrust of the cognitive-situated period, the researchers pursued two main objectives: (a) to relate the various intrinsic/extrinsic components established in motivational psychology to orientations developed in L2 research, and (b) to examine how the learners' level of self-determination is affected by various classroom practices.

With regard to the first issue, Noels and her colleagues found (for a review, see Noels, 2001b) that Gardner's integrative orientation was most strongly associated with the more self-determined forms of motivation (i.e., identified regulation and intrinsic motivation), although it did have modest correlations with the less self-determined orientations as well. Instrumental orientation, on the other hand, correlated highly with external regulation. Moreover, as Noels, Pelletier, Clément, and Vallerand (2000) concluded, the instrumental and the external regulation scales correlated in similar ways with the antecedent variables of 'perceived autonomy' and 'competence,' as well as with the consequence variables of 'intention to pursue language study' and 'anxiety.' Based on these findings, Noels (2003) proposed a larger motivation construct made up of three interrelated substrates. The first substrate includes *intrinsic reasons* inherent in the language learning process, such as whether learning the language is fun, engaging, challenging, or competence-enhancing. The second category includes *extrinsic reasons* for language learning lying on a continuum of self-determination, including external and internalized pressures; Gardner's instrumental orientation belongs to this group. The third substrate comprises *integrative reasons* relating to positive contact with the L2 group and perhaps eventual identification with that group.

With regard to examining environmental influences on learner self-determination, Noels and her colleagues found a consistent pattern (see Noels, 2001a): The more students perceived their teachers as controlling and as failing to provide instructive feedback, the less they were intrinsically motivated. Thus, perceptions of autonomy support and informative feedback from teachers enhanced the students' feelings of intrinsic motivation. Interestingly, the perception of *autonomy-supporting* vs. *controlling* teacher behavior turned out to be a more salient factor in learners than the more general perceptions of the teacher as *negative* vs. *congenial*; in fact, structural equation modeling showed that the former factors mediated the latter. A further intriguing finding in this respect has been that the directive influence of the language teacher's communicative/instructional style on the students' sense of self-determination (autonomy) and enjoyment did not reach significance with students who pursued learning primarily for extrinsic (instrumental) reasons. This indicated that learners who studied a language primarily because they *had to* were less sensitive to this aspect of teacher influence than those who did it of their own free will.

Table 4.2. Description of Noels, Pelletier, Clément and Vallerand's (2000) Language Learning Orientations Scale: Intrinsic Motivation, Extrinsic Motivation, and Amotivation

Subscale	DESCRIPTION AND EXAMPLE
Amotivation	A lack of motivation caused by the realization that *'there is no point...'* or *'it's beyond me...'* E.g., [Why are you learning the L2?] *Honestly, I don't know, I truly have the impression of wasting my time in studying a second language.*
External Regulation	The least self-determined form of extrinsic motivation, coming entirely from external sources such as rewards or threats (e.g., teacher's praise or parental confrontation). E.g., *Because I have the impression that it is expected of me.*
Introjected Regulation	Externally imposed rules that the student accepts as norms he/she should follow so as not to feel guilty (e.g., rules against playing truant). E.g., *Because I would feel guilty if I didn't know a second language.*
Identified Regulation	The person engages in an activity because he/she highly values and identifies with the behavior, and sees its usefulness (e.g., learning a language which is necessary to pursue one's hobbies or interests). E.g., *Because I think it is good for my personal development.*
Intrinsic Motivation: Knowledge	Doing the activity for the feelings associated with exploring new ideas and acquiring knowledge. E.g., *For the satisfied feeling I get in finding out new things.*
Intrinsic Motivation: Accomplishment	Sensations related to attempting to master a task or achieve a goal. E.g., *For the satisfaction I feel when I am in the process of accomplishing difficult exercises in the second language.*
Intrinsic Motivation: Stimulation	Sensations stimulated by performing the task, such as aesthetic appreciation or fun and excitement. E.g., *For the 'high' feeling that I experience while speaking in the second language.*

Noels and her colleagues (2000) also developed a valid and reliable measuring instrument assessing the various components of self-determination theory in L2 learning, the Language Learning Orientations Scale: Intrinsic Motivation, Extrinsic Motivation, and Amotivation. Table 4.2 presents descriptions of the constituent scales and sample items.

A recent study by Wu (2003) attempted to further situate the self-determination framework proposed by Noels and her colleagues by adding a new dimension to it, the immediate classroom environment. In a quasi-experimental study, the author examined the effect of a range of environmental variables on L2 intrinsic motivation and demonstrated that (a) providing young L2 learners with a predictable learning environment, moderately challenging tasks, necessary instructional support, and evaluation that emphasizes self-improvement are effective ways of developing students' perceived competence, and (b) giving them freedom in choosing the content, methods, and performance outcomes of learning, as well as providing integrative strategy training, lead to enhanced perceived autonomy. Perceived competence and autonomy, in turn, resulted in a significantly higher level of L2 intrinsic motivation.

Attribution Theory

Attribution theory has achieved a special status among contemporary motivation theories in psychology because this was the first theory that successfully challenged Atkinson's classic achievement motivation theory in the 1970s (for a review, see Dörnyei, 2001a). Subsequently, it became the dominant model in research on student motivation in the 1980s. The theory is also unique because it successfully links people's past experiences with their future achievement efforts by introducing *causal attributions* as the mediating link: As the main proponent of the theory, Bernard Weiner (1992), argued, the subjective reasons to which we attribute our past successes and failures considerably shape our motivational disposition underlying future action. If, for example, we ascribe past failure in a particular task to low ability on our part, the chances are that we will not try the activity ever again, whereas if we believe that the problem lay in our insufficient effort or the unsuitable learning strategies that we had employed, we are more likely to give it another try.

Because of the generally high frequency of language learning failure worldwide, attributional processes are likely to play an important motivational role in language studies, which was indeed demonstrated by Ushioda's (1996, 1998, 2001) interview study of Irish learners of French. In accordance with Weiner's theory, Ushioda found that positive motivational thinking involved two attributional patterns: (a) attributing positive L2 outcomes to personal ability or other internal factors (e.g., effort, perfectionist approach), and (b) attributing negative L2 outcomes or lack of success to temporary (i.e., unstable) shortcomings that might be overcome (e.g., lack of effort, lack of opportunity to spend time in the L2 environment).

Qualitative research by Williams and Burden (1999; Williams, Burden, & Al-Baharna, 2001) further confirmed the importance of motivation-enhancing attributions in school children's perceptions of their learning. Besides providing evidence that attributions play an important role in shaping learner motivation, the researchers also found that the range of attributional categories that the pupils cited was partly a function of their cultural background; for example, in Williams et al.'s (2001) sample of Arab students, the notion of 'luck' was never mentioned, and ability was cited very rarely either by students or teachers. On the other hand, their participants mentioned a wide range of attributional factors related to the classroom environment, circumstances, exposure to the language, interest, strategy use, and support from others. These findings confirm that the study of attributions is clearly an important line of investigation with much future scope.

Task Motivation

SLA researchers have been attracted to tasks because focusing on them allows to break down the complex and prolonged L2 learning process into discrete segments with well-defined boundaries, thereby creating researchable behavioral units. Thus, from this perspective, tasks can be seen to constitute the basic building blocks of instructed SLA. Accordingly, an interest in the motivational basis of language learning tasks can be seen as the culmination of the situated approach in L2 motivation research since L2 motivation can hardly be examined in a more situated manner than within a task-based framework (Dörnyei, 2002). Indeed, in a recent study, Kormos and Dörnyei (2004) emphasized that a focus on tasks as the unit of analysis brings to a head the recent shift from the macroperspective toward more situation-specific and process-oriented approaches in L2 motivation research, but as we concluded, hardly any empirical research has been conducted to examine the motivational basis of language learning tasks. This is in stark contrast with the abundance of research on cognitive operations underlying various aspects of task performance (Ellis, 2003; Skehan, 2003).

In the few studies that did look at task motivation, the construct was seen as a combination of generalized and situation-specific motives (Julkunen, 1989, 2001), corresponding to the traditional distinction between *state* and *trait* motivation. In a study specifically devoted to the analysis of the motivational characteristics of language learning tasks, I proposed

(Dörnyei, 2002) that task motivation may be more complex than the state–trait dichotomy because on-task behavior is embedded in a series of 'actional contexts' (e.g., going to a specific school, attending a particular class, taking up the study of a particular L2), each of which exert a certain amount of unique motivational influence. That is, it may be insufficient to assume that the learner enters the task situation with some 'trait motivation baggage' and to obtain a comprehensive picture of task motivation all we need to do is add to this 'baggage' the motivational properties of the instructional task. Instead, I believe that engaging in a certain task activates a number of different levels of related motivational mindsets or contingencies associated with the various actional contexts, resulting in complex interferences. Some empirical basis for this proposal has been supplied by a series of studies on the co-construction of motivation by participants in dyadic communicative tasks (Dörnyei, 2002; Dörnyei & Kormos, 2000; Kormos & Dörnyei, 2004; cf., also Edmondson, 2004).

The main question in understanding task motivation is how we operationalize the dynamic interface between motivational attributes and specific language behaviors. This question takes us to the third phase of L2 motivation research, the process-oriented period, described next, but for the sake of coherence I provide a brief summary here. In my view, the complex of motivational mindsets and contingencies activated during task performance feed into a dynamic *task processing system* that consists of three interrelated mechanisms: *task execution, appraisal,* and *action control* (see Fig. 4.2).

Task execution refers to the learners' engagement in task-supportive learning behaviors, following the action plan that was either provided by the teacher (through the task instructions) or drawn up by the student or the task team. *Appraisal* refers to the learner's continuous processing of the multitude of stimuli coming from the environment and of the progress made toward the action outcome, comparing actual performances with predicted ones or with ones that alternative action sequences would offer. The importance attached to the appraisal process coincides with Schumann's (1998) emphasis on 'stimulus appraisal.' Finally, *action control* processes denote self-regulatory mechanisms that are called into force in order to enhance, scaffold, or protect learning-specific action (for more details about motivational self-regulation, see the separate section below). Thus, task processing can be seen as the interplay of the three mechanisms: When learners are engaged in *executing* a task, they continuously *appraise* the process, and when the ongoing monitoring reveals that progress is slowing, halting, or backsliding, they activate the *action control* system to save or enhance the action. The process-oriented conception of motivation and the role of various action-control mechanisms will be analyzed in more detail later in this chapter.

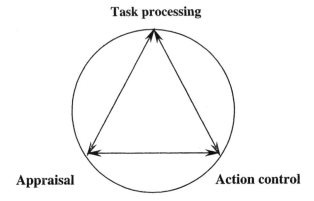

FIG. 4.2. Schematic Representation of the Three Mechanisms Making
Up The Task-Processing System.

Task motivation can also be connected to an intriguing motivational feature examined in motivational psychology by Csikszentmihalyi and his colleagues in great detail, the experience of *flow* (e.g., Csikszentmihalyi, 1990, 1997). As Egbert (2003) summarized in a recent pioneering study on the role of flow in SLA, the experiential state of flow involves a particularly intense focus and involvement in an activity, to the extent that we may even lose self-consciousness and a track of time amidst our absorption. Thus, flow can be seen as a heightened level of motivated task engagement, leading to improved performance on a task; in many ways it is the optimal task experience. From our current perspective, the important aspect of this line of research is that flow theory specifies the task conditions under which flow can occur. These, according to Egbert, can be organized along four dimensions: (1) there is a perceived balance of task challenge and participant skills during the task, (2) the task offers opportunities for intense concentration and the participants' attention is focused on the pursuit of clear task goals, (3) the participants find the task intrinsically interesting or authentic, and (4) the participants perceive a sense of control over the task process and outcomes. Thus, Egbert proposed that "teachers can theoretically facilitate the flow experience for students by developing tasks that might lead to flow" (p. 513) and she subsequently analyzed several computer-based and reading tasks that might be good candidates for supporting flow because they present a way for individuals to experience optimal levels of challenge, control, and interest.

The Process-Oriented Period

The cognitive–situated approach emerging in the 1990s soon drew attention to another, rather neglected, aspect of motivation: its *dynamic character* and *temporal variation*. As I argued elsewhere (Dörnyei, 2000b, 2001c), when motivation is examined in its relationship to specific learner behaviors and classroom processes, there is a need to adopt a *process-oriented approach/ paradigm* that can account for the daily ups and downs of motivation to learn, that is, the ongoing changes of motivation over time. Even during a single L2 class one can notice that language-learning motivation shows a certain amount of changeability, and in the context of learning a language for several months or years, or over a lifetime, motivation is expected to go through rather diverse phases. Looking at it from this perspective, motivation is not seen as a static attribute but rather as a dynamic factor that displays continuous fluctuation. As the following quote demonstrates, this characteristic of motivation is becoming a basic assumption in contemporary motivational psychology: "Many of the tasks faced by students extend over time, and as noted in chapter 1 of any Introduction to Motivation text, one of the prime characteristics of motivation is that it ebbs and flows" (Garcia, 1999, p. 231).

With language acquisition being a particularly lengthy learning process, the potential importance of a temporal perspective that includes the division of various motivational phases has not gone unnoticed in L2 research. Williams and Burden (1997, p. 121), for example, separated three stages of the motivation process along a continuum: "Reasons for doing something" → "Deciding to do something" → "Sustaining the effort, or persisting." As they argued, the first two stages involved *initiating* motivation whereas the third stage involved *sustaining* motivation. Similarly, Ushioda (1996, 2001) also emphasized that when it comes to institutionalized learning, the common experience appears to be motivational flux rather than stability, which highlights the "notion of a temporal frame of reference shaping motivational thinking" (Ushioda, 1998, p. 82). Finally, a recent study by Manolopoulou-Sergi (2004) made an interesting attempt to look at motivational variation according to the three main phases of SLA within an information-processing framework: Input, central processing, and output.

Next I present first a process model of L2 motivation that I developed with István Ottó to specify the components and mechanisms making up the L2 motivation process. Then I describe several recent empirical studies that were carried out in the process-oriented vein, looking at motivational evolution either in a school context or in the broader frame of the lifespan.

The Dörnyei and Ottó Model of L2 Motivation

In an attempt to operationalize the process-oriented conception of L2 motivation, István Ottó and I drew up a process model that describes some aspects of motivational evolution (Dörnyei & Ottó, 1998). This model and its further elaboration (Dörnyei, 2000, 2001) broke down the motivational process into several discrete temporal segments, organized along the progression that describes how initial *wishes* and *desires* are first transformed into *goals* and then into operationalized *intentions*, and how these intentions are *enacted*, leading (hopefully) to the accomplishment of the goal and concluded by the final *evaluation* of the process. In this process, at least three distinct phases can be separated (see Fig. 4.3 for more details):

1. *Preactional Stage:* First, motivation needs to be *generated*—the motivational dimension related to this initial phase can be referred to as *choice motivation,* because the generated motivation leads to the selection of the goal or task that the individual will pursue.

2. *Actional Stage:* Second, the generated motivation needs to be actively *maintained* and *protected* while the particular action lasts. This motivational dimension has been referred to as *executive motivation,* and it is particularly relevant to sustained activities such as studying an L2, and especially to learning in classroom settings, where students are exposed to a great number of distracting influences, such as off-task thoughts, irrelevant distractions from others, anxiety about the tasks, or physical conditions that make it difficult to complete the task.

3. *Postactional Stage:* There is a third phase following the completion of the action—termed *motivational retrospection*—which concerns the learners' *retrospective evaluation* of how things went. The way students process their past experiences in this retrospective phase will determine the kind of activities they will be motivated to pursue in the future.

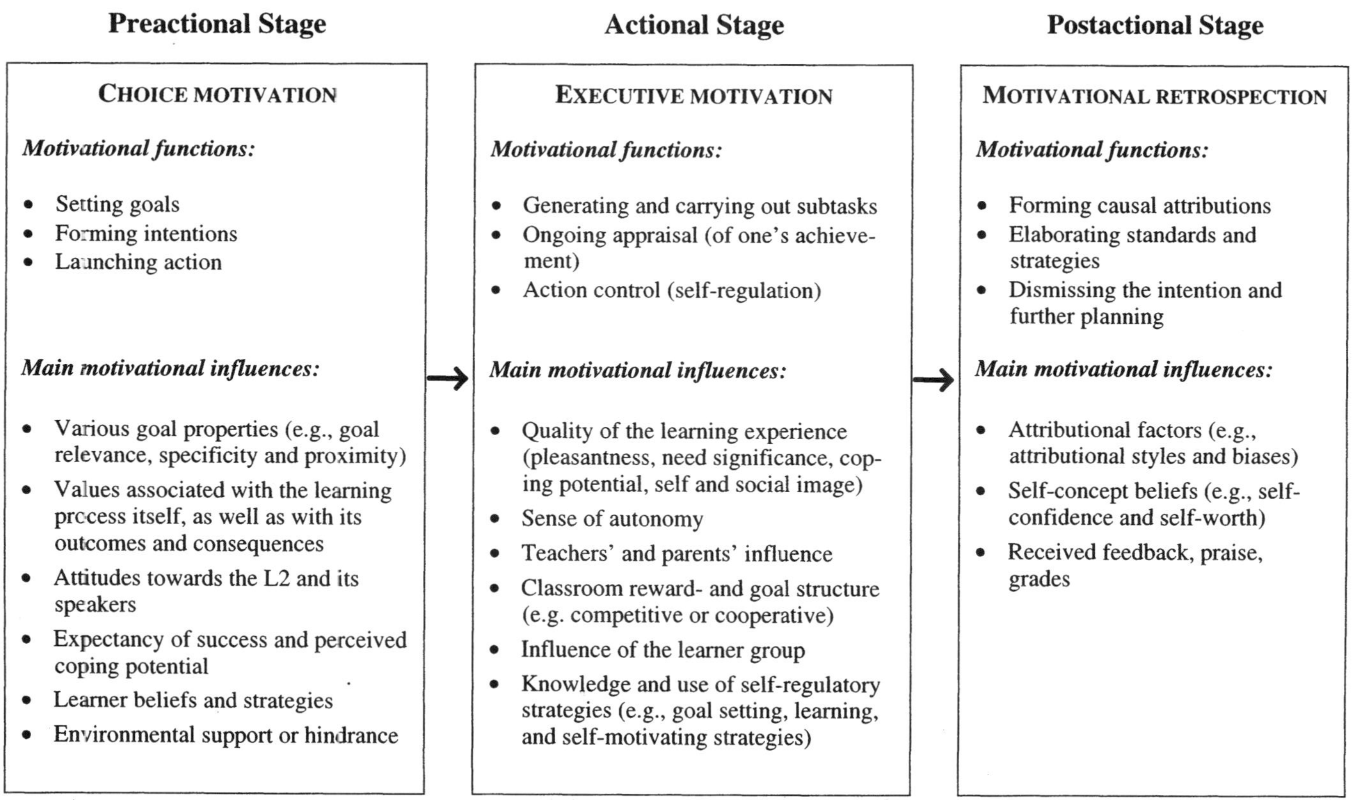

Preactional Stage

Actional Stage

Postactional Stage

CHOICE MOTIVATION

Motivational functions:

- Setting goals
- Forming intentions
- Launching action

Main motivational influences:

- Various goal properties (e.g., goal relevance, specificity and proximity)
- Values associated with the learning process itself, as well as with its outcomes and consequences
- Attitudes towards the L2 and its speakers
- Expectancy of success and perceived coping potential
- Learner beliefs and strategies
- Environmental support or hindrance

EXECUTIVE MOTIVATION

Motivational functions:

- Generating and carrying out subtasks
- Ongoing appraisal (of one's achievement)
- Action control (self-regulation)

Main motivational influences:

- Quality of the learning experience (pleasantness, need significance, coping potential, self and social image)
- Sense of autonomy
- Teachers' and parents' influence
- Classroom reward- and goal structure (e.g. competitive or cooperative)
- Influence of the learner group
- Knowledge and use of self-regulatory strategies (e.g., goal setting, learning, and self-motivating strategies)

MOTIVATIONAL RETROSPECTION

Motivational functions:

- Forming causal attributions
- Elaborating standards and strategies
- Dismissing the intention and further planning

Main motivational influences:

- Attributional factors (e.g., attributional styles and biases)
- Self-concept beliefs (e.g., self-confidence and self-worth)
- Received feedback, praise, grades

FIG. 4.3. A Process Model of L2 Motivation.

A key tenet of the process-oriented approach is that these three actional phases are associated with largely different motives. That is, people are influenced by a set of factors while they are still contemplating an action that is different from the motives that influence them once they have embarked on the activity. And similarly, when they look back at what they have achieved and evaluate it, again a new set of motivational components will become relevant. Thus, we can organize the manifold motives that are relevant to language learning by grouping them according to which actional phase they are related to. An important corollary of this perspective is that different motivational systems advocated in the literature do not necessarily exclude each other but can be valid at the same time if they affect different stages of the motivational process. I believe, for example, that the Canadian social psychological construct is effective in explaining variance in choice motivation but to explain executive motivation, more situated factors need to be taken into account.

The process model described above is a good starting point in understanding motivational evolution but it has two obvious shortcomings. First, it implies that the actional process in question is well-definable and has clear-cut boundaries. But where exactly does action start in an educational context? As already pointed out when discussing task motivation, the task-specific behavior characterizing a concrete learning activity is not entirely independent of the actional character of the whole course, and this behavioral domain is further embedded in the complex tapestry of other activities in the particular school. These actional contexts generate somewhat different motivational mind sets in the students, resulting in a task motivation complex that is made up of motivational influences associated with various levels of action-oriented contingencies or hierarchical action sequences.

The second problem is related to the fact that the actional process does not occur in relative isolation, without any interferences from other ongoing activities the learner is engaged in. Instead, people are typically involved in a number of parallel action processes, an issue already highlighted by Atkinson and Birch (1974) in their Dynamic Action Model more than 30 years ago. This multiple engagement means that various action episodes can be simultaneously active; for example, a new action may be initiated while the success of the previous action is still being evaluated. This is particularly valid for classroom contexts where student motivation and achievement are the product of a complex set of interacting goals and intentions of both academic and social nature (Juvonen & Nishina, 1997; Wentzel, 1999): Whereas academic motivation is—hopefully—an important facet of the learners' general disposition toward attending school, the classroom is also a social arena in which students go through some of the key developmental experiences in their lives, such as establishing friendships, falling in love, and experimenting with increasingly elaborate personal identities. Thus, academic goals will be accompanied by different social goals and practicing teachers know all too well how such social agendas can modify or disrupt the academic action sequence. However, hardly any research has been done to examine how people deal with multiple actions and goals, how they prioritize between them, and how the hierarchies of superordinate and subordinate goals are structured (cf. Boekaerts, 1998).

Empirical Studies on Motivational Evolution

The process-oriented conception of L2 motivation is a novel research paradigm and at the moment few of its tenets have been explicitly tested in L2 contexts. This does not mean, however, that motivational changes have not been documented in the past; they have, particularly the frequent phenomenon that motivation loses its intensity in school contexts over sustained periods. Koizumi and Matsuo (1993), for example, examined attitudinal and motivational changes of 296 Japanese 7th grade students learning English and reported a definite decrease over a period of seven months. After this period student motivation appeared to stabilize as learners started to develop realistic goals. Tachibana, Matsukawa, and Zhong (1996) investigated 801 Chinese and Japanese pupils and also found that the students' interest in learning English declined from junior to high school both in Japan and in China. Gardner, Masgoret, Tennant, and Mihic (2004) observed motivational changes over a period of one academic year in Canadian university students learning French and found a general tendency for the scores on the measures of language attitudes and motivation to decrease from the fall to the spring. Interestingly, situation-specific motives such as attitudes toward the learning situation displayed almost twice as big a change as more generalized motives such as integrativeness. In their Israeli study already mentioned, Inbar et al. (2001) found a consistent and significant small drop in motivation for all groups in all motivational dimensions. Finally, two separate studies, by Chambers (1999) and Williams, Burden, and Lanvers (2002), found that the motivation of British language learners declined between Year 7 and Year 9. Chambers summarized this as follows:

> Year 7 pupils are looking forward with enthusiasm to learning their subject. ... The scene is set for a very positive start. Two years later, the picture is not quite so encouraging. It seems that pupils' expectations are not matched by the reality. The honeymoon is over. The enthusiasm is on the wane. Pupils appear disgruntled. Something has gone wrong. (p. 81)

Recently, there have been a few data-based studies specifically addressing aspects of motivational change from a process-oriented paradigm. In a qualitative study, Ushioda (2001) interviewed 20 Irish young adult learners of French twice, with an interval of 16 months between the two sessions. The researcher's main interest was not so much to examine the magnitude but rather the quality of the motivational evolution. The interview data revealed definite changes in the temporal frame of reference that shaped the students' thinking, particularly with regard to the evolving nature of goal-orientation in the learners' motivational experience: Over the 16-month period learners appeared to have developed a clearer definition of L2-related personal goals.

The changing nature of L2 motivation has also been documented in studies focusing on longer periods in the learners' lifespan (e.g., Lim, 2002; Shedivy, 2004). The most systematic study of this sort to date has been carried out by Shoaib and Dörnyei (in press), who conducted qualitative interviews with 25 language learners to identify different motivational influences and various temporal patterns over a period of approximately two decades. Based on the learners' personal histories, we discovered a number of salient recurring temporal patterns and *motivational transformation episodes* in the learners' lives that resulted in the profound restructuring of their motivational disposition. Six such motivation-specific temporal themes were identified: (a) maturation and gradually increasing interest, (b) standstill period, (c) moving into a new life phase, (d) internalizing external goals and imported visions, (e) relationship with a significant other, and (f) time spent in the host environment.

Thus, while empirical results are still scarce, the available evidence indicates that examining the temporal progression of L2 motivation is a potentially fruitful research direction that can significantly enrich our understanding of the attitudinal/motivational basis of language learning.

NEW CONCEPTUAL ISSUES

We have seen in the previous sections that the study of L2 motivation has made considerable progress since the 1960s, adopting new research paradigms and approaches. The brief outline, however, could not give us more than a cursory overview of the specific issues and therefore in this section I highlight four conceptual developments which, I believe, may have a considerable bearing on future research.

Motivation and Group Dynamics

The discipline of group dynamics is a thriving interdisciplinary field in the social sciences, focusing on understanding the behavior of humans in various small group contexts such as sports teams, business committees, psychotherapy groups, or political task forces. Because contemporary education typically takes place in groups of various sizes, the principles of group dynamics are highly relevant to the study of institutional teaching/learning. This has been recognized by several recent publications in the L2 field that examined classroom life and processes from a group perspective (e.g., Dörnyei, 1997, in press; Dörnyei & Malderez, 1997, 1999; Dörnyei & Murphey, 2003; Ehrman & Dörnyei, 1998; Senior, 1997, 2002; Ushioda, 2003). It becomes clear from these analyses that the motivation of individual learners is significantly affected by the various groupings they are part of; as Ushioda (2003, p. 93) concluded, "The social unit of the classroom is clearly instrumental in developing and supporting the motivation of the individual." This social influence is well illustrated by everyday statements such as someone 'got into bad company' or 'you simply cannot teach in this class.'

Given the salient impact of learner groups on the members' learning behavior, in a recent summary I have argued (Dörnyei, in press) that to create a motivating classroom environment group issues need to be taken into account just as much as more traditional motivational concerns. It is my belief that group influences can be seen as a major aspect of the L2 motivation complex and the notion of *group norm* is in many ways the group equivalent of individual student motivation. 'Group norms' refer to the overt and covert rules and routines that help to prevent chaos in the group and allow everybody to go about their business as effectively as possible. They range from explicitly imposed school regulations to spontaneously and unconsciously evolved routines as a result of copying certain behaviors of some influential member or the leader, which are then solidified into unofficial but powerful norms of classroom existence. A negative example of such covert norms is the *norm of mediocrity*, which refers to the peer pressure put on students in many schools not to excel or else they may be called names such as 'nerd,' 'swot,' 'brain,' and so on. For a more detailed analysis of the motivational impact of the social group context, please refer to Dörnyei (2001c).

Demotivation

Although there are both positive and negative forces exerting their influence on ongoing student behaviors, past motivation research has typically overlooked the negative motives and conceptualized motivation as a kind of inducement, that is, as a force whose strength ranges on a continuum from zero to strong. This, however, is not in accordance with students and teachers' classroom experience that suggests that motivational influences that 'de-energize' action (Dörnyei, 2001c) are rather common. Drawing on the lessons of a large-scale longitudinal classroom investigation, Ushioda (2003) analyzed this dark side of student motivation as follows:

> The inevitable problems in classroom motivation arise when there is not a happy fusion between internal and external forces but a negative tension, where the latter dominate at the expense of the former. In other words, individual motivation becomes controlled, suppressed or distorted by external forces. As argued below, this may happen through negative influences in the classroom social dynamic, or through regulating forces in the educational system. ... Collective motivation can all too easily become collective demotivation, boredom, or at the far end of the spectrum, collective dissatisfaction or rebellion, often in the form of classroom counter-cultures defined by rejection of educational aims and values. (pp. 93-94)

Dörnyei (2001c) defined 'demotivation' as "specific external forces that reduce or diminish the motivational basis of a behavioral intention or an ongoing action" (p. 143). I argued that being demotivated does not necessarily mean that all the positive influences that originally made up the motivational basis of a behavior have been annulled; rather, it is only the resultant force that has been dampened by a strong negative component, while some other positive motives may still remain operational. This has been illustrated by Nikolov's (2001) study of demotivated language learners mentioned earlier. She found that although the learners in her sample all considered themselves unsuccessful, their attitudes toward knowing languages were positive. In this study the decisive force was related to negative experiences associated with the language classroom.

A review of the scarce literature on demotivation in the L2 field and in education in general reveals that the phenomenon is rather salient in learning environments and that teachers have a considerable responsibility in this respect: The majority of demotives identified in past research concern some aspects of classroom existence 'owned' by, or under the control of, the teacher (cf. Dörnyei, 2001c).

Motivational Self-Regulation

When we view motivation as a dynamic, continuously changing resultant of a variety of internal and external forces, it becomes clear that the internal monitoring, filtering, and processing mechanisms that learners employ in this dynamic process will have an important role in shaping the motivational outcome. It makes a great difference, for example, if someone consciously plays down any negative influences and focuses instead on forward-pointing and controllable aspects, thereby putting things in a positive light, or if the same person dwells in negative experiences without making an effort to move on. In chapter 6, I describe an important recent shift in educational psychology which has highlighted the importance of *learner self-regulation*, integrating the learners' proactive involvement in controlling the various facets of their learning in a broad and unified framework. The important point from our current perspective is that self-regulation has been conceptualized to also include *motivational* self-regulation besides the cognitive and metacognitive components.

The study of this motivational self-regulatory process goes back to Heckhausen and Kuhl's Action Control Theory (e.g., Heckhausen, 1991; Heckhausen & Kuhl, 1985; Kuhl & Beckmann, 1994), which formed the basis of the Dörnyei-Ottó process model of motivation (just described). As Pintrich (1999) summarizes in the conclusion of a special issue of the journal *Learning and Individual Differences* (Vol. 11/3), the renewed focus on the 'whole' person and how they control their own motivation, emotions, behavior (including choice, effort, and persistence), and their environment, has been a welcome addition to research on academic self-regulation. In the introduction of a special issue of the *International Journal of Educational Research* on the related topic of 'volition in education' (Vol. 33/7), Corno (2000) expresses a similar view, namely that volitional control over sustaining motivation and implementing goals is "critically important in education, not only as means to goals but as goals in themselves" (p. 659).

The basic assumption underlying the notion of motivational self-regulation is that students who are able to maintain their motivation and keep themselves on-task in the face of competing demands and attractions should learn better than students who are less skilled at regulating their motivation (in this respect, these strategies are very similar to the affective learning strategies discussed in chapt. 6). Learning, as Wolters (2003) pointed out, is an effortful process and academic tasks are fraught with obstacles that are likely to interfere with the students' initial motivational state; therefore their ability to remain in control of their attitudinal/motivational disposition should be seen as an important determinant of self-regulated learning and achievement. In addition to this consideration, Ushioda (2003) argued that a further function of motivational self-regulation is to help learners to 'step outside' certain maladaptive motivational belief systems and engage in constructive and effective thinking to regulate their motivation. In order for this to happen, learners must be brought to view their motivation as "emanating from within themselves, and thus to view themselves as agents of their own motivation and their own learning" (p. 98).

Empirical evidence for the role of motivational self-regulation has been provided by Wolters (1999), who found that the effective use of five motivational regulation strategies together explained approximately 22% of the variance in effort, and approximately 16% of the variance in the learners' grade-point average (GPA). The issue of self-motivational strategies is further analyzed and examples are provided at the end of this chapter when discussing the educational implications of motivation research.

Recently, Willis Edmondson (2004) put forward an interesting typology of six *motivational syndromes,* indicating six typical ways or scenarios whereby learners deal with motivational conflicts. By motivational conflict Edmondson means situations when the learner's internal motives clash with external demotivating conditions such as the lack of social acclaim (or success), social utility, and institutional support. Because these scenarios, then, concern strategic ways of dealing with partially learner-owned difficulties, they can be seen as linked to motivational self-regulation. The six syndromes are as follows: (1) *P.O.R. Syndrome* [Press On Regardless], involving persistence and maintained effort, (2) *T.O.Y. Syndrome* [Take Over Yours], involving a weaker version of the previous syndrome by also taking over some of the imposed learning goals/behaviors, (3) *I.K.B. Syndrome* [I Know Best], involving a confident, autonomous approach, (4) *G.Y.T. Syndrome* [Grit Your Teeth], involving an increased effort to do better, (5) *I.N.P. Syndrome* [I Need Pressure], involving a reliance on the environment for pressure to keep one going, and (6) *N.E.P. Syndrome* [No External Pressure], involving the opposite of the I.N.P. Syndrome as here the individual relies entirely on his or her internal resources. Edmondson suggests that the issue of which syndromes characterize an individual's learning is an ID variable that constitutes part of the individual's motivational profile.

The Neurobiology of Motivation

The final novel conceptual approach that I highlight in this chapter is the *neurobiological* investigation of motivation, introduced by John Schumann in the 1990s (for reviews, see Schumann, 1998, 1999, 2001a, 2001b; Schumann et al., 2004). As Schumann (2001a) argued, recent technological developments in brain scanning and neuroimaging have made the brain increasingly amenable to direct psychological investigation. This means that the various mental processes that have been by and large unobservable in the past might now receive direct empirical validation in neurobiological studies. What is particularly important from our perspective is that the first area of SLA that Schumann has examined from a neurobiological point of view is L2 motivation, and the result of this examination has been an intriguing motivation theory.

The key constituent of Schumann's theory is *stimulus appraisal,* which occurs in the brain along five dimensions: *novelty* (degree of unexpectedness/familiarity), *pleasantness* (attractiveness), *goal/need significance* (whether the stimulus is instrumental in satisfying needs or achieving goals), *coping potential* (whether the individual expects to be able to cope with the event), and *self and social image* (whether the event is compatible with social norms and the individual's self-concept). As Schumann has demonstrated, these appraisals become part of the person's overall value system through a special 'memory for value' module and thus stimulus appraisals are largely responsible for providing the affective foundation of human action. More specifically, Schumann et al. (2004) proposed that stimulus appraisals compute the emotional relevance and motivational significance of stimulus events in relation to information stored in the value memory, and the generated emotions (such as joy, fear, or anger) lead to action tendencies.

Schumann (2001b) has broadened his theory by outlining a conception of learning as a form of *'mental foraging'* (i.e., foraging for knowledge), which engages the same neural systems as the ones used by organisms when foraging to feed or mate, and which is generated by an incentive motive and potentiated by the stimulus appraisal system. Accordingly, Schumann et al. (2004) hypothesized a neural system for mental foraging in which the incentive motive or goal is held over time in the form of emotional memory or value memory, and appraisal information modulates the intensity of the incentive motive in relation to the current stimulus situation. This circuit is linked to brainstem motor nuclei, thereby enabling the generation of motor activity to achieve the organism's goal. Although Schumann's theory is based on the results of neurobiological research, he admits that there is as yet no direct evidence available that the proposed mechanisms do operate in SLA. However, indirect evidence for the role of stimulus appraisal and mental foraging in SLA can be found, Schumann argued, in autobiographies of L2 learners (Schumann, 1998; Schumann et al., 2004).

REFRAMING L2 MOTIVATION AS PART OF THE SELF-SYSTEM

Having offered an overview of the evolution of L2 motivation theory over the past decades and having highlighted some of the most promising new conceptual themes, in this section I would like to present a new conceptualization of L2 motivation that re-orients the concept in relation to a theory of self and identity. Three basic observations have led me to this major reformulation:

- Along with many other L2 scholars, I believe that a foreign language is more than a mere communication code that can be learnt similarly to other academic subjects; instead, it is also part of the individual's personal 'core,' involved in most mental activities and forming an important part of one's identity. Thus, I have become increasingly open to

paradigms that would approach motivation from a whole-person perspective.

- I have been intrigued by Robert Gardner's concept of 'integrativeness'
throughout my whole research career. Although Gardner's conceptualization of the concept makes sense in the multicultural context of Mont-
real, where it originated from, extending the relevance of integrativeness
to learning environments that are significantly different from this context (because, e.g., there is no real contact with L2 speakers available for
the learners) has not always been straightforward. Thus, I have been
trying to find a broader interpretation of the notion than was originally
offered by Gardner—the new paradigm I propose builds on the robust
body of past research but reinterprets the concept in a way that it goes
beyond the literal meaning of the verb 'integrate'.

- Empirical results concerning various dimensions of L2 motivation have
been relatively consistent with regard to identifying the range of factors
that play a decisive role in a learner's motivational disposition, but the
exact relationship between the key components in various studies has
displayed a variety that did not seem to add up to an obvious big picture.
The specific trigger for the proposed construct was provided by my empirical research with Kata Csizér (e.g., Dörnyei & Csizér, 2002; Csizér &
Dörnyei, 2005), in which we submitted the data obtained from a large-
scale motivation survey conducted in Hungary to a range of complex
multivariate statistical procedures. Structural equation modeling revealed
a consistent relationship in our dataset between the key variables of
integrativeness, instrumentality, attitudes toward L2 speakers, and
learning behavioral measures, and the emerging theoretical framework to
be presented in the following is an attempt to accommodate our findings.

In this section I first present evidence to support the case that the classic
concepts of integrativeness and integrative motivation need to be reinter-
preted. Then I go on to describe research in personality psychology concerning *possible* and *ideal selves*, which forms the theoretical basis of the
new model. Finally, I put the pieces together in an extended theory of L2
motivation, the *L2 Motivational Self System.*

The Need to Reinterpret 'Integrativeness'

If we look at the L2 motivation literature carefully, we find a certain amount
of ambivalence about Gardner's notion of 'integrativeness' and the 'integrative motive,' which sometimes amounts to a kind of 'love–hate' relationship
in researchers outside Gardner's Canadian circle. The concept is certainly an

enigma: It is without any doubt the most researched and most talked about notion in L2 motivation studies and yet it has no obvious equivalent in any other approaches in mainstream motivational and educational psychology. Partly for this reason and partly because the actual empirical findings did not always fit Gardner's original interpretation of the notion, several scholars in the past have questioned the validity and relevance of integrativeness. For example, a Canadian research team consisting of prominent motivational psychologists has stated:

> Although it was originally suggested that the desire for contact and identification with members of the L2 group [i.e., integrative orientation] would be critical for L2 acquisition, it would now appear that it is not fundamental to the motivational process, but has relevance only in specific sociocultural contexts. Rather, four other orientations may be seen to sustain motivation. (Noels et al., 2000, p. 60)

The four orientations—or learning goals—the researchers were advocating are *travel, friendship, knowledge,* and *instrumental orientation,* which echoes the findings of Clément and Kruidenier's (1983) seminal paper in the early 1980s that was the first 'insider challenge' to the integrative construct proposed by Gardner.

Other scholars arrived at a similarly critical perspective on different bases. For example, investigating language learning in Japan, McClelland (2000) called for a definition of 'integrativeness' that focuses on "integration with the global community rather than assimilation with native speakers" (p. 109), highlighting a "need to reappraise Gardner's concept of integrativeness to fit a perception of English as an international language" (ibid). Using path analysis, Yashima (2000) actually attempted this reappraisal and found that the results confirmed the "causal relations proposed in Gardner's model, although here integrativeness was replaced with two orientations [instrumental and intercultural friendship orientations] which had been operationally defined as most important in the Japanese English learning context" (p. 131). In a survey article reviewing motivation research in Japan, Irie (2003) also mentioned the ambiguous disposition toward integrative motivation:

> Most studies on Japanese university students report a factor indicating positive disposition toward native speakers and the cultures of the TL [target language] community. One can interpret this as a form of integrative motivation, and indeed researchers refer to the concept by acknowledging the similarity to Gardner's expanded definition: positive attitudes toward TL communities and TL speakers, without a desire to assimilate into them (Gardner, 1985, 2001a). However, the researchers avoid using integrative motivation as a label, as they believe the factor

does not fit the original definition. Another possible reason for avoiding the label is that in many studies the positive disposition factor included items on utilitarian interests, such as traveling, which blurred the distinction between integrative and instrumental motivation as pointed out by Dörnyei (1990, 1994a). (pp. 90–91)

Based on a recent qualitative study in Indonesia, Lamb (2004) drew a similar conclusion:

> Moreover, we have seen that an integrative and instrumental orientation are difficult to distinguish as separate concepts. Meeting with westerners, using computers, understanding pop songs, studying and traveling abroad, pursuing a desirable career—all these aspirations are associated with each other and with English as an integral part of the globalization processes that are transforming their society and will profoundly affect their own lives. (p. 15).

Finally, in an article focusing on the existence of integrative motivation in Taiwan, Warden and Lin (2000) did not succeed in identifying such a motive; as they summarized, "This preliminary study has discerned the existence of two motivational groups and two temporal orientations in the Taiwanese EFL environment. An integrative motivational group is notably absent" (p. 544). This result, in fact, is not unique, as several studies in the past, particularly in foreign language learning situations, failed to detect a motive that could be labeled as 'integrative' in Gardner's original sense. In light of these findings and because our own Hungarian data did not confirm the traditional content validity of the integrative concept either, Dörnyei and Csizér (2002) concluded:

> Although further research is needed to justify any alternative interpretation, we believe that rather than viewing 'integrativeness' as a classic and therefore 'untouchable' concept, scholars need to seek potential new conceptualizations and interpretations that extend or elaborate on the meaning of the term without contradicting the large body of relevant empirical data accumulated during the past four decades. (p. 456)

So, what does an integrative disposition involve? In broad terms, an integrative motivational orientation concerns a positive interpersonal/affective disposition toward the L2 community and the desire for affiliation with its members. It implies an openness to, and respect for, the other cultural group and its way of life; in the extreme, it might involve complete identification with the community and possibly even withdrawal from one's original group. Thus, a core aspect of the integrative disposition is some sort of a psychological and emotional *identification*. According to Gardner

(2001a), this identification concerns the L2 community (i.e., identifying with the speakers of the target language), but I argued over a decade ago (Dörnyei, 1990) that in the absence of a salient L2 group in the learners' environment (as is often the case in foreign language learning contexts in which the L2 is primarily learnt as a school subject) the identification can be generalized to the cultural and intellectual values associated with the language, as well as to the actual L2.

Thus, one way of extending the concept of 'integrativeness' is to talk about some sort of a virtual or metaphorical identification with the sociocultural loading of a language, and in the case of the undisputed world language, English, this identification would be associated with a non-parochial, cosmopolitan, globalized world citizen identity. In several parts of the world there is a clear indication that such a 'world identity' exists, and it is merely a terminological issue as to whether we label this a modified version of integrativeness or in some other way. Yashima (2000, 2004) for example talked about an 'international posture,' referring to a complex trait that includes an "interest in foreign or international affairs, willingness to go overseas to study or work, readiness to interact with intercultural partners and ... a non-ethnocentric attitude toward different cultures" (Yashima, 2000, p. 57). This variable appears to be similar to 'international orientation,' which Nakata (1995a, 1995b) found to be an important individual difference variable among Japanese learners, involving a general cosmopolitan outlook.

The World English identity is, of course, also related to instrumental aspects because the English-speaking world coincides with several of the technically most developed industrialized nations and therefore English has become the language associated with technological advances, for example computing and the Internet. This may explain the frequently observed blending of integrative and instrumental motives, which has been explicitly expressed by Kimura, Nakata, and Okumura (2001) when they talked about an 'Intrinsic-Instrumental-Integrative Motive.' The conceptualization of this global language identity is in line with psychological research on the effects of globalization: Lamb (2004) draws attention to Arnett's (2002) summary of the psychology of globalization, in which the author argues that "most people now develop a *bicultural identity*, in which part of their identity is rooted in their local culture while another part stems from an awareness of their relation to the global culture" (p. 777). Through the media, especially television but increasingly the Internet, young people in diverse countries "develop a global identity that gives them a sense of belonging to a worldwide culture and includes an awareness of the events, practices, styles and information that are part of the global culture" (ibid).

At this stage it is important to introduce the intriguing concept of the *'imagined community'* proposed by Bonny Norton (2001). Based on Wenger's (1998) notion of 'imagination' as a mode of belonging to a community, Norton conceptualizes the concept of 'communities of imagination' as being constructed by a combination of personal experiences and factual knowledge (derived from the past) with imagined elements related to the future. It appears that the notion of 'imagined community' lends itself to be used with regard to the various international or World English identities described above as these identities concern membership in a virtual language community. Indeed, Norton explicitly states that a learner's imagined community invites an "imagined identity" (p. 166). Looking at integrative motivation from this perspective, it can be viewed as the desired integration into an imagined L2 community.

While the concept of extended or metaphorical or imaginary integration does help to explain findings that are in many ways similar to the Canadian results but have been obtained in contexts without any realistic opportunity for direct integration, I would suggest that we can get an even more coherent picture if we leave the term 'integrative' completely behind and focus more on the identification aspects and on the learner's self-concept. An important theoretical strand in personality psychology which has elaborated on 'possible' and 'ideal selves' appears to be particularly relevant in this respect.

'Possible' and 'Ideal Selves'

Personality psychology, as we saw in chapter 1, has made considerable progress in understanding the structural basis of individual differences, and there have been substantial advances in the taxonomic efforts to chart the major and stable personality dimensions (cf. the Big Five model). These advances, according to Cantor (1990), have paved the way for paying more attention to questions about *how* these individual differences are translated into behavioral characteristics, examining the "'doing' sides of personality" (p. 735). Thus, over the past two decades self theorists have become increasingly interested in the active, dynamic nature of the self-system. As Markus and Ruvolo (1989) summarized, the traditionally static concept of self-representations was gradually replaced with a self-system that mediates and controls ongoing behavior, and various mechanisms, including 'self-regulation' (described earlier), have been put forward to link the self with action. As a result, recent dynamic representations of the self-system place the self right at the heart of motivation and action, creating an intriguing interface between personality and motivational psychology.

I believe that *possible selves* offer the most powerful, and at the same time the most versatile, motivational self-mechanism, representing the individuals' ideas of what they *might* become, what they *would like* to become, and what they are *afraid of* becoming. As Markus and Nurius (1986) described in their seminal paper that introduced the concept,

> The possible selves that are hoped for might include the successful self, the creative self, the rich self, the thin self, or the loved and admired self, whereas the dreaded possible selves could be the alone self, the depressed self, the incompetent self, the alcoholic self, the unemployed self, or the bag lady self. (p. 954)

Thus, possible selves are specific representations of one's self in future states, involving thoughts, images, and senses, and are in many ways the manifestations, or personalized carriers, of one's goals and aspiration (or fears, of course). As Markus and Nurius (1986) emphasize, possible selves are represented in the same imaginary and semantic way as the here-and-now self, that is, they are a *reality* for the individual. According to the scholars, it is a major advantage for framing future goals in this way—that is, in terms of self images—because this representation seems to capture some elements of what people actually experience when they are engaged in motivated or goal-directed behavior. Markus and Ruvolo (1989) state that by focusing on possible selves we are "phenomenologically very close to the actual thoughts and feelings that individuals experience as they are in the process of motivated behavior and instrumental action" (p. 217).

It is clear from the above description that positive 'possible selves' are closely related to 'visions.' Tim Murphey (1998) gives a fascinating account of the motivational disposition of a former Olympic athlete, Marilyn King, and of top sportspeople in general:

> Marilyn says now that most people think that Olympic athletes have a lot of *will-power* and *determination* and that's what enables them to work so hard. She says no, it's not that; it's the vision. It's the power of an image that inspires great passion and excitement—so much that you have enormous energy to do what you want. ... She started bringing together other ex-Olympians to find out if they had had similar experiences. She discovered that most Olympians had a very clear vision of what they wanted and that this vision was constantly present. The vision (or goal or outcome) also inspired great passion and excitement. The vision and the passion inspired them to take a lot of action, over and over again. To do something about it. (p. 62)

I believe that Marilyn King's vision can be seen as a possible self, and it certainly had a powerful motivational effect on her. This direct link between vision and action was very clearly depicted in her recollection of how she managed to get up at dawn for training. Her typical first reaction was *'Oh I'm too tired...,'* but as Murphey (1998, p. 62) describes, as she lay there, "the image of her walking into the Olympic stadium would pop into her head, and she would smile, and get excited! And she just couldn't stay in bed! She would get up and run!" (p. 62) This appears to be a perfect illustration of Markus and Ruvolo's (1989) claim that "imaging one's own actions through the construction of elaborated possible selves achieving the desired goal may thus directly facilitate the translation of goals into intentions and instrumental actions" (p. 213). A similar idea has been expressed by Wenger (1998) when he described the concept of 'imagination:'

> My use of the concept of imagination refers to a process of expanding our self by transcending our time and space and creating new images of the world and ourselves. Imagination in this sense is looking at an apple seed and seeing a tree. It is playing scales on a piano, and envisioning a concert hall. (p. 176)

Thus, possible selves give form, meaning, structure, and direction to one's hopes and threats, thereby inciting and directing purposeful behavior. The more vivid and elaborate the possible self, the more motivationally effective it is expected to be. Furthermore, research has shown that the impact of the self will be even stronger if a positive possible self is offset by a *feared* possible self in the same domain (cf. Carver, Reynolds & Scheier, 1994; Oyserman, Bybee, Terry, & Hart-Johnson, 2004). This makes sense: A positive image will be a stronger motivational resource if it is linked with representations of what could happen if the desired state should not be realized. Therefore, Markus and Ruvolo (1989) concluded that a dynamic balance between one's expected and feared selves in a given domain will create a more powerful motivational state than either an expected possible self or a feared self alone.

The educational relevance of possible selves has been documented by a number of studies (e.g., Oyserman, Terry, & Bybee, 2002; Oyserman et al., 2004; Yowell, 2002). They can act as 'academic self-guides,' and in this respect I found the concept of one type of possible self, the *ideal self*, particularly useful. It was introduced by Higgins (1987), referring to the representation of the attributes that someone would ideally like to possess (i.e., representation of hopes, aspirations, or wishes). Higgins also mentioned another self-guide that has particular relevance to future behavior strivings, the *ought self*, referring to the attributes that one believes one ought to possess (i.e., a representation of someone's sense of your duty, obligations, or responsibilities) and which therefore may bear little resemblance to desires or wishes. The motivational aspect of these self-guides is explained by Higgins's *self-discrepancy theory*, postulating that people are motivated to reach a condition where their self-concept matches their personally relevant self-guides. In other words, motivation in this sense involves the desire to reduce the discrepancy between one's actual and ideal or ought selves.

Although ideal and ought selves are similar to each other in that they are both related to the attainment of a desired end-state, Higgins (1998) emphasized that the predilections associated with the two different types of future selves are motivationally distinct from each other: Ideal self-guides have a *promotion* focus, concerned with hopes, aspirations, advancements, growth, and accomplishments; whereas ought self-guides have a *prevention* focus, regulating the absence or presence of negative outcomes, and are concerned with safety, responsibilities, and obligations. This distinction, Higgins adds, is in line with the age-old motivational principle that people approach pleasure and avoid pain.

Although I believe that the concept of ideal self may be useful when conceptualizing academic motivation, we should note that the ideal self theory is far from complete. Nasby (1997) points out, for example, that we still do not have an accurate description of the actual structures (e.g., associative networks, frames, lists of behaviors, propositions, prototypes) that describe the ideal self, even though different structures would entail different information-processing and self-directive properties. Neither is it clear how one's ideal self, which serves as a positive reference point, is related to the aspirations that others have about the particular individual. Higgins (1996) suggested that, to begin with, ideal self representations typically involve the standpoint of others and the person's own distinct standpoint develops only gradually.

Higgins (1987, 1996) emphasized that there are several types of self-representations beyond the ideal or ought self concepts and that not everyone is expected to possess a developed ideal or ought self guide. This lack of desired self guides would, then, explain the absence of sufficient motivation in many people, and this claim is also related to Markus and Nurius's (1986) argument that aspirations will only be effective in motivating behavior if they have been elaborated into a specific *possible* self in the working self-concept. Ruvolo and Markus (1992) provide empirical evidence that imagery manipulations (in their case, asking participants to imagine themselves as successful or unsuccessful before a task) increased the accessibility of possible selves and this was reflected in the subjects' performance. We come back to the question of the enhancement of self-representations at the end of this chapter when we consider the practical implications of increasing learner motivation by priming positive possible selves and by stimulating a desired end-state.

Integrativeness and the Ideal Language Self

In the multivariate statistical analysis of Hungarian school children's generalized motivational dispositions already mentioned briefly, Csizér and Dörnyei (2005) found that a latent factor that would have been traditionally identified as 'integrativeness' played a key role in mediating the effects of all the other attitudinal/motivational variables on two criterion measures related to motivated learning behavior, *intended effort* and *language choice* (see Fig. 4.4, for a schematic representation). Curiously, the immediate antecedents of this latent variable were *attitudes toward L2 speakers/community* and *instrumentality*; thus, our results indicated that 'integrativeness' was closely associated with two very different variables, faceless pragmatic incentives and personal attitudes toward members of the L2 community. I believe that applying the 'self' framework just described offers a good explanation of our findings. Looking at 'integrativeness' from the self perspective, the concept can be conceived of as the L2-specific facet of one's ideal self: If one's ideal self is associated with the mastery of an L2, that is, if the person that we would like to become is proficient in the L2, we can be described as having an integrative disposition.

This self interpretation of integrativeness is fully compatible with the direct relationship of the concept with 'attitudes toward members of the L2 community' in that L2 speakers are the closest parallels to the idealized L2-speaking self, which suggests that the more positive our disposition toward these L2 speakers, the more attractive our idealized L2 self. Earlier I introduced Norton's (2001) concept of the 'imagined community' and I believe that this concept can be meaningfully linked to the self approach: Our idealized L2-speaking self can be seen as a member of an imagined L2 community whose mental construction is partly based on our real-life experiences of members of the community/communities speaking the particular L2 in question and partly on our imagination. Thus, it is difficult to envisage that one can develop a potent ideal L2-speaking self while at the same time despising the people who speak the L2 in question.

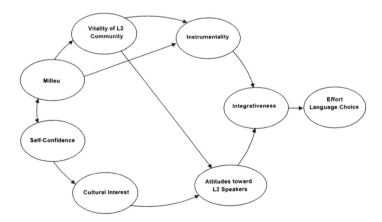

FIG. 4.4. Schematic Representation of the Interrelationships of the Motivational Variables and the Criterion Measures in Csizér and Dörnyei's (2005) Study.

The self interpretation also explains why instrumentality, the other main antecedent of integrativeness, correlated highly with integrativeness in the Csizér and Dörnyei (2005) study: Because the idealized language self is a cognitive representation of all the incentives associated with L2 mastery, it is also linked to professional competence. To put it broadly, in our idealized image of ourselves we may not only want to appear personally agreeable but also professionally successful. We should note here, however, that from a self perspective the term *instrumentality* can be divided into two types: Depending on the extent of internalization of the extrinsic motives that make up instrumentality, the concept can be related either to the 'ideal self' or to the 'ought self.' In the former case, instrumentality will be closely associated with the ideal L2 identity and will therefore contribute significantly to the learner's effort expenditure. On the other hand, non-internalized instrumental motives associated with the 'ought self,' that is, motives generated by a mere sense of duty or a fear of punishment, are more likely to have a short-term effect, without providing the sustained commitment that the successful mastery of an L2 requires. This division is in accordance with Higgins's (1998) distinction of a *promotion* versus *prevention* focus described above: Instrumental motives with a promotion focus (e.g., to learn English for the sake of professional advancement) are related to the ideal self, whereas instrumental motives with a prevention focus (e.g., study in order not to fail the test) are part of the ought self. Interestingly, a study by Kyriacou and Benmansour (1997) proposed a data-based five-factor construct that seems to reflect this duality well as it comprises a component labeled 'long-term instrumental motivation,' focusing on acquiring the L2 to enhance one's future professional career, and also a 'short-term instrumental motivation' factor, focusing on getting good grades.

Thus, instrumentality and the attitudes toward the L2 speakers constitute two complementary aspects of the ideal language self: its general agreeableness and its achievement-related effectiveness/competence. Within this framework what has traditionally been called 'integrativeness' refers to the overall driving force to approximate this idealized vision as much as possible. However, I do not think that the term *integrativeness* does justice to the broader interpretation of the concept described here; rather, I suggest that it be re-labeled as the *Ideal L2 Self.*

As noted earlier, the conception of the Ideal L2 Self does not conflict with Gardner's original notion of integrativeness related to an identification process; in fact, a model put forward by Tremblay and Gardner (1995) as an extension of Gardner's traditional construct indirectly confirms this conceptualization. The Tremblay and Gardner model proposes three main motivational facets: the first one is centered around 'Language attitudes,' a composite factor made up of 'Attitudes toward L2 speakers,' 'Integrative orientation,' 'Interest in foreign languages,' 'Instrumental orientation,' and 'Attitude toward the L2 course.' This core cluster is linked to 'Motivational behavior' (the third facet), through the mediation of three variables making up of the second facet: 'Goal salience,' 'Valence' (denoting an L2-learning related value component) and 'Self-efficacy.' The important aspect of the model from our current perspective is the 'Language attitudes' factor in the first facet, because this bears a close resemblance to the proposed concept of Ideal L2 Self in that it subsumes integrative orientation, instrumental orientation, and L2-speaker-related attitudes.

Thus, while the Ideal L2 Self perspective provides a good fit to the motivational data accumulated in the past and does not contradict the traditional conceptualizations of L2 motivation, it presents a broader frame of reference with increased capacity for explanatory power: Integrativeness seen as Ideal L2 Self can be used to explain the motivational set-up in diverse learning contexts even if they offer little or no contact with L2 speakers (e.g., in typical foreign language learning situations where the L2 is primarily a school language), and it would also be suitable for the study of the motivational basis of language globalization, whereby international languages, and World English in particular, are rapidly losing their national cultural base and are becoming associated with a global culture. That is, the Ideal L2 Self perspective offers a paradigm that can explain the 'integrativeness enigma' that has emerged in various data-based studies (reviewed above). One indication that this is a realistic prospect has been offered recently by Yashima, Zenuk-Nishide, and Shimizu (2004), who argued as follows:

> Those who are conscious of how they relate themselves to the world tend to be motivated to study English as they probably visualize 'English-using selves' clearly. The 'possible selves' and 'ideal selves' Dörnyei (2003b) cited in his discussion might be helpful for understanding the motivation process of Japanese learners. … Is it possible to hypothesize that learners who clearly visualize 'possible' or 'ideal' English-using selves are likely to make an effort to become more proficient and develop WTC and engage in interaction with others using English? (pp. 142–143)

The answer to Yashima et al.'s question is affirmative, as evidenced by Masgoret and Gardner's (2003) meta-analysis of 75 empirical studies conducted by Gardner and his associates in the social psychological vein. The researchers found that that integrative orientation displayed an overall pattern of higher correlations with criterion measures than instrumental orientation in both foreign and second language contexts.

The L2 Motivational Self System

The Ideal L2 Self perspective creates links with two important recent conceptualizations of L2 motivation by Noels (2003) and Ushioda (2001). It appears that the various models converge in a broad pattern of three main dimensions of L2 motivation, and if we compare this pattern with Gardner's original theoretical model we also find striking similarities. I have labeled the emerging new motivation construct, to be described below, the *L2 Motivational Self System.* Let us look at this system in more detail.

As discussed earlier, based on her systematic research program to examine the L2 relevance and links of self-determination theory, Kim Noels (2003) suggested a larger motivation construct made up of three interrelated types of orientations: (a) intrinsic reasons inherent in the language learning process, (b) extrinsic reasons for language learning, and (c) integrative reasons. Using qualitative rather than quantitative methods, Ushioda (2001) has identified a more complex construct which, however, is conceptually related to the one offered by Noels. Her findings pointed to eight motivational dimensions, which can be grouped in three broad clusters which correspond closely to Noels's framework: The first cluster concerns the *actual learning process* (subsuming the following components: Language-Related Enjoyment/Liking, Positive Learning History, and Personal Satisfaction); the second cluster corresponds to the dimension that Ushioda labeled *External Pressures/Incentives*; the third cluster is made up of four constituents, forming a board *integrative* dimension: Personal Goals, Desired Levels of L2 Competence (consisting of language-intrinsic goals), Academic Interest (which had the greatest contribution from interest in French literature), and Feelings about French-speaking Countries or People.

In an attempt to synthesize these two paradigms with my own research findings, I would like to propose a new *L2 Motivational Self System,* which is a broad construct of L2 motivation, made up of three dimensions:

(1) *Ideal L2 Self,* referring to the L2-specific facet of one's ideal self: If the person we would like to become speaks an L2, the *Ideal L2 Self* is a powerful motivator to learn the L2 because of the desire to reduce the discrepancy between our actual and ideal selves. This dimension is related to Noels' integrative category and the third cluster formed of Ushioda's motivational facets.

(2) *Ought-to L2 Self,* referring to the attributes that one believes one *ought to* possess (i.e., various duties, obligations, or responsibilities) in order

to *avoid* possible negative outcomes. This dimension corresponds on the one hand to Higgins' ought self and thus the more extrinsic (i.e., less internalized) types of instrumental motives, and on the other hand to the 'extrinsic' constituents in both Noels' and Ushioda's taxonomies.

(3) *L2 Learning Experience,* which concerns situation-specific motives related to the immediate learning environment and experience. Although Csizér and Dörnyei's (2005) study only concerned generalized (i.e., non-situation-specific) motives and therefore did not offer information about this dimension, past research conducted in the spirit of the situated approach described earlier has provided ample evidence of the pervasive influence of executive motives related to the immediate learning environment and experience. This dimension corresponds to Noels' intrinsic category and the first cluster formed of Ushioda's motivational facets.

Ushioda (2001) summarized her findings as follows: "We can classify all the factors in each language learner's motivational configuration as either *causal* (deriving from the continuum of L2-learning and L2-related experience to date) or *teleological* (directed toward short-term or long-term goals and future perspectives)" (p. 107). This summary fits the proposed construct closely, because the *Ideal* and the *Ought-to L2 Selves* are by definition teleological, concerning future motivational perspectives (as they concern imagined future end-states) and the *L2 Learning Experience* component is the causal dimension. It is interesting that Ushioda found that the future-oriented dimension of motivational goals/incentives and the past/present-oriented perception of the learning experience are in a complementary relationship: In her study, students with positive learning experiences tended to emphasize intrinsic motivational factors whereas participants with less illustrious learning histories tended to define their motivation principally in terms of particular personal goals or career plans. This would suggest that there may be two potentially successful motivational routes for language learners, either fueled by the positive experiences of their learning reality or by their visions for the future.

Finally, let us compare the proposed system to Robert Gardner's conceptualization of the integrative motive (cf. Fig. 4.1). At first sight there is little resemblance but if we take into account that the 'motivation' subcomponent is associated to a considerable degree with motivated behavioral measures and that Gardner has recently attached a possible instrumental motivational link to the Motivation subcomponent, we find striking similarities: The model suggests, in effect, that motivated behavior (i.e., the Motivation subcomponent) is determined by three major motivational dimension: Integrativeness, Instrumentality, and the Attitudes toward the learning situation, which corresponds closely with the proposed L2 Motivational Self System.

Temporal aspects of the L2 Motivational Self System

Although I have demonstrated that the L2 Motivational Self System is in accordance with some of the most influential lines of thoughts in L2 motivation research, further research is needed to establish its compatibility with the process-oriented conception of L2 motivation (described earlier). The L2 Learning Experience dimension is undoubtedly related to executive motives associated with the actional stage of motivated behavior, and the Ideal and Ought-to L2 Selves are by definition involved in pre-actional deliberation, but it needs to be specified how the latter two components relate to motivational processing occurring during the actional and post-actional phases of the motivational process. Ushioda (2001) suggested that motivational change entails the evolving nature of goal-orientation, that is, achieving a clearer definition of L2-related personal goals. Within a self framework this would correspond to the elaboration of the Ideal L2 Self and perhaps the internalization of the Ought-to L2 Self.

A possible promising inroad into understanding the interface of the Ideal L2 Self and the actional phase of motivation opens up if we consider Norton's (2001) concept of 'imagined communities' discussed earlier. Analyzing the stories of two immigrant language learners in Canada, Norton described their 'imagined communities' as follows:

. When Katarina and Felicia entered their language classrooms, they not only saw a classroom with four walls, but envisioned a community that transcended time and space. Thus although these learners were engaged in classroom practices, the realm of their community extended to the imagined world outside the classroom—their imagined community. (p. 164)

Norton argued that while Katarina and Felicia were actively engaged in classroom practices, the realm of their community extended beyond the four walls of the classroom; that is, they were operating at the interface of reality and imagination. However, in their case some serious problems occurred because their imagined communities were not accessible to the teacher, who, in each case, focused her energy on practices of engagement, rather than on practices of the imagination. As Norton concludes, it was for this reason that Katarina and Felicia ultimately withdrew from their ESL classes. This is a notable insight that offers a way of combining the imagined and the social aspect of classroom reality, leading to the pedagogical recommendation that teachers should encourage learners to think of themselves as living in multiple communities, including the classroom community, the target language community, and the imagined community.

Norton (2001) also highlighted Wenger's (1998) proposal of three modes of belonging to a community: *engagement, imagination,* and *align-*

ment. The conceptualization of imagination and alignment can lead us to a better understanding of how ideal self images are realized in concrete situations, because, as Norton explained, "imagination does not necessarily result in the coordination of action. It is here that the notion of alignment becomes central, because it is through alignment that learners do what they have to do to take part in a larger community" (p. 164). The author argued that the concept of 'investment' deserves special attention in this respect because this can capture the learner's active process of promoting belonging to the imagined community (see also Pittaway, 2004).

Finally, it may also be useful to consider Wenger's (1998) conceptualization of 'alignment' more closely. It reflects people's coordinating their "energy and activities in order to fit within broader structures and to contribute to broader enterprises" (p. 174). Thus, alignment concerns motivated behavior whereby participants coordinate their energies, actions, and practices. It directs and controls energy, bringing into the picture, in Wenger's words, a "scope of action writ" (p. 179). The crucial question from our perspective is how imagination and alignments interact. Wenger gave some general guidelines when he stated that imagination can change both our understanding of alignment and our ability to control it because imagination helps to build a picture of how our part fits.

L2 MOTIVATION AND SLA RESEARCH   •

Before we look at the practical, pedagogical implications of L2 motivation research, let us examine a curious situation that characterizes the position of motivation research within the broader domain of SLA. Although the study of language learning motivation has undoubtedly been one of the most developed areas within SLA research, it has virtually no links with other SLA research traditions, resulting in what appears to be a total lack of integration of motivation research into the traditional domain of applied linguistics. What is the reason for this puzzling isolation? One obvious cause may be the different scholarly backgrounds of the researchers working in the two areas. L2 motivation research has been initiated and spearheaded by *social psychologists* interested in second languages, whereas the scholars pursuing the mainstream directions of SLA research have been predominantly *linguists* by training. I suspect, however, that this is only part of the answer, and some of the reasons are inherent to the past practice of motivation research.

In my view, the crux of the problem is that SLA research, naturally, focuses on the development of language knowledge and skills and therefore analyses various language processes from a situated, process-oriented perspective. This perspective, however, has been largely incompatible with the product-oriented approach adopted by traditional motivation research, especially within the social-psychological paradigm. Broadly speaking, the main questions motivation researchers have traditionally asked are these:

- *What are the motivational characteristics of the students who decide to study an L2?*

- *How do different types of motivational dispositions affect L2 learning achievement?*

That is, the traditional motivational focus has involved matching motivational conditions and learning outcomes. In contrast, and again broadly speaking, the main question SLA researchers seek to answer is this:

- *How does the acquisition of a second language take place?*

That is, SLA researchers have concentrated on the process of language development in learners who have already made a commitment to L2 learning, without being too concerned about what exactly initiated this process. Edmondson (2004) called this view the *enabling function of motivation*, explaining it as follows:

> It hypothesizes that some minimal motivational profile is a necessary precondition for acquisition. Roughly, we can't do it, unless we 'put our minds to it,' and this enabling function can be translated metaphorically as the lowest tolerable rheostat setting, in Stevick's terms, or a slightly porous affective filter in Krashen's terminology. (p. 4)

Thus, traditional L2 motivation researchers were not particularly interested in the process of language learning because for them the focal issues of SLA were rather irrelevant—if one is interested in the social foundation of intercultural communication and affiliation, then the developmental order of various morphological features of the L2, to give only one example, is likely to seem unimportant. And, similarly, traditional SLA researchers have not been particularly interested in motivation—if one is interested in interlanguage development, then learning about the attitudinal orientations of ethnolinguistic communities is rather unhelpful. Thus, the two different research perspectives have prevented any real communication between the two camps.

Recently, however, the prospects for some real integration between the study of L2 motivation and mainstream SLA have improved considerably for at least two reasons. First, as argued in the Introduction of this volume, there has been a changing climate in applied linguistics, characterized by an increasing openness to the inclusion of psychological factors and processes into research paradigms. Second, the introduction of the process-oriented approach to motivation research has created a research perspective that is not unlike the general approach of SLA research, thereby enabling scholars coming from the two traditions to look at their targets through the same lens. This potential interface still does not automatically guarantee integration. For real integration to take place, L2 motivation research needs to meet a final criterion, namely that it should focus on specific *language behaviors* rather than general learning outcomes as the criterion measure. To exemplify this, instead of looking, for instance, at how the learners' various motivational attributes correlate with language proficiency measures in an L2 course (which would be a typical traditional design), researchers need to look at how various motivational features affect learners' specific learning behaviors during the course, such as their increased willingness to communicate in the L2, their engagement in learning tasks, or their use of certain learning/communication techniques and strategies. The viability of such an approach has been shown by Markee's (2001) intriguing study in which he related conversation analytical moves in interlanguage discourse to underlying motivational themes.

EDUCATIONAL IMPLICATIONS: DEVISING MOTIVATIONAL STRATEGIES

The cognitive-situated period of L2 motivation research shifted the attention to classroom-specific aspects of motivation and created a fertile ground for educational implications directly relevant to classroom practice. In conclusion to this chapter, I discuss three areas where recent advances have generated material that can promote the effectiveness of instructed SLA: (a) the systematic development of *motivational strategies* that can be applied by the teacher to generate and maintain motivation in the learners, (b) the formulation of *self-motivating strategies* that enable the learners to take personal control of the affective conditions and experiences that shape their subjective involvement in learning, and (c) the study of *teacher motivation*. The description of these themes is followed by a final section that examines how the newly proposed L2 Motivational Self System can enrich our understanding of the practical aspects of L2 motivation.

Devising Motivational Strategies

Given the widespread problems observed with regard to the insufficient commitment and enthusiasm of language learners, as well as the high rate of language learning failure, L2 teachers have traditionally been on the lookout for techniques they can apply to enhance student motivation. In 2001, I felt the time was ripe to summarize the relevant developments within both the L2 field and educational psychology, and the richness of what I found was frankly astonishing: There is a wealth of materials that classroom practitioners can apply to promote their motivational teaching practice and to create a motivating classroom environment (Dörnyei, 2001a, in press). Therefore, an unexpected new challenge arose: the need to organize the possible motivational strategies in a structure that offers a wide range of options for teachers to choose from yet which avoids being daunting and making readers feel how complex the domain is and how much they are *not* doing. The final framework I came up with was based on the Dörnyei-Ottó process model described earlier and consisted of four main dimensions (see Fig. 4.5):

1. *creating the basic motivational conditions,*
2. *generating initial student motivation,*
3. *maintaining and protecting motivation,*
4. *encouraging positive retrospective self-evaluation.*

In Dörnyei (2001a) these motivational facets are further broken down to concrete motivational strategies and techniques, covering a wide range of areas from 'Making the teaching materials relevant to the learners' through 'Setting specific learner goals' to 'Increasing learner satisfaction.' In the concluding chapter of that book I proposed a selective and stepwise approach to broadening one's motivational repertoire: It was argued that in developing a motivation-sensitive teaching practice it is not the quantity but the *quality* of the selected strategies that matters. Accordingly, we should aim at becoming *good enough motivators* rather than striving unreasonably to achieve 'Supermotivator' status. A few well-chosen strategies that suit both the teacher and the learners might take one beyond the motivational threshold, creating an overall positive motivational climate in the classroom. Some of the most motivating teachers often rely only on a few basic techniques.

Devising Action Control and Self-Motivating Strategies

The bottom box in Figure 4.5 contains a strategic area, 'Promoting self-motivating strategies,' which is different from the other motivational scaffolding techniques in that it passes the ownership of motivation from the teacher to the students: By applying self-motivating strategies, learners assume responsibility and regulatory control of their own motivational disposition. Because contemporary learning theories in educational psychology presume an active contribution of the learner as an agent in constructing knowledge (cf. McGroarty, 1998, 2001), a shift toward a conception of motivation that is at least partly owned by the learner makes intuitive sense. It is important to realize, however, that learners will not automatically take ownership of their motivational disposition but need to be supported in this process. In particular, their awareness needs to be raised about the variety of the potential mental reinforcers they can apply.

How can we describe the possible self-motivating strategies? Most psychological investigations in this area go back to Kuhl's (1985) pioneering conceptualization of *action control mechanisms*, which constitute a subclass of *self-regulatory strategies* concerning the learners' motivational regulatory function (see chapt. 6). Based on Corno (1993), Corno and Kanfer (1993), and Kuhl (1987), I divided self-motivating strategies into five main classes (Dörnyei, 2001a):

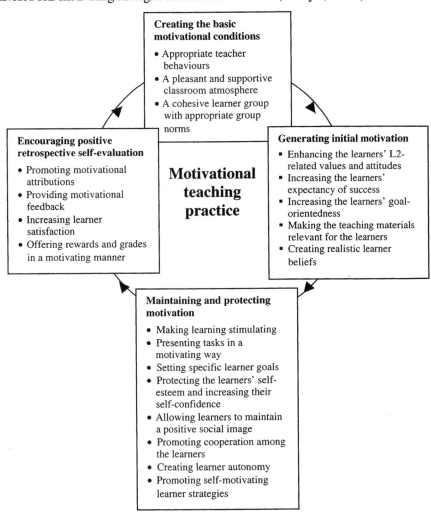

Creating the basic motivational conditions

- Appropriate teacher behaviours
- A pleasant and supportive classroom atmosphere
- A cohesive learner group with appropriate group norms

Encouraging positive retrospective self-evaluation

- Promoting motivational attributions
- Providing motivational feedback
- Increasing learner satisfaction
- Offering rewards and grades in a motivating manner

Motivational teaching practice

Generating initial motivation

- Enhancing the learners' L2-related values and attitudes
- Increasing the learners' expectancy of success
- Increasing the learners' goal-orientedness
- Making the teaching materials relevant for the learners
- Creating realistic learner beliefs

Maintaining and protecting motivation

- Making learning stimulating
- Presenting tasks in a motivating way
- Setting specific learner goals
- Protecting the learners' self-esteem and increasing their self-confidence
- Allowing learners to maintain a positive social image
- Promoting cooperation among the learners
- Creating learner autonomy
- Promoting self-motivating learner strategies

FIG. 4.5. The Components of Motivational L2 Teaching Practice.

1. *Commitment control strategies* for helping to preserve or increase the learners' original goal commitment (e.g., keeping in mind favorable expectations or positive incentives and rewards; focusing on what would happen if the original intention failed).

2. *Metacognitive control strategies* for monitoring and controlling concentration, and for curtailing unnecessary procrastination (e.g., identifying recurring distractions and developing defensive routines; focusing on the first steps to take in a course of action).

3. *Satiation control strategies* for eliminating boredom and adding extra attraction or interest to the task (e.g., adding a twist to the task; using one's fantasy to liven up the task).

4. *Emotion control strategies* for managing disruptive emotional states or moods, and for generating emotions that are conducive to implementing one's intentions (e.g., self-encouragement; using relaxation and meditation techniques).

5. *Environmental control strategies* for eliminating negative environmental influences and exploiting positive environmental influences by making the environment an ally in the pursuit of a difficult goal (e.g., eliminating distractions; asking friends to help one not to allow to do something).

Chapter 6 presents an instrument developed by Tseng, Dörnyei, and Schmitt (in press) to measure students' self-regulatory capacity in the area of vocabulary learning following the taxonomy just discussed, and the results of the validation of this scale provided empirical confirmation of the soundness of the system.

Recently, Wolters (2003) offered a different system of macrostrategies for the regulation of motivation. This taxonomy, which is an extension of his earlier work (Wolters, 1999), is not exhaustive but, as the author argued, is merely intended to substantiate the motivational self-regulatory process. Wolters identified eight key strategic ways in which students can regulate their motivation:

- *Self-consequating:* Identifying and administering self-provided extrinsic rewards or punishments for reinforcing one's desire to reach particular goals associated with completing an academic task. The rewards can be concrete such as buying an ice-cream or more subtle such as making self-praising verbal statements.

- *Goal-oriented self-talk:* Using subvocal statements or thoughts designed to increase one's desire to complete a task. This self-talk is similar to the self-reinforcing verbal statements mentioned above but the content goes beyond mere praises. Instead, students intensify their focus by elaborating on or making salient various reasons for persisting with the task, thereby 'talking themselves into' increased performance.

- *Interest enhancement:* Increasing one's intrinsic motivation by using strategies that promote the immediate enjoyment or situational interest of an activity, for example by turning the task into a game.

- *Environmental structuring*: Decreasing the possibility of off-task behavior by reducing the probability of encountering distractions or reducing the intensity of distractions.

- *Self-handicapping:* Manufacturing obstructions before or during a task to make the task more difficult. By doing so, students in effect create a kind of 'win-win' situation for themselves because if they fail, they can use the obstacle as a mitigating circumstance, and if they succeed against the odds, that puts them in a particularly good light.

- *Attribution control:* As Wolters (2003) points out, self-handicapping entails the students' *a priori* manipulation of the causal attributions that they can make once the outcome of an academic task has been obtained. Causal attributions, however, can also be manipulated after task completion in a way that they positively impact motivation by the purposeful selection of causal explanations that put students in a positive light.

- *Efficacy management:* Monitoring, evaluating, and purposefully controlling one's own self-efficacy for tasks by applying one of three methods: (a) *proximal goal setting*—that is, breaking complex tasks into simpler and more easily completed segments, associated with straightforward, specific, and short-term goals, (b) *defensive pessimism*—highlighting one's level of unpreparedness or lack of ability in order to increase anxiety that will strategically increase one's effort to prepare, and (c) *efficacy self-talk*—engaging in thoughts or subvocal statements, such as "You can do it!" to increase one's perceived self-efficacy.

- *Emotion regulation:* Regulating one's emotional experience in a constructive way, for example by reducing negative affective response or using wishful thinking.

It is obvious that the two taxonomies outlined above overlap. For example, Wolters' 'Interest enhancement' appears to be akin to my 'Satiation control,' and his concepts of 'Environmental structuring' and 'Emotion regulation' seem to correspond closely to my 'Environmental control' and 'Emotion control.' This shows that, similarly to learning strategies, the key issue in this domain is not necessarily the exact list or taxonomy of the relevant mechanisms but rather the underlying capacity that leads learners to apply such mechanisms. This selection and internalization process can be scaffolded by using the same approaches as described with learning strategies (see chapt. 6).

Teacher Motivation

The increased shift toward examining classroom-based motivation in the 1990s drew attention to a rather overlooked motivational area, the *motivational characteristics of the language teacher.* There is no doubt that teacher motivation is an important factor in understanding the affective basis of instructed SLA, since the teacher's motivation has significant bearings on the students' motivational disposition and, more generally, on their learning achievement. Furthermore, the study of teacher motivation can help us understand a looming crisis in the field of education in general: the growing disillusionment of teachers of all subject matters and the growing rate of their leaving the profession in many parts of the world. For example, a recent survey in England that involved more than 70,000 practicing teachers (GTCfE, 2002) found that 34% of them did not expect to be a teacher in five years' time and 56% claimed that their level of morale/motivation was lower than when they first became teachers. Not surprisingly, then, only 50% of the sample said that they would consider a career in teaching if they had the choice again. These figures reflect a broad, worldwide tendency and the situation of language teachers is in no way better than that of their colleagues in other subject areas (cf. Dörnyei, 2001c; Pennington, 1995).

Prompted by these considerations, in my 2001 monograph on motivation (Dörnyei, 2001c) I devoted a whole chapter to the question of *teacher motivation.* I stated there that very little work had been done on the topic in the L2 field and that this was also true of educational psychology in general. During the past few years we have conducted extensive research on the topic at the University of Nottingham, which also included comprehensive literature searches (see, e.g., Gheralis-Roussos, 2003; Shoaib, 2004). These confirmed that there is indeed very little published work on the motivation of language teachers (for valuable exceptions, see Doyle & Kim, 1999; Jacques, 2001; Kassabgy, Boraie, & Schmidt, 2001; Kimura, 2003; Pennington, 1992, 1995; Pennington & Ho, 1995), and only a limited amount of rigorous scientific research has been conducted in educational psychology on the topic. However, as we have found, there is a large body of relevant work that is hovering somewhere in between research, teaching methodology, and popular educational non-fiction. Although these studies may not meet standard research requirements, in their multitude they add up to a fairly consistent overall picture about the factors that motivate and demotivate teachers. What we need now is empirical L2-specific research that examines in a systematic way which aspects mentioned in these studies are valid and reliable characteristics of language educators. This is clearly a fertile ground for future investigations.

Practical Implications Related to the L2 Motivational Self System

The conceptualization of L2 motivation from a self perspective opens up a whole new avenue for promoting student motivation by means of increasing the elaborateness and vividness of self-relevant imagery in the students. This is, in fact, similar to the promotion of commitment control strategies just described, but our more detailed understanding of the nature of possible selves offers a rich and systematic source of motivational ideas. According to past theorizing by Markus and her colleagues (Markus & Nurosis, 1986; Markus & Ruvolo, 1989; Ruvolo & Markus, 1992; Oyserman & Markus, 1990), the following conditions can be seen to increase the motivational power of a possible self:

- *The possible self needs to exist.* Not everyone can easily generate a highly successful possible self and therefore the strength of the motivation resulting from the desire to reduce the discrepancy between one's actual and ideal L2 self will be dependent on the learner's ability to develop a salient vision of oneself as an attractive, competent, and successful L2 user.

- *The possible self needs to be primed.* Each individual has a number of different self-representations concerning different content areas as well as different types of hopes and fears, and the working self-concept, which is the accessible and functional self-concept of the moment, is a "biased sample from the universe of one's self-representations" (Ruvolo & Markus, 1992, p. 98). For a particular self-representation such as the Ideal L2 Self to become active, it needs to be triggered by some relevant event or needs to be consciously invoked by the individual as a response to an event.

- *The possible self needs to be associated with relevant procedural knowledge.* A desired end-state will have an impact on behavior only if the individual can personalize it by building a bridge of self-representations between one's current self and the hoped-for self. That is, the more elaborate a possible self in terms of concrete and relevant action plans, scripts, and strategies, the more effectively it can function as a regulator of instrumental action.

- *The possible self should be offset by a countervailing possible self in the same domain.* Positive expected selves will be maximally effective if they are linked with representations of what could happen if the desired state was not realized.

These four principles can serve as general guidelines for the development of specific classroom techniques. A recent study by Oyserman et al. (2002) provided empirical evidence that it is possible to design an intervention that promotes the development of detailed and academically focused possible selves in school learners which, in turn, increase their engagement in school. With regard to L2 learning, several motivational strategies identified in the literature (cf. Dörnyei, 2001a) can be fitted into the self framework, but Murphey's (1998, chapt. 15) unique analysis of "Passion, vision, and action" shows that by focusing on the vision aspect we can design some powerful novel motivational practices. It also seems highly likely that if we approach the promotion of a motivational teaching practice from a self perspective, the importance of social mediation—either as a result of the teacher's explicit modeling function or of the more indirect role of the peer group—will gain particular prominence (cf. Dörnyei, 2001c; Dörnyei & Murphey, 2003; Ushioda, 2003).

CONCLUSION

What kind of conclusion can be drawn about the state of the art of L2 motivation research? A rather mixed one. On the one hand, the past 15 years have revitalized the field both in terms of theoretical content and research volume: The paradigm shift from the macro- to the microperspective had a liberating effect on L2 motivation research, leading to an unprecedented boom in the field, with almost 100 new studies published in the 1990s alone. On the other hand, with regard to the main question as to whether the field can accommodate the concept of motivation in its psychological richness, the jury is still out. Not unlike the situation during the 1960 through 1990 period, when the main advances originated from a few, mainly Canadian research laboratories, we find today that a limited number of research centers are pushing the field forward. It may, unfortunately, not be an exaggeration to say that the majority of applied linguists still think of L2 motivation as the sum of integrative and instrumental motivation. We must, of course, quickly add that because of the broad domain of L2 studies and applied linguistics and because of the relatively low number of academic departments and positions specialized in this field worldwide, except for a few lucky subareas the whole field is rather thinly covered by research.

In this chapter I took a broad-angled perspective on the field of L2 motivation research, trying to describe where it came from and which direction it is moving in. In this final summary let me highlight two trends that I personally find the most promising. First, similarly to several other ID factors, recent developments in L2 motivation research have offered the possibility of a closer and more organic integration with other areas of the study of SLA. Thus, I can foresee several studies in the future investigating various applied linguistic areas using motivational factors and profiles as meaningful independent background variables, and similarly there are likely to be many more motivational studies that use elaborate SLA processes as reference points or criterion measures.

Second, as Cantor (1990) so clearly summarized, recent advances in personality psychology have successfully charted the major and stable dimensions of personality (e.g., the Big Five model—see chapt. 2) and these efforts to establish the structural basis of individual differences have paved the way for a new shift in the field, characterized by an emphasis on process, more specifically on the 'doing' side of personality. This new shift has resulted in an increased convergence of the concepts of personality and motivation, as both are now seen as active antecedents of behavior. The L2 Motivational Self System outlined in this chapter is in accordance with this new development and, I believe, it offers increased explanatory power with regard to variations in L2 learning. It seems to me that 'World English learning' is becoming a prominent and distinct subarea in human education, and due to the all-encompassing relevance of World English in a globalized world, the success of this process will partly be a function of the language aspect of the individual's global identity. Thus, whether or not we are motivated to learn English—and if we do, how much—is becoming increasingly a personality issue that can be captured by the proposed self perspective.

This latter point also concerns a more general question: In the light of the global status that English has attained, it may be reasonable to consider the usefulness of introducing a two-tier approach to L2 motivation, focusing on *world-language-learning* vs. *non-world-language-learning* separately (cf. Dörnyei & Csizér, 2002). It may well be the case that the proposed L2 Motivational Self System is more relevant to the understanding of the former than the latter process, but there is clearly a need for further research before we can draw any firm conclusions in this respect.

5

Learning Styles and Cognitive Styles

There is a considerable body of literature discussing the role of *learning styles* in SLA and most of these studies treat the concept as an important, although somewhat underresearched, topic. However, the uninitiated reader would find only very few clues in the published L2 literature that indicate that the area is a real quagmire: There is a confusing plethora of labels and style dimensions; there is a shortage of valid and reliable measurement instruments; there is a confusion in the underlying theory; and the practical implications put forward in the literature are scarce and rather mixed, and rarely helpful. So why talk about learning styles? Why devote a whole chapter to them? The answer is that there is something genuinely appealing about the notion and what scholars are hoping is that the current confusion is merely due to our insufficient knowledge rather than the scientific inadequacy of the concept. In many ways, Peter Skehan's evolving view on styles illustrates the situation well; talking about the most well-known learning style construct, *field dependence–independence*, Skehan concluded in 1989:

> Interesting though the underlying hypothesis may be, the research results are not encouraging. Field independence looks to be a seam which has been mined for all the value that is going to be found. (p. 115)

In 1998 he admitted a shift in his view:

> I concluded some years ago that 'the field independence construct is one that has been mined for all it is worth' (Skehan 1989, p. 115), and suggested that investigators turn their attention to other issues. It is interesting to see, several years later, that the situation is nothing like so clear-cut. Since then, the stakes in FD/I [field dependence–independence] research have got rather higher. (p. 240)

Quite recently, however, he again expressed a more skeptical prognosis of the field, while still maintaining that the 'jury is still out:'

> it appears from a review of findings on style that such concepts may not deserve high research priority, but they have not been eliminated as po-

120

tentially relevant second language linked measures. What is now needed is more evidence of educationally linked applications of such concepts. If such evidence is forthcoming, style concepts may become more central in SLA once again. (Dörnyei & Skehan, 2003, p. 607)

In this chapter I look into the learning style issue and show that the controversial situation concerning styles is not confined to L2 studies only but a similar picture emerges in the field of educational psychology; as Snow et al. (1996) summarized in their summary of individual differences in the *Handbook of Educational Psychology*, "No category we have covered contains a more voluminous, complex, and controversy-laced literature than that of personal styles" (p. 281). In a review article Richard Riding, one of the main authorities in cognitive style research, went even further when he claimed that "The area of style research generally has a poor reputation" (2000a, p. 316). As he explained, this is because this research area has suffered from a number of serious problems, particularly with respect to four key aspects:

Workers in this area have been remiss in that they have: generated a large and bewildering array of labels purporting to being different styles, used ineffective and questionable assessment methods, not made a clear distinction between style and other constructs such as intelligence and personality, and have been slow to demonstrate the practical utility of style. (Riding, 2000b, p. 368)

Yet, the curious fact is that many educational psychologists, including Riding himself, still believe in the concept, or at least give it the benefit of the doubt, trying at the same time to tighten up its theoretical underpinnings. Let us also start our overview of this intriguing and controversial topic by looking at some basic concepts. Firstly, what exactly are learning styles?

WHAT ARE LEARNING STYLES?

As is the case with a number of ID variables that turn out to be problematic under close scrutiny, *learning styles* can initially be defined in a seemingly straightforward and intuitively convincing manner. According to the standard definition, they refer to "an individual's natural, habitual, and preferred way(s) of absorbing, processing, and retaining new information and skills" (Reid, 1995, p. viii); thus, they are "broad preferences for going about the business of learning" (Ehrman, 1996, p. 49). In other words, the concept represents a profile of the individual's approach to learning, a blueprint of the habitual or preferred way the individual perceives, interacts with, and responds to the learning environment. These definitions make intuitive sense:

Few would question that different learners can approach the same learning task in quite different ways and it is also a logical assumption that this variation in approach is not infinite but is characterized by systematic patterns. These patterns, then, can be rightfully called 'learning styles.'

Learning styles are an appealing concept for educationalists because—unlike abilities and aptitudes—they do not reflect innate endowment that automatically leads to success. That is, styles are not yet another metaphor for distinguishing the gifted from the untalented but rather they refer to *personal preferences*. These preferences are typically bipolar, representing a continuum from one extreme to another (e.g., being more global vs. being more particular) and no value judgment is made about where a learner falls on the continuum: One can be successful in every style position—only in a different way. Thus, ideally, the concept of learning styles offers a "value-neutral approach for understanding individual differences among linguistically and culturally diverse students" (Kinsella, 1995, p. 171). In reality, however, this neutral status does not always apply to all the style dimensions because certain learning styles correlate more highly than others with desired aspects of language performance in specific settings.

Basic Conceptual Issues

Let us look at some recurring issues in the conceptualization of styles. First, what is the relationship between learning styles and learning strategies? The two concepts are thematically related since they both denote specific ways learners go about carrying out learning tasks. According to Snow et al. (1996), the main difference between the two concepts lies in their breadth and stability, with a style being a "strategy used consistently across a class of tasks" (p. 281). In agreement with this claim, Riding (2000a) added that styles probably have a physiological basis and are fairly fixed for the individual, whereas strategies may be learned and developed in order to cope with situations and tasks. Sternberg and Grigorenko (2001) highlighted the difference between the degree of consciousness involved in applying styles and strategies: Styles operate without individual awareness, whereas strategies involve a conscious choice of alternatives. As the authors conclude, although the two terms are often mixed up, "strategy is used for task- or context-dependent situations, whereas style implies a higher degree of stability falling midway between ability and strategy." (p. 3)

On the whole, the argument that styles are stable and have a cross-situational impact sounds convincing but if we take a closer look we find that there is a definite interaction between styles and situations; as Ehrman (1996) put it succinctly, "Just as situations determine which hand to use (write with one hand, grip jars to open with the other), so they also have considerable influence on choice of learning strategies associated with one learning style or another" (p. 53). Furthermore, the stability aspect of styles has also been questioned when researchers found that early educational experiences do shape one's individual learning styles by instilling positive attitudes toward certain sets of learning skills and, more generally, by teaching students how to learn (Kolb, Boyatzis, & Mainemelis, 2001).

We also get on shaky ground when we try to analyze what exactly the term 'preference' means when we talk about styles being 'broad learning preferences.' How much do these 'preferences' determine our functioning? Ehrman (1996) suggested a relatively soft interpretation of 'preference' by equating it with 'comfort zones:' "For most of us, a preference is just that— something we find more comfortable but can do another way if circumstances require it" (p. 54). As she explained, however, for a minority learning styles are more firmly set and are therefore more than mere preferences. They do not have the flexibility to change or shift their employed style according to the demands of the situation, and this may land them in trouble. According to Ehrman, a learning style, then, can range from a mild preference to a strong need.

Finally, how do learning styles relate to personality? This, again, is a source of controversy, because some well-known psychological constructs are sometimes referred to as learning styles and sometimes as personality dimensions. The dimension of extraversion–introversion is a good example, as this popular dichotomy, first brought into wide use by Swiss psychologist Carl Jung, can be found in almost every personality and learning style taxonomy. In fact, Ehrman, Leaver, and Oxford (2003) concluded in a recent overview of ID variables that the influence of personality variables on learning styles has increased greatly in recent years, promoted by the use of the 'Big Five' personality model and the Myers-Briggs Type Indicator (MBTI; cf. chapt. 2). For this reason, Ehrman (1996) actually characterized certain learning styles as 'personality-based learning styles,' which are personality dimensions that have cognitive style correlates.

I believe that the above outline of various style issues conveys well the general impression one gains when dealing with learning styles, namely that they are elusive, 'halfway' products: They refer to preferences, but these can be of varying degree; they are related to learning strategies but are somewhat different from them as they fall midway between innate abilities and strategies; they appear to be situation-independent but they are not entirely free of situational influences; and some style dimensions are also listed as major components of personality. Indeed, learning styles appear to have very soft boundaries, making the category rather open-ended, regardless of which perspective we approach it from. Ehrman et al.'s (2003) summary of the use of the term is, regrettably, valid: "the literature on learning styles uses the terms learning style, cognitive style, personality type, sensory preference, modality, and others rather loosely and often interchangeably" (p. 314).

The natural question to ask, then, is this: Do learning styles really exist? Are they independent individual difference factors or is the term merely a convenient way of referring to certain patterns of information-processing and learning behaviors whose antecedents lie in a wide range of diverse factors, such as varying degrees of acquired abilities and skills, idiosyncratic personality traits, and different exposures to past learning experiences (Dörnyei & Skehan, 2003)? The honest answer, I believe, is that we are not absolutely sure. We still do not know enough about the exact psychological mechanisms that make up the process that we usually conveniently refer to as 'learning' to be able to say that learning styles have definite neuropsychological validity and relevance to this process. The problem is that learning—and consequently the related concept of learning styles—is associated at the same time with perception, cognition, affect, and behavior, and a term that cuts across these psychologically distinct categories does not lend itself to rigorous definition.

One way forward, however, is to make a clear distinction between learning styles and cognitive styles. Although these terms have too often been used in the literature in an interchangeable manner, they are not the same. As Rayner (2000a) summarized, if learning style is represented as a profile of the individual's approach to learning, this profile can be seen to comprise two fundamental levels of functioning: The first is cognitive, referring to a stable and internalized dimension related to the way a person thinks or processes information; the second is the level of the learning activity, which is more external and embraces less stable functions that relate to the learner's continuing adaptation to the environment. It follows from this distinction that the core of a learning style is the 'cognitive style,' which can be seen as a partially biologically determined and pervasive way of responding to information and situations; and when such cognitive styles are specifically related to an educational context and are intermingled with a number of affective, physiological, and behavioral factors, they are usually more generally referred to as learning styles (Brown, 2000). In our quest for understanding the nature of learning styles, therefore, we need to take a step back and start with the analysis of cognitive styles.

COGNITIVE STYLES

Cognitive styles are usually defined as an individual's preferred and habitual modes of perceiving, remembering, organizing, processing, and representing information. As just argued, the advantage of focusing on cognitive styles prior to learning styles is that the former are devoid of any educational and situational/environmental interferences, thereby allowing for a 'purer' definition. Yet, as we will see next, this is still only a partial solution to the style ambiguity because we still find an unspecified or 'fluid' relationship between cognitive styles and personality on the one hand, and cognitive abilities on the other. Thus, cognitive styles are typically identified as being in a "conceptual gray area" (Hampson & Colman, 1994, p. x) between personality and intelligence, and are expected to explain variance beyond both of these variables. This latter point is crucial: Interest in the notion of cognitive styles originally developed, and has been maintained, by the recognition that conventional ability tests explain only part of the variance in people's performance; and, as Sternberg and Grigorenko (2001, p. 1) ask, "If abilities are only part of the answer to understanding how and why people differ in their performance, what might the rest of the answer be?"

Thus, scholars interested in individual variation in cognitive processing have traditionally identified two classes of relevant factors: those related to ability and those to style. According to Messick (1994), abilities refer to the content and level of cognition (the questions of *What?* and *How much?*), whereas cognitive styles refer to the manner or mode of cognition (the question of *How?*). That is, ability is associated with the *level* of performance (e.g., more intelligent people produce better work), whereas style focuses on the *manner* of performance (e.g., some people prefer to process information by means of visual input such as written texts, and others prefer audio input, such as listening to lectures). A second difference between styles and abilities is that abilities are unipolar (ranging from 'little' to 'more'), whereas most styles are bipolar (forming a continuum between two poles with specific characteristics). Finally, ability is associated with a straightforward value direction in that high amounts of ability are always preferable to low amounts, whereas for cognitive styles neither end of the style continuum is considered better per se. This would mean, in practical terms, that although both style and ability affect student task performance, the increase of ability improves task performance for all students, whereas the effect of style depends on the nature of the task—if a course includes a range of different tasks, students at both ends of the style continuum will have the chance to excel (Riding, 2000b).

Research on cognitive styles goes back to the end of the 19th century when scholars noticed that some people had a predominantly verbal way of representing information in thought, whereas others were more visual or imaginal (cf. Riding, 2000a). There have been ongoing investigations on styles ever since, but style research got seriously embraced only in the 1940s and 1950s, when Witkin and his colleagues initiated work on the study of *field dependence–independence* (see later in detail). During the subsequent decades, scholars identified an ever-increasing number of cognitive style dimensions (well over 20 in total), but the validity of such an extensive range of styles became the subject of a great deal of debate at the end of the 20th century, with some scholars claiming that the different style labels did not reflect genuine differences and therefore most identified styles could be grouped into far fewer principal cognitive style dimensions (Riding, 2000a). The most well-known such parsimonious theory, offered by Riding and his colleagues, is described in a separate section below.

Problems with the Notion of Cognitive Style

Although the theoretical basis of cognitive styles is more solid than that of learning styles, even cognitive styles have been subject to a lot of criticism, which never allowed for the concept to take a substantial place in mainstream cognitive psychology. As one of the main champions of cognitive style research, Richard Riding (2000b, p. 365), openly admitted:

> In the past, the study of cognitive style has been rightly criticized for being vague and superficial. It has suffered from a number of serious problems, particularly with respect to there being too many labels purporting to being different styles, the use of ineffective assessment methods, and the lack of a clear distinction between style and other constructs such as intelligence and personality.

The crux of the problem is that style research in the past has not been able to demonstrate sufficiently that the notion of cognitive style is a theoretical construct in its own right, and thus the concept has become, in Sternberg and Grigorenko's (2001) words, too 'instrument-bound.' That is, a style was what a particular style questionnaire measured. And since most researchers produced their own idiosyncratic instruments, resulting in their own idiosyncratic style conceptualizations, these overlapping concepts could not converge sufficiently, thereby creating a rather confused and confusing overall picture. This was coupled with the fact that many of the actually identified and measured style dimensions were not sufficiently separate from certain ability and personality characteristics, a problem that lead to the fall of even the most famous cognitive style dimension, field dependence–independence (as it was found to correlate excessively with spatial intelligence). As a result, several authorities in the field (e.g., Carroll, 1993) eventually rejected the construct of cognitive style as a misguided illusion (cf. Riding, 2000b; Yates, 2000).

In an analysis of the reasons for the untimely demise of styles research, Sternberg (2001) concluded that the main problem has been that the styles literature has failed to provide a common conceptual framework for scholars that would have allowed successful communication among them. Indeed, the range of metaphors used in the literature is diverse, which has resulted in a "kind of balkanization of research groups, and balkanization always has led to division and, arguably, deaths of a thousand cuts" (p. 250). Within the field of L2 studies, Griffiths and Sheen (1992) also stated in a passionate article that the fact that after three decades of research on cognitive styles it is still contested whether these styles actually exist indicates the ultimate weakness of the concept and therefore its research should be abandoned. This is a valid point, but so is Carol Chapelle's (1992) response that we simply cannot afford ignoring such a potentially useful concept as cognitive style which expresses "some of our intuitions about students" and which facilitates "appreciation for the divergent approaches to thinking and learning" (p. 381).

Riding's System

As just mentioned, Richard Riding has been one of the main international proponents of cognitive style research. Aware of the manifold problems that this research domain has struggled with, Riding has proposed a powerful and parsimonious system of cognitive styles that, in his and his followers' view, remedies the shortcomings of past styles research while maintaining the attractive features of the concept. The proposed taxonomy postulates only two superordinate style dimensions that subsume most of the previously proposed constructs (for a summary, see Table 5.1):

- *Wholist–Analytic Style* dimension, determining whether individuals tend to organize information as an integrated whole or in discrete parts of that whole (i.e., take a whole view or see things in parts).

- *Verbal–Imagery Style* dimension, determining whether individuals are outgoing and inclined to represent information during thinking verbally or whether they are more inward and tend to think in mental pictures or images; in other words, *verbalizers* are superior at working with verbal information, whereas *imagers* are better at working with visual or spatial information.

Table 5.1. List of the major cognitive style constructs that Riding's two fundamental style dimensions subsume (adapted from Riding & Rayner, 1998)

The wholist–analytic dimension

Field dependence–independence	Individual dependence on a perceptual field when analyzing a structure or form which is part of the field.
Leveling–sharpening	A tendency to assimilate detail rapidly and lose detail or emphasize detail and changes in new information.

Impulsivity–reflectiveness	Tendency for a quick vs. deliberate response.
Converging–diverging thinking	Narrow, focused, logical, deductive thinking rather than broad, open-ended, associational thinking to solve problems.
Holist–serialist thinking	The tendency to work through learning tasks or problem solving incrementally or globally and assimilate detail.
Concrete sequential/concrete random/abstract sequential/abstract random	The tendency to learn through concrete experience and abstraction either randomly or sequentially.
Assimilator–explorer	Individual preferences for seeking familiarity or novelty in the process of problem-solving and creativity.
Adaptors–innovators	Adaptors prefer conventional, established procedures, whereas innovators favor restructuring or new perspectives in problem solving.
Reasoning–intuitive active–contemplative	Preference for developing understanding through reasoning or by spontaneity/insight and learning activities which allow active participation or passive reflection.

The verbal–imagery dimension

Abstract versus concrete thinker	Preferred level and capacity of abstraction.
Verbalizer–visualizer	The extent to which verbal or visual strategies are used in thinking and to represent knowledge.

As Riding (2002) described, *wholists* tend to see a situation as a whole, are able to have an overall perspective, and appreciate the total context. Wholists therefore are 'big picture people' and therefore they can also easily lose sight of the details. When presented with a prose passage for recall, for example, wholists will do best when the title of the passage is given before rather than after the passage is presented because this title will provide them with an overall thematic orientation. *Analytics,* on the other hand, see a situation as a collection of parts, often focusing on one or two aspects only, and therefore providing the title of the reading passage will not enhance their performance substantially. Their strength is that they can separate out a situation into its parts, which allows them to come quickly to the heart of any problem. They are also good at seeing similarities and detecting differences. The danger for analytics, on the other hand, is that they may get the particular aspects that they focus on out of proportion, and thus may not get a balanced view.

The *verbal–imagery* style dimension concerns the way information is represented as well as the external and internal focus of attention. The former aspect refers to the extent to which one constructs mental pictures when reading or thinking, rather than thinking in words. The latter aspect has implications for social relationships: *Verbalizers* tend to focus outward and prefer a stimulating environment, whereas *imagers* tend to be more passive with an inward focus, content with a static environment. Of course, most people are somewhere in between the two extremes with regard to the two style dimensions, often being able to benefit from the advantages of both. And, to complicate things further, the two style dimensions interact with each other, resulting in various combination patterns.

The validity of these dimensions has been greatly increased by the development of a computerized instrument, the Cognitive Styles Analysis, that provides relatively direct measures for each of the two dimensions (see later in detail). Empirical research using this instrument has revealed that the dimensions are independent of one another, are separate from intelligence, and are independent of, but interacting with, personality (Riding, 2000a).

KOLB'S MODEL OF LEARNING STYLES

Having reviewed briefly a 'pure' cognitive style system, let us now return to the broader issue of learning styles. There are a number of competing models in the literature, but the theory proposed by Kolb (1984; Kolb et al., 2001) as part of his broader experiential learning theory is one that has been widely endorsed by both researchers and practitioners. Furthermore, as is the case with Riding's construct, Kolb's theory is also accompanied by an established measuring instrument, the 'Learning Style Inventory' (see later).

Kolb's learning style construct is based on the permutation of two main dimensions, *concrete* vs. *abstract thinking* and *active* vs. *reflective information processing*. An orientation toward *concrete thinking* focuses on being involved in experiences and dealing with immediate human situations in a personal way, emphasizing feeling as opposed to thinking. An orientation toward *abstract conceptualization* focuses on using logic, ideas, and concepts, emphasizing thinking as opposed to feeling. An orientation toward *active experimentation* focuses on actively influencing people and changing situations; it emphasizes practical applications as opposed to reflective understanding. An orientation toward *reflective observation* focuses on understanding the meaning of ideas and situations by carefully observing and impartially describing them; it emphasizes understanding as opposed to practical application. Based on the combination of the two style continuums, four basic learner types, or learning style patterns, emerge:

- *Divergers* (concrete & reflective) have received their label because they prefer concrete situations that call for the generation of ideas, such as a brainstorming session. This does not mean they are abstract thinkers; just the opposite, they are down-to-earth people who learn best through concrete experience and like to look at concrete situations from many points of view in a reflective manner. They are also interested in other people and are fairly emotional in their dealings with them. They have broad cultural interests and often specialize in the arts. In classroom situations they prefer to work in groups.

- *Convergers* (abstract & active) are abstract thinkers who generate ideas and theories. They are, however, not detached from reality as they are interested in active experimentation to find practical uses for their schemes. They are good at solving specific problems, especially if the tasks are technical rather than interpersonal or social in nature. In formal learning situations, people with this style prefer experiments and simulations, laboratory assignments, and practical applications.

- *Assimilators* (abstract & reflective) are also abstract thinkers but their strength is not in dreaming up ideas and then actively trying to put them into test, like that of the *convergers*, but rather, as the name suggests, assimilating disparate observations in a reflective manner, that is, understanding a wide range of information and putting it into a concise and logical form. People with this style embody best the stereotype of the 'aloof academic,' as they are less interested in people than in abstract concepts and find it more important that a theory has logical soundness than practical value.

- *Accommodators* (concrete & active) are the most hands-on learners: They like concrete experience and active experimentation, and they are stimulated by challenging experiences even to the extent of taking risks. They often follow their 'gut' feelings rather than logical analysis. No wonder that this learning style is effective in action-oriented careers such as marketing or sales. In formal learning situations they like to work with others on active projects and enjoy field work.

As I was preparing the above summary of the main facets of Kolb's four learning styles/types, I caught myself saying after each style, *'Yes, that's me!'* This experience, which I believe I share with many others, is related to two broader issues. One issue is that we should not forget that the four types are the 'pure' and extreme cases, whereas people typically display some sort of a combination of these, and in an ideal situation they can even benefit from all the four. The other issue is that the narrative descriptions that often accompany various learning style dimensions can be deceptive in the sense that people often read them in a somewhat selective manner, focusing only on the aspects that characterize them, although the style as a whole may not match their learning approach. Therefore, for learning styles to be usable in a scientifically rigorous manner, they need to be operationalized in a measurable way and not merely in descriptors of the style categories. In other words, the way to really see which style category we fall under should not happen by merely matching style descriptors with our self-image but rather through using a measuring instrument. Thus, the existence of accurate measuring tools is the prerequisite to the recognition of the validity of various style theories and this is where cognitive and learning styles so often fall short of the mark. Let us next look at the assessment issue in some detail.

ASSESSING COGNITIVE AND LEARNING STYLES

The assessment of cognitive and learning styles is undoubtedly the Achilles heel of the concept. In a review of the area, Irvine (2001) stated rather disappointedly that "the enforced conclusion one may have to accept with reluctance is that the means of pursuing, in operational form, the elusive pimpernel of an acceptable measurement protocol for style is not available" (p. 274). He found this all the more disconcerting as in their everyday lives people do not seem to have any trouble identifying various style characteristics. As he pointed out, "the notion of style is so intuitively certain in ordinary people untrammeled by psychologists' preoccupations with measurement, that professional entertainers make a good living by mimicking styles among the great, the good, the bad, and the ugly" (p. 274). So, if this claim is true and style is relatively easy to capture and imitate, why is it so difficult to measure?

We can answer this question in at least two ways. On the one hand, we must recognize that there are some style instruments that appear to do a reasonably good job. Two of the best known ones, Riding's Cognitive Styles Analysis (CSA) and Kolb's Learning Style Inventory (LSI), are examined in some detail next. On the other hand, we may also want to consider Chapelle's (1992) summary: "I believe that the most important and relevant human constructs are those which are neither interesting to 'authorities' nor measurable at present" (p. 381). That is, it could be the case that although learning styles are valid and important psychological entities, measurement theory has not as yet developed the right methodology to capture them. In the history of physics, for example, we find several examples when a theory was proposed well before the adequate measuring procedures and instruments had been developed to verify it.

When it comes to cognitive and learning styles, currently we know only of two established ways of assessing them: either by relying on the learners' own self-reports on how they perceive their cognitive functioning, or by asking learners to perform mini-information-processing tasks and then making inferences from their performances. Kolb's LSI is a good example for the first type and Riding's CSA for the second (the Embedded Figures Test, which has traditionally been used to measure field dependence–independence, is also a test of performance belonging to the second category and it will be discussed later in this chapter). Interestingly, Rebecca Oxford and her colleagues have been experimenting since the 1990s with a qualitative approach to infer language learners' style preferences by eliciting thematic student essays in several locations around the world and then submitting these narratives to content analysis (e.g., Oxford, 1999d; Oxford, 2001; Oxford & Massey, in press). This is a real innovation in the area of style assessment, resulting in fresh insights into the learners' perceptions of the impact of their styles, as well as the mismatches between their and their teachers' styles, on their learning process (see later in more detail).

Kolb's Learning Style Inventory (LSI)

The original LSI instrument was a nine-item self-description questionnaire. Each item asked the respondent to rank-order four words in a way that best described their learning style. One word in each item corresponded to one of the four learning modes—concrete experience (e.g., "feeling"), reflective observation (e.g., "watching"), abstract conceptualization (e.g., "thinking"), and active experimentation (e.g., "doing"). The most recent version of the instrument, Version 3 (Kolb, 1999), has 12 items and the actual wording has been changed from single words to short statement format, as illustrated in Table 5.2.

The initial validation of the LSI scales was carried out with a sample of 1,933 participants. As Kolb (1984) reports, the theoretical assumption that the 'abstract' and 'concrete thinking' categories were opposite ends of a continuum was born out by significant negative correlation (-0.57) between the two orientations. Similarly, there was also a significant negative correlation (-0.50) between 'active' and 'reflective information processing' orientations. On the other hand, there was no substantial intercorrelation between the components associated with the two different dimensions.

Although the LSI scales are theoretically well-founded and have good psychometric properties, the big question still remains: Are the attributes that the scales measure indices of learning styles or something else? Kolb et al. (2001) offered some evidence of the ambiguous nature of this issue because, as they summarized, the main dimensions of the LSI correlate signifi-

---

Table 5.2. Sample items from Kolb's (1999) Learning Style Inventory (Version 3: LSI3)

The four statements in both sample items need to be rank-ordered according to how they refer to the respondents. Thus, four marks are to be given to the statement that is most true and one to the one that is least appropriate.

When I learn:
_____ I like to deal with my feelings
_____ I like to watch and listen
_____ I like to think about ideas
_____ I like to be doing things

I learn best from:
_____Observation
_____Personal relationships
_____Rational theories
_____A chance to try out and practice

---

cantly with certain components of the Myers-Briggs Type Indicator (MBTI), which is primarily a personality type inventory, although as was pointed out in chapter 2, various psychological types display a strong link with certain learning styles and therefore the MBTI is often cited when discussing learning styles (cf. Ehrman, 1996).

A further problem with self-report measures such as the LSI is that the actual items usually focus on behavioral correlates of assumed style characteristics (Riding, 2000b); in other words, respondents are not asked about their style features but rather about typical behaviors associated with these style features. The item "I write lists of everything I need to do each day" from the Learning Style Survey (Cohen, Oxford, & Chi, 2002; see Table 5.5) is a good example of this. While behavioral self-report items are not necessarily an inappropriate way of obtaining an index of an underlying trait, problems start when researchers correlate the test results with behavioral criterion measures, such as the learners' performance. As Riding pointed out, this creates a circularity of correlating, in effect, behavior with behavior, in contrast to identifying fundamental sources of style that can be seen to affect behaviors.

Riding's Cognitive Styles Analysis (CSA)

Currently the CSA (Riding, 1991) appears to be one of the most accurate instruments to measure styles for a number of reasons: First, it focuses on cognitive styles rather than learning styles, which allows it to target a narrower and more precisely definable domain. Second, it does not utilize the introspective self-report format that the LSI is an example of, but rather tests respondent performance directly. Third, the reliability of the test is greatly enhanced by the fact that it is computer-based. The CSA assesses both ends of the *wholist-analytic* and *verbal-imagery* dimensions, and comprises three subtests:

- *Subtest 1, Verbal-Imagery dimension:* Students are presented a number of statements (48 in total), one at a time, which require a simple true or false response by pressing a button on the keyboard. Half of the statements are about conceptual categories (e.g., "table and chair are the same type"); the other half describe the appearance of objects ("snow and chalk are the same color"). Half of the statements of each type are true, the other half false. This subtest is based on the assumption that *imagers* respond more quickly to visual items because they find it easier to represent the information in terms of visual images, whereas *verbalizers* are at an advantage with the conceptual items because the conceptual category membership is verbally abstract in nature and cannot be represented in visual form. The computer automatically records the response time to each statement and uses this information to calculate a ratio of verbal response time to visual response time. A low ratio corresponds to a *verbalizer* and a high ratio to an *imager*, with the intermediate position being described as *bimodal*. Because both types of item require reading, factors such as reading speed and ability are inherently controlled for by the calculation of the ratio.

- *Subtest 2, Wholist dimension:* Students are presented pairs of complex geometrical figures side by side on the screen (a total of 20 pairs) and they have to decide about each pair whether they are identical or not. *Wholists* are assumed to respond more quickly because their natural tendency to focus on the whole picture corresponds to the task of absorbing the whole shapes.

- *Subtest 3, Analytic dimension:* This subtest is similar to the previous one in presenting a pair of geometrical shapes at a time (20 times), but this time the question is whether the first figure, which is a relatively simple geometrical shape (e.g., a square or a triangle), is contained within the second, more complex figure. *Analytics*, who are more inclined to focus on details, respond more quickly because the task requires the larger shape to be broken down into its constituent parts. Once again, the computer records the response times and calculates the wholist–analytic ratio.

Throughout the test the testees are not made aware that the assessment uses response time, because the intention is that they undertake the tasks in a relaxed way that reflects their usual manner of processing information. And because the final indices are based on ratios, the actual response speed does not influence the style result.

Riding and Rayner (1998) emphasized several positive features of the CSA: (a) It is an objective test in the sense that it is objectively scored and the respondents are not aware of the real focus of the assessment; (b) both ends of the style continuums are assessed, which makes it distinct from measuring abilities; (c) because of the limited and simple language it involves, its use is versatile across age and proficiency groups; and (d) the computerized format creates a context-free character, which allows it to be used across situations and cultures. Furthermore, Riding (2001) reported statistical evidence that the two dimensions are unrelated to one another and show no age or gender differences. What is just as important, the scales appear to be unrelated to intelligence, which supports the fact that the styles measured are not simply subtypes of ability. Finally, although correlations of some magnitude were found between certain personality dimensions and the CSA scales, the overall pattern appeared to point to a model in which physiologically based personality sources are independent of cognitive style but are moderated by style in their effect on behavior.

Recently, Peterson, Deary, and Austin (2003a) examined the reliability of the CSA by comparing performance on the original CSA test and a new parallel version. They concluded that in its present form the test was not sufficiently reliable or internally consistent. However, the authors added that when the CSA was doubled in length, the wholist-analytic dimension of cognitive style preference became a more stable and reliable measure. Not surprisingly, Riding (2003) questioned these findings because he claimed that Peterson et al.'s study was not executed properly. And again unsurprisingly, Peterson et al. (2003b) maintained that their original concerns were valid.

COGNITIVE AND LEARNING STYLES IN L2 STUDIES

Styles research in the L2 field offers a mixture of good and bad news. On the positive side is the fact that there has been a longstanding research interest in language learning styles and several instruments have been developed and used to understand the role of learning styles in SLA. Reid's (1995, 1998) two anthologies of relevant articles and instruments offer a good overview of the early research, and Bailey et al. (2000), Ehrman and Leaver (2003), and Ehrman et al. (2003) summarize the research of the 1990s. The negative aspect is that hardly any attempt has been made to address the issue of the various conceptual ambiguities and difficulties associated with the notion of learning styles in the psychological literature, as if authors had been oblivious to the problematic nature of the concept; this is illustrated well by the fact that the terms *learning styles* and *cognitive styles* have either not been distinguished properly in the L2 literature or have been used in an interchangeable manner. This problem has been augmented by the fact that empirical studies conducted on L2 learning styles have typically produced weak, mixed, or at best moderate results, as a consequence of which there has been a gradual loss of interest in language learning style research in the second half of the 1990s. However, this situation may be changing for the better because there has been a renewed interest since the late 1990s in designing learning style constructs in several different parts of the world.

The following discussion is largely chronological. I first discuss the research into *field dependence–independence* and then the area of *sensory preferences*. This will be followed by an overview of the best known language learning styles batteries and constructs, and through their description the other major learning style dimensions that have featured in L2 research. Two of these constructs, a recently developed theory by Ehrman and Leaver (2003) and a theoretical proposal by Skehan (1998), are examined in separate sections. Finally, the chapter concludes by looking at the controversial issue as to whether the notion of learning styles has any real practical relevance to classroom practitioners.

Field Dependence–Independence in L2 Studies

The initial momentum in L2 styles research was generated by the conceptualization of *field dependence–independence* (FD/I) and this style construct has received the greatest amount of attention in L2 studies ever since. Psychological research on FD/I was initiated by Herman Witkin over thirty years ago and was originally associated with visual perception: It was noticed that people could be categorized in terms of the degree to which they were dependent on the structure of the prevailing visual field. Some people are highly dependent on this field, which in practical terms means that they cannot see inconspicuous things right in front of their nose—for example, they are hopeless when looking for some small object (such as a nail) dropped on the floor. Field-independent people on the other hand are free— or independent—of the influence of the whole field when they look at the parts and therefore can notice details that their field-dependent counterparts simply cannot 'see.' Thus, field-independent people make perfect scouts, for example, as they can notice an enemy's camouflage against its natural background. Our varying capacity to perceive the details of a field is so well known that magazines regularly include visual tasks along the 'spot the difference/similarities' line or publish complex pictures in which the readers must find embedded figures or shapes.

The FD/I style distinction, however, is more than a mere perceptional characteristic as it is assumed to affect the individual's whole behavior in a similar way to Riding's wholist–analytic style (which is thought to subsume FD/I). Sternberg and Grigorenko (2001) argued that field independence is almost always the preferable style, and indeed, as Johnson, Prior, and Artuso (2000) summarized, much of the literature on the construct reports that field independents tend to outperform field dependents on cognitive tasks. This makes intuitive sense because field independents, by definition, are better at focusing on some aspects of experience or stimulus, separating it from the background, and analyzing it unaffected by distractions. However, it has also been proposed that when the target of our attention is a complex domain such as language with its prominent cognitive, affective, and social dimensions, being able to focus on the background, that is, the whole situation, can have its advantages (Chapelle, 1995). Field dependents are more responsive as they interact with the environment and, thus, tend to have a stronger interpersonal orientation and greater alertness to social cues than field independents. As Ehrman (1996) reported, already Witkin and his colleagues noticed in their initial research that field independents were often characterized by social detachment, task orientation, and a lack of interest in what was important to most others. Brown (2000) called this aloof characteristic a 'cognitive tunnel vision' and related it to the saying, 'You can't see the forest for the trees.'

Thus, in L2 studies field dependence may not necessarily be a disadvantage because the accompanying social sensitivity can be a real asset in certain tasks; for example, in Johnson et al.'s (2000) study, the researchers found that field dependents, as opposed to field independents, performed better on L2 tasks that emphasized communicative rather than formal aspects of language proficiency. Other researchers, however, found that field independents had an overall advantage at various aspects of SLA (for reviews, see Brown, 2000; Chapelle, 1995; Hoffman, 1997), which could be related to their ability to separate the essential from the inessential, as well as a greater capacity to channel attention selectively and to notice important aspects of language. Skehan (1998) summarized the emerging consensus well:

> In sum, the FI individual benefits from the way he or she processes information but is seen to avoid situations in which language is actually going to be used for communication. FD individuals, while comfortable and sensitive in communication situations, are not seen to be effective

information processors, and so, although provided with more information to work with, will exploit it less. From this one can infer that FI individuals should do better on non-communicative, more cerebral tests, while FD individuals should excel in more communicative situations, when what is assessed is language use rather than language-like use. Clearly, this is a comprehensible and attractive 'package,' whose lures have engaged the attentions of many researchers. (pp. 238–239)

We should note, however, that this clear-cut and seemingly straightforward and logical pattern is partly the result of speculation and wishful thinking, because the actual research results are far from being strong, and are often nonsignificant or conflicting (cf. Ellis, 1994). This has led Griffiths and Sheen (1992) to launch a critical attack on the whole line of FD/I research in SLA, claiming that "field dependence/independence does not have, and never has had, any relevance for second-language learning" (p. 131), a view that is echoed by some other researchers such as Ellis (1994). In a less pessimistic response to Griffith and Sheen, Chapelle (1992) acknowledged that past research—both in cognitive psychology and in L2 studies—had suffered from a number of conceptual and measurement problems, but she believed that the construct had such great potential that it should not simply be dismissed. Indeed, we need to recognize that even if the construct does exist, it would be difficult to produce consistently strong results in its support because of its interaction with situational and task constraints, other personality and style characteristics, as well as with various learning approaches and strategies. Of course, these difficulties are not unique to FD/I but characterize the study of cognitive/learning styles in general, and the fact that they are mentioned with regard to this particular construct is only due to the prominence of FD/I among the various style dimensions.

Let us conclude this section by addressing yet another problem concerning FD/I, one that has probably played the most important role in discrediting the concept among researchers, namely its strong association with ability, which led to the allegation that this cognitive style was simply a disguised measure of intelligence (cf. Dörnyei & Skehan, 2003). Sternberg and Grigorenko (2001) reported on several studies that provided evidence that field independence was consistently correlated with verbal and performance aspects of intelligence and was essentially indistinguishable from spatial ability. Furthermore, research on the heritability of the construct also pointed to the conclusion that a significant portion of the genetic variance in FD/I was explainable by genetic variation in intelligence. Consequently, Sternberg and Grigorenko's summary was rather grim: "Thus, the preponderance of evidence at this point suggests that field independence is tantamount to fluid intelligence" (p. 7).

Although this analysis by two leading cognitive psychologists is rather conclusive and does not bode well for the long-term survival of FD/I, let me mention a further point that may actually cancel out some of the negative evidence and which also illustrates the complexity of the cognitive style issue. This point concerns the measurement of field dependence–independence. We need to realize that in research studies whenever data-based results are mentioned, the target construct in question (in our case FD/I) is necessarily equated with the scores on a particular measuring instrument. But what if the construct is valid but the instrument is not and it is this measurement deficiency which distorts the picture? As described next, there are indications that this might indeed be the case with regard to FD/I, suggesting that we need to be careful not to confound the FD/I construct with the test measures.

FD/I is typically measured by means of the Embedded Figures Test (EFT) or its group version, the GEFT. These are paper-and-pencil instruments which require students to attempt to discern simple geometric figures from more complicated patterns. As Riding (2000a) argued, it was assumed in these tests that field-independent individuals would be able to complete tasks more quickly than field-dependent ones; however, the tests do not include any subtests on which the field-dependent individuals are likely to outperform the field-independent ones, and therefore the overall test score is more like an ability score, ranging from bad to good, than a bipolar cognitive style score. This ability aspect of the EFT/GEFT is further augmented by the fact that the testtakers' test performance is likely to be affected by their general ability or intelligence scores, rendering the test a disguised ability measure. If this is so, as Skehan (1998) concluded, then the EFT and the GEFT achieve their predictive power not from any style dimension, but because they contain scope for traditional intelligence to operate. In this case, the correlation between FD/I as measured by EFT/GEFT and language proficiency would be due to the inbuilt intelligence component. This was exactly the case in a study by Hansen and Stansfield (1981), where the moderate positive correlations between field independence and Spanish proficiency scores were substantially weakened when the students' scholastic ability was statistically removed from the equations: only one of the original six proficiency measures, the score on a cloze test, maintained significance.

Sensory Preferences

The learning style dimension that most language teachers, and even many language students, would be familiar with is the categorization of *sensory preferences* into 'visual,' 'auditory,' 'kinesthetic,' and sometimes 'tactile' types. This dimension concerns the perceptual modes or learning channels through which students take in information; certain aspects of this dimension are also covered by Riding's 'verbal-imagery' style dimension. Let us look at the four preference types:

- *Visual learners* outnumber all the other three groups; Oxford (1995) reported that in her experience as many as 50% to 80% of people in any class would say they are predominantly visual. As the term suggests, these learners absorb information most effectively if it is provided through the visual channel. Thus, they tend to prefer reading tasks and often use colorful highlighting schemes to make certain information visually more salient. We need to be careful not to equate automatically the visual style with the unconditional love of the written word. As Kinsella (1995) pointed out, some visual learners may be overwhelmed by extensive printed material and require a less verbal presentation of information through media such as pictures, graphs, charts, and other graphic forms. In general, visual learners like visual stimulation such as films and videos, and if some large chunk of information is presented orally (e.g., in a lecture) their understanding is considerably enhanced by a handout and various visual aids, such as overhead transparencies, as well as by taking extensive notes.

- *Auditory learners* use most effectively auditory input such as lectures or audiotapes. They also like to 'talk the material through' by engaging in discussions and group work. They benefit from written passages to be read out and they often find that reciting out loud what they want to remember (even telephone numbers or dates) is helpful. Not surprisingly, they find teaching tapes very useful and, as Ehrman (1996) observed, they prefer oral practice without their books.

- *Kinesthetic* and *tactile learners* are often grouped together under the 'haptic' style category and this is understandable because the two style preferences are somewhat related although not identical. The kinesthetic style refers to learning most effectively through complete body experience (e.g., whole-body movement), whereas tactile learners like a hands-on, touching learning approach. The key issue for the former group is movement, while for the latter the manipulation of objects. Kinesthetic learners thus require frequent breaks or else they become fidgety—sitting motionless for hours is a real challenge for them. They often find that walking around while trying to memorize something helps. Tactile learners enjoy making posters, collages, and other types of visuals, building models, and they also happily engage in creating various forms of artwork. For them conducting a lab experiment may be a real treat.

The different sensory preferences do not exclude each other. For example, successful learners often use both visual and auditory input, but they usually display slight preferences, or *modality strengths,* one way or the other. As students grow older, those with mixed modality strengths have a decidedly better chance of success than do those with a single modality strength because they can process information in whatever way it was presented (Kinsella, 1995).

Assessing Language Learning Styles

There have been a number of published instruments available for teachers and researchers to measure L2 learning styles. They all follow a self-report format in which respondents are to indicate their answers by marking one of the options on a rating scale. The tests vary in how much reliability and validity data have been reported about them by the authors but it is fair to say that most of them have been developed for practical rather than research purposes, that is, to raise language learners' awareness of style issues in general and of their own style preferences in particular. Thus, these batteries have normally not been fine-tuned for scientific measurement purposes by submitting them to the kind of rigorous standardization process that is a requirement in psychology for an instrument to become admissible. The following section presents a sample of the best known or most recent tests. Describing their components also offers a good opportunity for introducing the various style dimensions they cover.

Perceptual Learning Style Preference Questionnaire and Learning Style Indicator

Joy Reid's (1995) Perceptual Learning Style Preference Questionnaire (PLSPQ; originally developed in 1984) was the first learning style measure widely known in the L2 field. Although the author is an L2 researcher and the instrument has been used with L2 learners, it is in fact not L2-specific, as the items do not mention any subject matter. It consists of 30 randomly ordered statements for six learning style preferences: visual, auditory, kinesthetic, tactile, group learning, and individual learning. It uses 5-point Likert scale items ranging from 'strongly agree' to 'strongly disagree,' focusing on behavioral preferences (e.g., "I learn more by reading textbooks than by listening to others"). The instrument is very user-friendly, with an accompanying self-scoring sheet and a short explanation of learning style preferences that also contains practical suggestions for learners. Table 5.3 presents a sample item from each scale.

Wintergerst, Itzen, and DeCapua (2001) reported on a series of validation studies of the PLSPQ that involved confirmatory factor analysis and follow-up interviews containing direct and open-ended questions. The researchers found that some items in the survey were not clear measures of the learning styles they intended to measure, and the results of the PLSPQ and the subsequent oral interviews contradicted each other on several points. However, after they ran a factor analysis of the PLSPQ items (and deleted six original items), Wintergerst et al. managed to obtain a simple three-factor solution, and the multi-item scales that were based on this factor structure displayed adequate internal consistency reliability. They labeled the three scales as follows: (a) Group Activity Orientation, referring to a student's preference of learning best when he/she is interacting or working with one or more students in a learning situation, (b) Individual Activity Orientation, referring to a student's preference of learning best when he/she is working alone in a learning situation, and (c) Project Orientation, referring to a student's preference of learning best when he or she is involved in hands-on activities or when working with materials in a learning situation. Because the authors viewed the reduced PLSPQ item pool and their reinterpretation of its internal structure to represent a new instrument, they called it the Learning Style Indicator. Wintergerst, DeCapua, and Verna (2003) provided further evidence in support of the reliability and validity of this diagnostic tool.

Table 5.3. Sample items from Joy Reid's Perceptual Learning Style Preference Questionnaire (Reid, 1995, pp. 202-207)

Visual preference
- I learn more by reading textbooks than by listening to others.

Auditory preference
- I learn better in class when the teacher gives a lecture.

Kinesthetic preference
- When I do things in class, I learn better.

Tactile preference
- I enjoy making something for a class project.

Group preference
- I learn more when I study with a group

Individual preference

> • When I study alone, I remember things better.

Style Analysis Survey and Learning Style Survey

Rebecca Oxford's (1993; reprinted in Oxford, 1999d; Reid, 1995) Style Analysis Survey (SAS) is similar to the PLSPQ in that although it has been devised by an L2 expert and has primarily been used with L2 learners, the items themselves are non-subject-specific. The similarities do not end here: Both tests consist of 5 parts, but the SAS is more complex and with its 110 items is considerably longer than the PLSPQ. Section 1 of the SAS targets sensory preferences similarly to the PLSPQ, but the other four sections focus on other established personality/style characteristics: extraversion vs. introversion, intuitive vs. concrete/sequential, closure-oriented vs. open, global vs. analytic. Table 5.4 provides a brief description and a sample item for each

---

Table 5.4. Description of Oxford's (1993) Style Analysis Survey

I. How I use my physical senses to study or work (30 items)

- Visual, auditory, hands-on — This section is similar to the corresponding parts of the PLSPQ.

II. How I deal with other people (20 items)

- Extroverted — Turning outward and gaining energy from the external world.
  E.g., *"Wherever I go, I develop personal contacts."*
- Introverted — Turning inward for our sense of wholeness and self-esteem.
  E.g., *"In a large group, I tend to keep silent."*

III. How I handle possibilities (20 items)

- Intuitive-random — Thinking in abstract, future-oriented way, willing to rely on hunches, inspiration, and imagination for perceiving reality.
  E.g., *"I have a vivid imagination."*
- Concrete-sequential — Being concerned with facts and preferring them to be presented in a step-by-step, organized fashion.
  E.g., *"I behave in a down-to-earth way."*

IV. How I approach tasks (20 items)

- Closure-
  oriented
  Having a need for clarity and preferring to plan ahead and follow instructions without any improvisation.
  E.g., *"I make lists of things I need to do."*

- Open
  Preferring spontaneity, flexible situations without concern for deadlines.
  E.g., *"I like to just let things happen, not plan them."*

V. How I deal with ideas (20 items)

- Global
  Focusing on the big picture and following instincts or guesswork in distilling the main principles of a certain material.
  E.g., *"I can summarize information rather easily."*

- Analytic
  Preferring to work our way through the material systematically and breaking units apart to understand them.
  E.g., *"I use logical analysis to solve problems."*

Table 5.5. Description of Cohen, Oxford, and Chi's (2001) Learning Style Survey

---

I. How I use my physical senses (30 items): Similar to Section I of SAS.

II. How I expose myself to learning situations (12 items): Similar to Section II of SAS.

III. How I handle possibilities (12 items): Similar to Section III of SAS.

IV. How I deal with ambiguity and deadlines (8 items): Similar to Section IV of SAS.

V. How I receive information (10 items)

Global
Being comfortable getting the gist or main idea and communicating even if we don't know all the words of concepts.
E.g., *"I prefer short and simple answers rather than long explanations."*

Particular
Focusing more on details and remembering specific information about a topic well.
E.g., *"I need very specific examples in order to understand fully."*

VI. How I further process information (10 items)

Synthesizing
Being able to summarize material well and enjoy guessing meanings and predicting outcomes.
E.g., *"I can quickly paraphrase what other people say."*

| Analytic | Being able to pull ideas apart and do well on logical analysis tasks; having a tendency to focus on grammar rules.
E.g., *"I'm good at solving complicated mysteries and puzzles."* |

VII. How I commit material to memory (6 items)

| Sharpener | Tendency to notice differences and seek distinctions among items as we commit material to memory.
E.g., *"As I learn new material in the target language, I make fine distinctions among speech sounds, grammatical forms, and words and phrases."* |
| Leveler | Tendency to clump material together in order to remember it, by eliminating or reducing differences, and by focusing almost exclusively on similarities.
E.g., *"I ignore distinctions that would make what I say more accurate in the given context."* |

VIII. How I deal with language rules (6 items)

| Deductive | Preference to go from the general to the specific and to start with rules and theories rather than with specific examples.
E.g., *"I like to start with rules and theories rather than specific examples."* |
| Inductive | Preference to go from specific to general and prefer to begin with examples rather than rules or theories.
E.g., *"I like to learn rules of language indirectly by being exposed to examples of grammatical structures and other language features."* |

IX. How I deal with multiple inputs (6 items)

| Field-independent | Preference to separate or abstract material from within a given context.
E.g., *"I not only attend to grammar but check for appropriate level of formality and politeness."* |
| Field-dependent | Tendency to deal with information in a more holistic way.
E.g., *"It is a challenge for me to both focus on communication in speech or writing while at the same time paying attention to grammatical agreement (e.g., person, number, tense, or gender)."* |

X. How I deal with response time (6 items)

| Impulsive | Tendency to react quickly in acting or speaking without thinking the situation through.
E.g., *"I jump in, see what happens, and make corrections if needed."* |

Reflective	Tendency to think things through before taking action rather than trusting our gut reactions. E.g., *"I need to think things through before speaking or writing."*

XI. How literally I take reality (4 items)

Metaphoric	Preference to learn material by conceptualizing aspects of it, such as the grammar system, in metaphorical terms. E.g., *"I find that building metaphors in my mind helps me deal with language (e.g., viewing the language like a machine with component parts that can be disassembled).*
Literal	Preference for a relatively literal representation of concepts. E.g., *"I take things at face value, so I like language material that says what it means directly."*

style dimension. Respondents give their answers on 4-point rating scales with 'never' and 'always' as the two poles. The SAS is also a user-friendly test, with a self-scoring sheet, explanations about the results, and some practical tips and suggestions.

Cohen, Oxford, and Chi's (2001) Learning Style Survey (LSS) is a further improvement on the SAS. The authors attempted to enhance the quality of the original instrument in two ways: First, they increased the breadth of the test by including several additional style dimensions. In this work they drew on Ehrman and Leaver's (2003; Ehrman, 2001) theoretical construct that is described in the next section. Second, they set out to devise an instrument that would be more focused on language-related issues than the previously published style batteries were. As a result of their effort, the LSS displays the following changes relative to the SAS: (1) It contains more facets—11 instead of 6 components—but the total number of items did not increase, which was achieved by shortening some scales. (2) It contains some L2-learning-specific items, mixed with non-subject-specific ones, and even the latter have been generally revised (partly drawn on the Ehrman and Leaver's 'E&L Construct'—see below). (3) The rating scale has been changed from a 4- to a 5-point format. (4) The 'global–analytic' dimension has been changed for 'global–particular.' Table 5.5 provides details about the test; the component descriptions are partly based on the information material accompanying the battery.

Cohen and Oxford (2001) developed a simplified version of the LSS for young learners. This test contains only 51 items in four subscales: (1) How I use my physical senses (sensory preferences), (2) how I expose myself to learning situations (extroverted vs. introverted), (3) how I approach tasks (closure-oriented vs. open), and (4) how I receive information (global vs. particular).

The Ehrman & Leaver Construct

In cooperation with Rebecca Oxford, Betty Lou Leaver, and other colleagues, Madeline Ehrman has been generating high quality work on personality and language learning styles since the early 1990s (e.g., Ehrman, 1990, 1993, 1996, 1998, 1999, 2001; Ehrman & Leaver, 2003; Ehrman & Oxford, 1990, 1995; Ehrman et al., 2003; Oxford, Ehrman & Lavine, 1991), and recently she and Leaver have devised a new learning style measure that is based on a novel approach to understanding styles. This complex battery has an elaborate underlying theoretical construct and has undergone extensive field-testing and validation at the Foreign Service Institute. Therefore it represents a serious attempt to reconceptualize cognitive styles in the service of language learning and warrants a closer inspection.

The *E&L Construct*, as Ehrman and Leaver (2003; Ehrman, 2001) have named their new system, is similar to Riding's theory in that it reorganizes a number of established style dimensions under a new, comprehensive, and parsimonious construct. However, unlike Riding's taxonomy, here only one superordinate style dimension is provided, with the two poles labeled *ectasis* and *synopsis* (see Fig. 5.1 for a summary). The main difference between the two extremes is that an *ectenic* learner wants or needs conscious control over the learning process, whereas a *synoptic* learner leaves more to preconscious or unconscious processing.

The complete system is made up of 10 subdimensions, and many of those are similar to the ones targeted by Cohen et al.'s Learning Style Survey (which, as just mentioned, has drawn on the E&L Construct). However, while in the case the LSS only brief explanatory notes are available (geared at the testtakers), Ehrman and Leaver (2003) provided a detailed rationale and theoretical explanation of the E&L Construct. As they pointed out, all the 10 subscales of the E&L Construct represent established style dimensions with a body of relevant literature available for each, although one dichotomy, the *analogue–digital dimension*, has not been applied to learning contexts before. Let us briefly consider each subscale (for more details, see Ehrman & Leaver, 2003; Leaver et al., in press):

- *Field dependent–independent* and *field sensitive–insensitive:* Field dependence–independence has been discussed in a separate section before; although the terms *(in)dependence* and *(in)sensitivity* have often been used in the literature in an interchangeable manner, Ehrman and Leaver distinguish them to the extent that they constitute two different scales in the overall construct. Based on Ehrman (1998), field dependence–independence refers to the preference for selection and prioritization vs. treating the whole context as the same, whereas field sensitivity–insensitivity concerns the preference for considering materials in a situated manner and being aware of their position in their broader context. Thus, field sensitivity relates to foreground and background together whereas field dependence treats the foreground and the background as the same. Field-sensitive learners prefer to address material as part of the context in contrast to their field-insensitive counterparts, who make little or no use of the context.

- *Random (non-linear) vs. sequential (linear):* This dimension relates to how the learner processes information. Random learners follow their own, internally developed and idiosyncratic order of processing (which may seem random to others), whereas sequential learners prefer a step-by-step, externally provided order of processing (such as the units in a syllabus).

- *Global–particular:* This dimension is well encapsulated by the top-down vs. bottom-up processing metaphor.

- *Inductive–deductive:* Inductive learners start with the details and facts, then form hypotheses, and finally test them; deductive learners start out with rules or theories and then try to apply them to examples.

- *Synthetic–analytic:* Synthetic learners like to use pieces to build new wholes, whereas analytic students like to disassemble wholes into parts to understand their componential structure.

- *Analogue–digital:* Analogue learners prefer to use metaphors, analogies, and conceptual links among units and their meanings, whereas digital learners take a more surface approach, characterized by a literal and logical understanding of what they can hear or see.

- *Concrete–abstract:* Concrete learners prefer a relationship with direct experience to the extent of sensory contact, whereas abstract learners may have more interest in the system underlying language than in the actual language of communication.

- *Leveling–sharpening:* This dimension concerns how people perceive, store, and retrieve information. Levelers often blur things together and form a generalized image, whereas sharpeners notice small differences and store them as salient attributes in their memories.

- *Impulsive–reflective:* Impulsive learners tend to respond rapidly, often acting on gut, whereas reflective learners prefer to think things through before they respond. Ehrman and Leaver emphasized that this is a real style dimension—rather than an ability continuum in which impulsive is inefficient and reflective efficient—in the sense that both poles can be beneficial or dysfunctional.

The E&L Construct has been operationalized by the Ehrman & Leaver Learning Style Questionnaire. This instrument contains 30 items using a 9-point semantic differential scale format and provides a rich set of data about an individual in the form of an emerging profile, which has the advantage both of generality and specificity. Table 5.6 presents 10 sample items from the test and Figure 5.1 contains a sample scoring grid. As Ehrman and Leaver (2003) explained, the synoptic–ectenic construct level can be used when a learner has a clear set of preferences tending to the right or the left of the chart (as is the case in the sample grid), which allows for a concise description. At the same time, the profile can also yield a more elaborate portrayal of an individual through the interplay of the ten subscales. However, because of the intercorrelation of the subscales, the multiplicity of profiles still falls within the same relatively standardized system.

Table 5.6. Sample items from the Ehrman & Leaver Learning Style Questionnaire

1 When I work with new material in context, in stories or articles or at least sentences, I often pick up new words, ideas, etc. that way, without planning in advance. You could say I make a lot of use of a floodlight to learn.

I don't usually get much from the context unless I pay close attention to what I'm doing. I certainly wouldn't describe myself as someone who learns by osmosis. It usually has to be out there in black and white.

Most like this ___ ___ ___ ___ ___ ___ ___ ___ ___ Most like this
               1   2   3   4   5   6   7   8   9

2 When working with new material with additional subject matter around it, I comfortably find and use what is most important. I also like out-of-context material like grammar rules. You could say I make a lot of use of a spotlight to learn.

When there is a lot of information that comes with what I need to learn, it's hard to tell what's most important. It all seems to fall together sometimes, and it's hard work to sort things out.

Most like this ___ ___ ___ ___ ___ ___ ___ ___ ___ Most like this
               1   2   3   4   5   6   7   8   9

3 I like to reduce differences and look for similarities. I notice mostly how things are similar, and I level out differences.

I like to explore differences and disparities among things and tend to notice them quickly.

Most like this ___ ___ ___ ___ ___ ___ ___ ___ ___ Most like this
               1   2   3   4   5   6   7   8   9

4 I tend to be most aware of and interested in the big picture; I notice the

I notice specifics and details quickly; I tend to be aware of the trees before the

4   I tend to be most aware of and inter-   I notice specifics and details quickly; I
    ested in the big picture; I notice the   tend to be aware of the trees before the
    forest before the trees; I start with the   forest. I begin with the details to work
    main points and work down to the de-   up to the main points.
    tails.

    Most like this __ __ __ __ __ __ __ __ __ Most like this
                     1   2   3   4   5   6   7   8   9

5   I react quickly, often acting or speak-   I tend to think about things before I do
    ing without thinking about it.   or say them.

    Most like this __ __ __ __ __ __ __ __ __ Most like this
                     1   2   3   4   5   6   7   8   9

6   I understand best by assembling what   I understand best by disassembly of
    I'm learning into a whole, synthesizing   learning into its component parts,
    information.   analyzing information.

    Most like this __ __ __ __ __ __ __ __ __ Most like this
                     1   2   3   4   5   6   7   8   9

7   I tend to learn things through meta-   I like things that can be counted and
    phors and associations with other   that say what they mean directly. I
    things. I often learn through stories or   take things at face value.
    example cases.

    Most like this __ __ __ __ __ __ __ __ __ Most like this
                     1   2   3   4   5   6   7   8   9

8   To learn, I like to interact with the   I like to learn through concepts and
    world and learn through application of   ideas and from formal renditions of
    knowledge, especially when I can   knowledge like theories and models.
    touch, see, or hear it.

    Most like this __ __ __ __ __ __ __ __ __ Most like this
                     1   2   3   4   5   6   7   8   9

9   I learn best when I can work out for   I learn best when there is a sequence
    myself the best sequence to use, even   of steps provided, so I can do things in
    if it's different from the one in the   order. Textbooks and lesson plans
    book or lesson.   really help me.

    Most like this __ __ __ __ __ __ __ __ __ Most like this
                     1   2   3   4   5   6   7   8   9

10 When I learn, I mostly start with ex-   When I learn, I mostly start with rules
    amples or my experience and make   and generalizations and apply them to
    generalizations or rules.   my experience to learn.

    Most like this __ __ __ __ __ __ __ __ __ Most like this
                     1   2   3   4   5   6   7   8   9

[1: Field (in)sensitivity, 2: Field (in)dependence, 3: Leveling–sharpening,
4: Global– particular, 5: Impulsive–reflective, 6: Synthetic–analytic,
7: Analogue–digital, 8: Concrete–abstract, 9: Random–sequential,
10: Inductive–deductive]

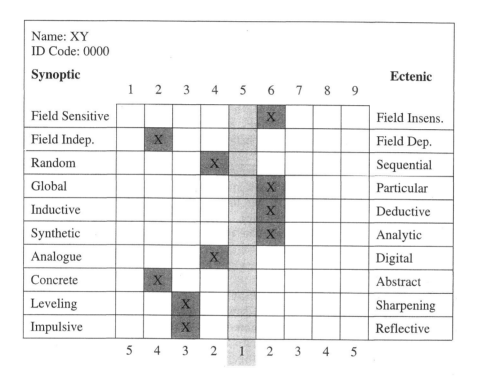

FIG. 5.1. Sample scoring grid for the E&L Construct. (Ehrman & Leaver, 2003)

Skehan's Conceptualization of a Learning Style Construct

The final model of learning styles to be presented in this chapter has been proposed by Peter Skehan (1998). This approach is unique because its starting point has not been styles research in cognitive or educational psychology but rather results obtained in the field of linguistics. The main claim that overarches the whole of Skehan's cognitive theory of L2 learning and processing is that learners can be characterized by a 'dual-coding' approach to language learning and performance, made up of a rule-based system and a memory-based system. Extending this insight further, and based on research on language aptitude (Skehan, 1986; Wesche, 1981), Skehan proposed that there are two types of learners, *analysis-oriented* and *memory-oriented*. As he explains, high-analysis learners develop organized and rule-based representations of language, engaging in regular restructuring and complexification of the underlying interlanguage system. They would value and strive for accuracy—for this reason Scovel (2001) called them 'grammarians' in contrast to the 'chunkers,' who are at the other end of Skehan's sliding scale and who try to associate clusters of words or phrases with certain meanings or situations. High memory learners do not use a complex analytic system for effective communication, particularly because they do not value form highly, but rather they store a wide range of lexicalized exemplars in their memory systems to be mobilized for communication in real time.

It is clear from this description that the system Skehan (1998) outlined may not be a stylistic issue at all. The two dimensions—analysis-oriented and memory-oriented—look much like abilities in the sense that we can talk about learners with low and high levels of these attributes, with the high level being, presumably, better than the low. Skehan readily acknowledges that one possible explanation for this differentiation is ability-based, assuming that the approach a particular learner takes is constrained or motivated by his or her underlying ap-titudinal strengths and weaknesses. For example, someone with a natural endowment of a good memory will be naturally more inclined to use it in his or her language operations. Skehan also mentioned a second alternative explanation, whereby it is the language task characteristics that influence representational and processing outcomes. From our current point of view, Skehan's third possible explanation is the most interesting, as this is style-based. According to this interpretation, analysis-orientation and memory-orientation are natural preferences: Some learners prefer to concentrate their attention on form and systematic rules, whereas others prefer to prioritize communication and the assembly of lexical phrases.

Our previous overview of the various, and largely non-language-specific, stylistic constructs shows that several established cognitive style dimensions bear a resemblance to Skehan's proposed styles; for example, ectenic learners would be more analysis-oriented in nature than their synoptic counterparts. Interestingly, we also find that a number of L2 studies in the past have identified certain L2 speaker variables that are similar to Skehan's constructs (for a review, see Kormos, 1999). For example, in his pioneering work in this area, Krashen (1978) distinguished between two types of L2 speakers: *monitor-under-users* and *monitor-over-users*, and two years later Seliger (1980) also identified two similar learner groups in terms of their speaking habits: *low input generators* (corresponding to monitor-over-users in Krashen's terminology) and *high input generators* (monitor-under-users in Krashen's terminology). Speakers in the latter group were found to speak fast, did not worry about making mistakes, and did not repair their utterances frequently; in this sense they are similar to Skehan's memory-oriented type. Low input generators, on the other hand, tended to speak more slowly and expressed their message more precisely than high input generators. These students seemed to be disturbed by mistakes and made frequent attempts to correct them; therefore they correspond to the analysis-oriented learners in Skehan's framework.

Finally, in a study of the self-correction behavior of Hungarian learners of English, Kormos (1999) found that the amount of attention available for monitoring was unrelated to the level of L2 competence. She explained this finding by assuming an underlying style-like learner trait, thereby providing further support to Skehan's style-based approach:

> The results described above reveal that this lack of change might be due to the fact that each speaker has a steady disposition concerning the allocation of attention to monitoring. This means that there might be an individual trait that determines how L2 learners generally decide to allocate attention in speech processing, and this trait may not be subject to modification in the language learning process. Due to the effect of this individual difference variable, certain L2 speakers pay more attention to monitoring at the expense of the other production processes of the utterance. (pp. 218-219)

Thus, although more research evidence is needed to test and fine-tune Skehan's theoretical proposal, the available data points to the possibility of identifying some cognitive styles that are closely related to second language acquisition and use. This would be a welcome development because almost all the learning style dimensions conceptualized in the L2 field are rather language-independent, as evidenced by the fact that most of the items in the style batteries could be used for any subject matter. This is not necessarily a problem because it is clear that linguistic operations are part of a broader cognitive system and therefore style characteristics affecting the whole system are likely to have a direct bearing on the language subarea as well. Yet, genuine language processing and representational styles would offer more straightforward explanations about certain individual L2 learner differences, somewhat similarly to the fact that language aptitude factors exceed general aptitude (i.e., intelligence) factors in their explanatory power with regard to SLA achievement. Genuine L2 styles would also have increased face validity, which would make it easier for teachers to recognize and deal with them, and thus the practical use of the construct would be enhanced.

PRACTICAL IMPLICATIONS

The discussion so far has, hopefully, shown that the concept of cognitive and learning styles is potentially important from a theoretical and research perspective. But does the notion have any practical value? That is, can it be used in any way to promote the effectiveness of instructed SLA? The honest answer is yes and no. An increased awareness of learner styles both in the learners and the teachers can have some educational potential but there are also some serious problems concerning any real practical applications. Let us start by considering the positive features.

In her book on understanding second language learning difficulties, Ehrman (1996) justified the extensive treatment of learning styles by claiming that "Learning style mismatches are at the root of many learning difficulties" (p. 50). Indeed, the general assumption shared by the advocates of learning style research is that a more principled teaching approach that would take into account the impact of various style characteristics on learning could reduce or even remove many mismatches and can thus enhance learning effectiveness.

What kind of mismatches are we talking about? We can conceive of at least six types of possible style conflict:

1. Mismatch between the student's learning style and the teacher's teaching style, a conflict that has been dramatically termed a *style war* by Oxford et al. (1991).

2. Mismatch between the student's learning style and the syllabus, for example when the latter does not cover grammar systematically, although analytic learners would need that.

3. Mismatch between the student's learning style and the language task, for example when a visual student participates in a task that involves receiving auditory input (e.g., from a tape).

4. Mismatch between the student's learning style and his or her beliefs about learning, for example when an analysis-oriented learner believes that rote learning is the most effective learning method (whereas that method would suit a memory-oriented learner better).

5. Mismatch between the student's learning style and the learning strategies applied, for example when a field independent learner tries to apply social strategies, or a global learner uses bottom-up reading strategies.

6. We can even conceive of a mismatch between the student's learning style and his or her abilities, for example when an ectenic learner has underdeveloped grammatical sensitivity.

So, there is no doubt that some sort of style harmony would be beneficial in many respects for teachers and learners alike. The question, then, is whether this is feasible. Let us look at how the proponents of a more style-based instruction envisage creating this harmony in practical terms.

• The most common and somewhat simplistic recommendation is that teachers can modify the learning tasks they use in their classes in a way that may bring the best out of particular learners with particular learning style preferences. Of course, the problem is that learners are not homogeneous in their style preferences, to which the commonsense answer is that teachers should "strive for a balanced teaching style that does not excessively favor any one learning style—or rather that tries to accommodate multiple learning styles" (Peacock, 2001, p. 15).

- A second option, mentioned by Oxford and Anderson (1995), is that by getting students to take a learning style questionnaire and by discussing the results with them we can help them to identify their own learning styles and to recognize the power of understanding their language learning styles for making learning more effective. A description of several practical adaptations of this approach in four countries (Egypt, Hungary, Russia, and Spain) can be found in Reid et al. (1998).

- It would also be beneficial for teachers to find out about their own learning styles because, as Kinsella (1995) pointed out, although the maxim that teachers teach the way they were taught has some truth in it, it is probably more accurate to say that teachers teach the way they learned best. She argued that many teachers, either consciously or unconsciously, select methods that reflect their own preferred ways of approaching academic tasks. This, however, as Oxford and Anderson (1995) argued, might not be helpful to all the students and an awareness in the teachers about how their preferred styles compare to the styles of their students might be beneficial.

- We can also help students learn how to operate outside their preferred styles, a phenomenon that is often referred to as *style stretching*. As learners become aware of their own learning style preferences, they may become open to guidance in structuring their classroom work and home assignments along lines that begin in their comfort zones and gradually stretch them out of this zone (Ehrman, 1996). Cohen (2002) also suggested that learners can be 'brought on board' in this way, that is, learners over time can be encouraged to engage in style-stretching so as to incorporate approaches to learning they were resisting in the past. Because of the complex nature of language and because of its manifold representations in the real world, it is a reasonable assumption that students who can operate in a range of styles in a situation-specific and flexible manner are likely to become more effective learners.

- A further way of empowering students is to teach them learning strategies that would suit their styles. One approach involves what Andrew Cohen (1998, 2002; Cohen & Dörnyei, 2002) has termed *Styles- and strategies-based instruction* (SSBI), which includes the teacher's assisting learners to develop an awareness of their own preferred learning styles, then determine the nature of their current learner strategy repertoire, and finally, to complement their strategy repertoire with additional strategies that match their styles. As Cohen (2002) argued, this is a particularly fruitful area and "The future looks bright for SSBI work" (p. 59).

- In principle, we can also imagine streaming learners according to their learning style preferences and then develop special syllabuses for the different tracks.

Although all these (and presumably several other) options are theoretically feasible ways of using learner styles, I believe we also need to be frank about the severe problems that arise in this respect and which have, by and large, prevented styles so far from becoming accessible and practical for classroom use. Let us start with some words of caution by Reid (1995), who pointed out that the complicated and fragmented nature of the area of learning styles with the proliferation of often overlapping terminology confuses classroom teachers (and we can add, even researchers themselves to the extent that—as we have seen—several of them have proposed abandoning styles research). If we add to this what Ehrman (1996) emphasized, namely that the classification into distinct styles in itself is merely a convenient oversimplification of a more complex picture, we can see that an average classroom practitioner may currently be ill-prepared to meaningfully deal with the style issue. Of course, in an ideal world in which teacher training would include a much more prominent psychological component, teachers could follow Ehrman's (1996) own practice: She believes that different individuals make different style dimensions important and therefore when she decides which style model to apply as a conceptual tool with an individual she takes into account the particular learner's features.

In a refreshingly down-to-earth analysis of the possible educational applications of learning styles, Yates (2000) warned us that the idea that we can create instructional programs or plan curriculum variations to match our students' cognitive style characteristics reflects a "visionary position that, unfortunately, is neither viable nor justified. It is unrealistic for a classroom teacher to classify students into cognitive style categories to be used to pre-scribe differential educational experience" (p. 359). Thus, the author continues, it is usually impractical or even unfair to attempt to vary our lesson plans in response to assessments of certain individual differences. However, Yates did recommend one powerful tool a teacher can use in a style-sensitive manner: *time management*.

> In teaching contexts, time is the one effective vehicle we have in striving to accommodate for the individual response. ... we can vary presentation times, speed of presentation, time devoted to direct modeling, thinking time, wait-time in questioning, time spent in revision and remediation, and time allocated for extended practice (i.e., independent enrichment and elaboration work). (p. 360)

That is, in Yates's (2000) view, the most effective way for teachers to demonstrate awareness of learning styles is to be sensitive to the students' differential time requirements in coping with certain types of tasks. As he concluded, the idea that different students need varying amounts of time to achieve certain learning objectives is one of the most basic but at the same time rather neglected principles of educational psychology.

Whereas few would disagree that time management is an important issue and that it can be used to cater for learning style differences, we need to ask whether there are really no more specific lessons we can learn from styles research. It is true that the heterogeneous nature of style distribution and the complex interference of several coexisting learning styles might make style-based instruction a far too complex issue for ordinary teachers to handle. Yet, I also believe that there are some broad and strong tendencies in terms of our students' style preferences that could be better taken into consideration. For example, Kinsella (1995) pointed out that in U.S. secondary schools roughly 90% of traditional classroom instruction for adolescents appears to cater for the competent auditory learner whereas in Oxford's (1995) experience, the proportion of real auditory learners is less than half of the total population. Learning style research has clearly demonstrated the need for a more balanced mixture of instructional input, with the materials presented visually as well as verbally, and reinforced through writing, drawing, or speaking activities.

A further practical and forward-pointing research direction has been offered by Oxford (1999d): In a qualitative study of written student narratives, the researcher identified specific types of style conflict between teachers and students. Four conflict types, in particular, appeared in the data: (a) students who disliked ambiguity and whose closure needs were ignored, (b) introverted students coping with extroverted teachers who 'entertained' the class, (c) global, intuitive-random students dealing with analytic, concrete-sequential details provided by the teacher, and (d) students whose sensory preferences were thwarted. The attraction of this approach is that it specifies concrete issues to deal with, making it thus possible to devise specific troubleshooting strategies addressing these conflict situations. I believe that a set of such tried and tested strategies would be a welcome addition to any language teacher training program. (For an interesting follow-up to this study in which the style conflict data is examined in light of Bakhtin's theories, see Oxford & Massey, in press.)

These examples illustrate that it may be possible for future research to come up with style-based teaching suggestions that are both useful and doable; for the time being, however, Peacock's (2001) recommendation seems reasonable: An obvious way to decrease the mismatch between teachers' and students' learning styles is to become more willing to involve learners in planning lessons and tasks, and more generally, to give them more control over their learning.

Finally, schooling in the 21st century could include, almost as a routine, some sort of an individualized consultation process for students about their learning styles. Ehrman and Leaver (2003) described how such a process has been successfully implemented in the language instruction at the Foreign Service Institute. There the procedure consists of four steps:

1. Students are first invited to a voluntary consultation, aimed at improving learning effectiveness both for those who are having difficulties and those who think they are doing fine.

2. Once a student has decided to take advantage of this offer, he or she completes a diagnostic learning style questionnaire.

3. The third step is the interpretation of the questionnaire results. At the FSI, this is first done in group sessions so the counselors do not have to repeat the same information for each student, and then in individual sessions to apply the generalizations to the student's own situation.

4. The final step is the follow-up, whereby a designated Learning Consultant makes sure that the recommendations made during the consultation process are put into practice. Students are then welcome to return for follow-up consultations with a counselor on any emerging issue.

CONCLUSION

As I was working on this chapter, an image started to form in my mind: I realized that the intricate tapestry of cognitive and learning styles could be compared to the complex patterns of colors around us. We live in a gaudy world with an infinite variety of shades of colors. Yet, we can sense that beneath this seemingly endless color complexity there is a simpler system, and it has indeed been found that all the colors in the spectrum are made up of only three basic primary colors. The quest for cognitive styles is not unlike the initial search for these primary colors. Although some definite progress has been made in identifying certain building blocks in the complex of human style characteristics, we still do not know for certain as to whether we have got the *primary styles*. For example, in the world of colors, green appears to be a basic constituent and yet we now know that it is a derivative, a secondary color, made up of two basic colors, blue and yellow. What we need to decide about the various overlapping style dimensions is which of them are blue and yellow, and which are some sort of green combinations of the two.

We can even take the color metaphor one step further to explain the difference between cognitive and learning styles. It appears to me that cognitive styles can be seen as equivalents of the colors proper, whereas learning styles are the manifestations of the colors in the real world, involving the texture of the background material and the paint, the size and the format of the colored shape, and the interrelationship of various colors forming color schemes. In the graphic arts there has actually been at least one attempt to grasp the 'learning styles system' of colors: At the beginning of the 20th century, the staff of the famous Bauhaus art school in Germany, which included world-famous artists such as Paul Klee and Wassily Kandinsky, developed and taught the principles of a 'color theory,' which related certain shapes and properties to colors. For example, a yellow triangle was seen by Kandinsky to represent the highest intellect and a blue circle spiritual feelings. Although the powerful paintings of Klee and Kandinsky have in many ways validated their theory indirectly, color research is still an active and ongoing field, looking for scientific verification of certain regularities that artistic sensitivity can detect. With regard to learning styles, several intuitively appealing systems have been developed that cut through the areas of cognitive styles, abilities, and personality, but we still lack a rigorous validation of the proposed constructs.

Thus, I believe that the best summary of the position of language learning styles in the broader field of SLA is that they constitute an as yet unrealized potential. The problem is that this was exactly the view expressed by several scholars in the 1980s and 1990s; reading the literature I came across Rod Ellis's (1994) conclusion and found that it perfectly encapsulated my current stance, which indicates how little has changed during the past decade. So let me conclude this chapter with Ellis's words:

> At the moment there are few general conclusions that can be drawn from the research on learning style. Learners clearly differ enormously in their preferred approach to L2 learning, but it is impossible to say which learning style works best. Quite possibly it is learners who display flexibility who are most successful, but there is no real evidence yet for such a conclusion. One of the major problems is that the concept of 'learning style' is ill-defined, apparently overlapping with other individual differences of both an affective and a cognitive nature. It is

unlikely that much progress will be made until researchers know what it is they want to measure. (p. 508)

6

Language Learning Strategies and Student Self-Regulation

As seen in the Introduction of this book, language learning strategies have traditionally been included in the taxonomy of individual differences. Yet on a closer look they may not be ID factors at all. After all, language learning strategies constitute an aspect of the learning process rather than being learner attributes proper. This is very clearly expressed in Cohen's (1998) definition, according to which learning strategies are "learning processes which are consciously selected by the learner" (p. 4), and it is also reflected in virtually all other definitions of the concept which equate learning strategies with the learners' actions/behaviors and thoughts aiming at facilitating learning. And let's face it: actions and thoughts are not individual differences.

At this point we could conclude this chapter saying that the notion of learner strategy is irrelevant to the general theme of this book. However, it is worth digging a bit further before we draw our conclusion, because, as we will see, learning strategies are immensely ambiguous phenomena and nothing is clear-cut about them. Thus, for example, we saw in chapter 5 that learning styles and learning strategies are interrelated concepts, differing primarily in their breadth and stability, with a style being a "strategy used consistently across a class of tasks" (Snow et al., 1996, p. 281). It has also been widely observed that some school children are more inclined to use learning strategies than others: In a seminal paper on self-regulated learning, Philip Winne (1995) portrayed these learners as students "calling on a library of information and applying a suite of varied skills during studying activities in which achievements are forged" (p. 173). He continued, when these learners begin to study, they:

> set goals for extending knowledge and sustaining motivation. They are aware of what they know, what they believe, and what the differences between these kinds of information imply for approaching tasks. They have a grasp of their motivation, are aware of their affect, and plan how

to manage the interplay between these as they engage with a task. They also deliberate about small-grain tactics and overall strategies, selecting some instead of others based on predictions about how each is able to support progress toward chosen goals. (p. 173)

Similarly to Winne, Randi and Corno (2000) also highlighted the existence of such 'self-regulated learners,' who "seek to accomplish academic goals strategically and manage to overcome obstacles using a battery of resources" (p. 651). And as they concluded, "Self-regulation is both an aptitude for and a potential outcome of schooling" (ibid). Interestingly, this view has also been expressed with regard to language learning strategies by Chamot and Rubin (1994): "The good language learner cannot be described in terms of a single set of strategies but rather through the ability to understand and develop a personal set of effective strategies" (p. 372). Thus, there seems to be an agreement that there is some sort of a trait-like strategic potential that enable certain learners to become effective strategy users. Let us not go as yet into the question of what factors or attributes this strategic capacity subsumes—the main point for now is that these observations create another strong link between learning strategies and ID factors. Therefore, I suggest that we suspend the dismissal of learning strategies from the domain of individual differences and delay any judgment about them until the conclusion of this chapter. Let us, then, start our exploration of this area with a basic question: Do language learning strategies exist?

DO LEARNING STRATEGIES EXIST?

Intuitively, I have always believed in the existence and significance of learning strategies and yet I became increasingly puzzled over the years about the lack of an unambiguous theoretical definition of the learning strategy construct. And, similarly to learning styles, most of the relevant literature in the L2 field seems to skip over this 'shortcoming' and pretends that with regard to learning strategies everything is more or less okay. Well, it is not, so let us examine the problem.

According to a current and comprehensive definition of learning strategies offered by Oxford (1999b, p. 518), the construct refers to

specific actions, behaviors, steps, or techniques that students use to improve their own progress in developing skills in a second or foreign language. These strategies can facilitate the internalization, storage, retrieval, or use of the new language.

Definitions of learning strategies do not come any better than this, as attested to by the fact that a recent definition from educational psychology by one of the most influential American strategy experts, Claire Weinstein (Weinstein, Husman, & Dierking 2000, p. 727), covered the same aspects: "Learning strategies include any thoughts, behaviors, beliefs, or emotions that facilitate the acquisition, understanding, or later transfer of new knowledge and skills."

Although these definitions appear to be logical and exhaustive, they leave several issues open. The most fundamental one is this: What exactly is the difference between engaging in an ordinary learning activity and a strategic learning activity? That is, what is the difference between the processes of *learning* and *learning strategy use*? For example, if someone memorizes vocabulary by simply looking at a bilingual vocabulary list, most people would say that this is an example of learning. But if the person applies some color marking code to highlight the words in the list which he or she still does not know, suddenly we can start talking about strategic learning. But what is the difference? The color code?

In his comprehensive book *Strategies in Learning and Using a Second Language,* Andrew Cohen (1998) offered a more specific definition of language learning strategies:

> Language learning strategies include strategies for identifying the material that needs to be learned, distinguishing it from other material if need be, grouping it for easier learning (e.g., grouping vocabulary by category into nouns, verbs, adjectives, adverbs, and so forth), having repeated contact with the material (e.g., through classroom tasks or the completion of homework assignments), and formally committing the material to memory when it does not seem to be acquired naturally (whether through rote memory techniques such as repetition, the use of mnemonics, or some other memory technique). (p. 5)

Although this definition is refreshing in its concreteness, it does not help us to distinguish normal learning behaviors and strategic learning behaviors: all the processes mentioned by Cohen can also apply to 'ordinary' learning without any strategic element.

So what are the distinguishing features of learning strategies? Weinstein et al. (2000) offered three critical characteristics: *goal-directed, intentionally invoked,* and *effortful.* The problem with these intuitively appealing attributes is that they can also be true about *hard and focused* learning in general. Does that mean that hard and focused learning is by definition strategic? To show that this is not an unreasonable question, let me quote Macaro (2001), who also tentatively raised the same issue: "An interesting practice-related avenue to pursue is whether what we mean by *effort* when doing a language task simply means the effective deployment of a range of strategies in a task" (p. 264). However, if we define the strategic quality of learning with goal-oriented, intentionally evoked, and effortful behavior then we, in effect, equate 'strategic' with 'motivated,' because goal-oriented, intentionally evoked, and effortful are three key features of motivation (cf. chapt. 4).

Cohen (1998) highlighted a further important aspect of learning strategies, the *element of choice*. He argued that it is an essential feature of these strategies that they are voluntarily employed by the learner. Although this is clearly important in distinguishing learning strategies from creative teacher-owned tasks that the learner engages in, choice is still not enough to distinguish strategies from non-strategies because students tend to make several choices concerning their learning process that are not strategic in the strict sense, that is, which do not necessarily involve appropriate and purposeful behavior to enhance the effectiveness of learning. Examples of such behavior include choosing the time to do home assignments; selecting a pen for doing a writing task; choosing a partner whom one likes for pairwork; performing a classroom task in a way that it will impress one's girlfriend or boyfriend, and so on—the point is that while these acts can be strategic, the learner can also engage in them without necessarily wanting to improve the effectiveness of his/her learning.

I believe the best way of distinguishing between normal learning activities and learning strategy use has been proposed by Riding and Rayner (1998). They argued that an activity becomes strategic when it is particularly *appropriate* for the individual learner, in contrast to general learning activities which a student may find less helpful. Accordingly, learners engage in strategic learning if they exert purposeful effort to select and then pursue learning procedures that they believe will increase their individual learning effectiveness. The same idea has been expressed more technically, from an information-processing perspective, by Winne (2001), who distinguished between *tactics* and *strategies*. A tactic, according to Winne, is a "particular form of schema that is represented as a rule in IF-THEN form, sometimes called a condition-action rule" (p. 159). A strategy is a broader design or plan for approaching a high-level goal and it coordinates a set of tactics. Winne argued that the actual student response only becomes strategic if it matches the IF condition in the pursuit of a goal, that is, if it is appropriate for the particular purpose.

This approach of defining strategies in terms of *appropriateness* appears to be simple but comprehensive. It does, however, raise two new problems: First, the term 'appropriate' is rather fluid and it is not easy to imagine how it can be operationalized in an actual research design. Second, and more importantly, learning strategies conceptualized in this vein can only be defined relative to a particular agent, because a specific learning technique may be strategic for one and non-strategic for another depending on the person's IF condition and how the specific tactic or strategy offers a personally effective response to that. Interestingly, in a recent study Ehrman, Leaver, and Oxford (2003) came to the same conclusion:

A given learning strategy is neither good nor bad; it is essentially neutral until it is considered in context. A strategy is useful under these conditions: (a) the strategy relates well to the L2 task at hand, (b) the strategy fits the particular student's learning style preferences to one degree or another, and (c) the student employs the strategy effectively and links it with other relevant strategies. (p. 315)

This relativity is not necessarily a problem but it does go against the standard view in the field; for example, this conception would disqualify several learning strategy inventories which start out with a list of preconceived strategies and learners are asked about the extent of their use of these; if a specific learner behavior only becomes a strategy when a learner endorses it as personally relevant and appropriate, such questionnaire items do not make much sense as they usually posit a rating scale ranging from 'not used or endorsed' at one end, which does not apply to strategies conceived in this way.

In summary, at this stage of our discussion we cannot offer a watertight definition of 'learning strategies.' I consider this issue further in a later section and describe there how scholars in educational psychology have gone around the definition problem without giving up the essence of strategic learning. First, however, we take a diachronic view of how the study of language learning strategies evolved in the past and what characterizes the field today.

LEARNING STRATEGIES IN L2 STUDIES

Three books published at the beginning of the 1990s by O'Malley and Chamot (1990), Oxford (1990), and Wenden (1991) indicated that the concept of *language learning strategy*—reflecting the learners' proactive contribution to enhancing the effectiveness of their own learning—had reached mainstream recognition in the L2 field. Indeed, right from its introduction into L2 research in the late 1970s, the notion of learning strategy was intuitively appealing to researchers and it was also embraced with enthusiasm by language teachers. The initial phase of strategy research focused primarily on what could be learned from the 'good language learner,' that is, what characteristics made some learners more successful than others when it came to attaining an L2 (e.g., Naiman et al., 1978; Rubin, 1975; Stern, 1975; Wong-Fillmore, 1979; for a review, see MacIntyre & Noels, 1994; for a new perspective, see Norton & Toohey, 2001). The results indicated in a fairly consistent manner that it was not merely a high degree of language aptitude and motivation that caused some learners to excel but also the students' own active and creative participation in the learning process through the application of individualized learning techniques.

Following this early research, the study of language learning strategies was taken up by a number of scholars in the 1980s, and by 1987 Wenden and Rubin had been able to compile a rich collection of research studies on learner strategies which underlined the important role these strategies played in the acquisition of an L2. The publication of the three summary books mentioned above further added to the general momentum, so that in an article describing a social psychological model of strategy use published in the mid-1990's, MacIntyre (1994) started his discussion by stating that "One of the most fertile areas of research in language learning in recent years is the topic of language learning strategies" (p. 185).

As Dörnyei and Skehan (2003) concluded, it may seem peculiar in retrospect that virtually nobody examined the theoretical soundness of the concept of learning strategy critically, particularly given that the definitions offered in the L2 literature were rather inconsistent and elusive; for example, Ellis (1994) concluded in his overview of SLA that "Definitions of learning strategies have tended to be *ad hoc* and atheoretical" (p. 533). Oxford (1989) provided a seemingly straightforward functional definition for language learning strategies—"behaviors or actions which learners use to make language learning more successful, self-directed, and enjoyable" (p. 235)—but when she described the scope of these strategies in her well-known taxonomy (Oxford, 1990), she also included cognitive and affective strategies that involved mental processes rather than 'behaviors or actions.' To eliminate this inconsistency, the 1990 volume simply replaced the phrase 'behaviors and actions used by the learner' with the more general 'steps taken by the learner,' which could accommodate both behavioral and mental steps.

An alternative definition of language learning strategies was offered by O'Malley and Chamot (1990), according to which these strategies involve "special thoughts or behaviors that individuals use to help them comprehend, learn, or retain new information" (p. 1). This conceptualization differed from Oxford's functional definition in that it highlighted the *cognitive* aspects of strategy use. Although the cautious wording of the definition did actually allow learning strategies to be 'behaviors,' the addition of 'thoughts' was an important alteration, as was the restriction of the purpose of strategy use to comprehending, learning, and retaining new information. All these reflected the fact that O'Malley and Chamot attempted to ground learning strategy research in Anderson's (1983, 1985) general cognitive psychological theory. However, when the authors listed concrete examples of learning strategies, we find an inventory that is not at all dissimilar to Oxford's (1990). To eliminate the problematic issue of the interrelationship between 'behaviors and thoughts' in their definition,

O'Malley and Chamot (1994) followed a strategy similar to Oxford's (1990) by replacing these words with the more general 'methods and techniques that individuals use' formula.

Taxonomies of Language Learning Strategies

The initial research effort generated two well-known taxonomies of language learning strategies, by Oxford (1990) and by O'Malley and Chamot (1990). Oxford's taxonomy was made up of six strategy classes: *cognitive*, *memory*, *metacognitive*, *compensation*, *affective*, and *social strategies*. Before we describe these categories, let us look into two issues. First, this division included 'compensation' (i.e., communication) strategies, which are related to language *use* rather than language *learning*. Although it is clear that language use leads to various opportunities for language acquisition, and therefore the competent employment of communication strategies does promote L2 proficiency, it has been argued by many (e.g., Cohen, 1998; Ellis, 1994; Selinker, 1972; Tarone, 1981) that the two processes are so different both in terms of their function and their psycholinguistic representation that they are best kept separate. In a recent article, Hsiao and Oxford (2002) admitted that the distinction was heuristically valuable but they also added that in actual practice it might be difficult to separate learning the L2 from using the L2. The second issue concerns the separation of cognitive and memory strategies as if they were independent categories of equal status. Although this is obviously not the case and memory strategies constitute a subclass of cognitive strategies (which was also confirmed in a study by Purpura, 1999), this separation was motivated by the observation that most memory strategies (especially mnemonic devices such as imagery, rhyming, and keyword) are associated with shallow processing, whereas most cognitive strategies are associated with deep processing (Oxford, personal communication, July 29, 2004).

The taxonomy of O'Malley and Chamot (1990) is quite similar to the one proposed by Oxford (1990). They distinguish three main classes of strategy, *cognitive strategies* (that correspond to Oxford's 'cognitive' and 'memory' categories), *metacognitive strategies* (that have a direct equivalent in Oxford's system), and *social/affective strategies* (that correspond roughly to Oxford's 'social,' 'affective' and 'communication' categories). The odd one out in O'Malley and Chamot's taxonomy is clearly the last group, 'social/ affective strategies,' which includes diverse behaviors such as 'cooperation,' 'questioning and clarification,' and 'self-talk.' These strategies are not related to the cognitive theoretical basis outlined by the authors, and they admittedly represent a "broad grouping" (p. 45), a miscellaneous category that appears to have been introduced simply to accommodate all the strategies that did not fit into the first two types but which could not be left out either. Indeed, Hsiao and Oxford's (2002) empirical analysis confirmed that the explanatory power of the O'Malley-Chamot model increased if the social/affective strategies were further differentiated into social and affective strategies.

Thus, the strategy systems proposed by Oxford (1990) and O'Malley and Chamot (1990) are highly compatible (for a detailed comparison, see Hsiao & Oxford, 2002), particularly if we make three changes on the basis of the arguments just described: (a) exclude communication strategies from the scope of learning strategies, (b) combine Oxford's memory and cognitive strategies, and (c) separate O'Malley and Chamot's (1990) social/affective strategies. The resulting typology comprises the following four main components:

1. *Cognitive strategies*, involving the manipulation or transformation of the learning materials/input (e.g., repetition, summarizing, using images).

2. *Metacognitive strategies*, involving higher-order strategies aimed at analyzing, monitoring, evaluating, planning, and organizing one's own learning process.

3. *Social strategies*, involving interpersonal behaviors aimed at increasing the amount of L2 communication and practice the learner undertakes (e.g., initiating interaction with native speakers, cooperating with peers).

4. *Affective strategies*, involving taking control of the emotional (affective) conditions and experiences that shape one's subjective involvement in learning.

Recent Research on Language Learning Strategies

Although the theoretical inconsistencies surrounding the learning strategy literature in general had been known since the early days, it was not at all unreasonable that the L2 field showed remarkable tolerance of these shortcomings. After all, learning strategies represented one of the most promising topics in the broader field of educational psychology in the 1980s and—what was just as important—research studies that included language learning strategies as either dependent or independent variables tended to produce interesting results (for reviews, see Chamot, 2001; Cohen, 1998; Oxford, 1993, 1996). There was an increasing body of research evidence that learning strategies played an important role in L2 attainment and their study offered a glimpse into the subtle mechanisms that constituted the complex process of learning. This was a particularly welcome development for many because the complex of learning had been long seen as a metaphorical 'black box:' we could describe what went in (input) and measure what came out (output) without having much of an understanding of what was going on inside. Learning strategies offered the potential of becoming floodlights into this box. The practical significance of this recognition was also augmented by the emerging view that learning strategies could be specifically taught to language learners (see below for details).

Thus, strategy research flourished and several high-profile researchers invested time and energy in its pursuit over the years; as a result, this line of investigation became well represented at international conferences and in academic journals, and before long it reached a critical mass which, to a certain extent, 'justified itself.' Any doubts about the validity of the construct were easily shrugged off by saying that significant developments are often accompanied by a theoretical muddle that will eventually be cleared away by the subsequent restructuring of our existing knowledge. Peter Skehan's summary of the learning strategy research at the end of the 1980s (Skehan, 1989) illustrated this ambivalent but optimistic research climate well:

> If, now, we review the whole of the learner-strategies research, we have to say that the area is at an embryonic stage. Conflicting results and methodologies proliferate. There are few hard findings. Even the causal role and intervention potential of strategies could be disputed. ... Yet the area of research has considerable attractions. A lot of useful and suggestive research has now been reported. There are the beginnings of systematicity in the categorization schemes for strategies, so that new investigators need not gather information blindly. ... This suggests that we are ready for the first attempts at theorizing within the learner-strategies field. (p. 98)

Fifteen years later we can conclude that the necessary theoretical clarification about the nature of the learning strategy concept did not happen, which resulted in a marked shift in the evolution and status of the notion of learning strategy both in educational psychology and L2 research. In the former field, the term *learning strategy* was first marginalized and then virtually abandoned by the research community in favor of the more versatile concept of *self-regulation*. In the L2 field the concept has increasingly shifted from the basic research domain into the more applied realm of language teaching methodology (although, for exceptions, see Griffiths, 2003; Lan & Oxford, 2003; Purdie & Oliver, 1999; Purpura, 1997, 1999; Wakamoto, 2000; Yamamori, Isoda, Hiromori, & Oxford, 2003; Yang, 1999). However, before looking at these developments in detail, let us consider some of the achievements of strategy research along with the critical issue of its assessment.

Learner Variation in Strategy Use

The most fruitful research direction in the area of learning strategies has focused on the systematic variation in the strategy use of certain groups of learners. In the light of the theoretical ambiguities surrounding learning strategies this is understandable: Although we may not know what a particular strategy score might imply with regard to SLA, if we compare the mean scores of two groups of learners and we find significant differences between them, we can draw conclusions about the difference in the scores. Several grouping variables have been applied over the years, with gender and cultural/ethnic background being the most extensively researched ones.

Learning strategies across cultures. In the preface of a book entirely devoted to the study of cross-cultural perspectives of language learning strategies, Oxford (1996b) argued that because language learning is fully situated within a given cultural context, various cultural beliefs, perceptions, and values significantly affect the strategies students adopt. This may be partly due to ethnicity-based variation in the students' learning styles as well as differences in formal and informal educational experiences. This claim has received clear evidence in a study conducted by Levine, Reves, and Leaver (1996) in Israel, which compared the learning strategies of immigrants from the former Soviet Union to the strategies used by people who had lived in Israel for at least five years. Immigrant students tended to show a preference for such traditional strategies as memorizing grammar rules, rote learning, repeatedly writing down words, or doing grammar exercises from a textbook or workbook, in contrast to the old-timers' preference for more communicative approaches, including taking risks in the use of new structures and words. As the authors concluded, the finding confirmed the hypothesis that "learners studying in a highly structured and uniform educational system would develop learning strategies reflecting that system" (p. 45). In the same volume, Bedell and Oxford (1996) provided a comprehensive review of the literature on the strategy use of learners from a wide range of ethnolinguistic contexts, and they concluded that learners often—although not always—behave in certain culturally approved and socially encouraged ways as they learn. However, the authors also emphasized that culture should not be seen as a strait jacket that binds students to a particular set of learning strategies all their lives: Through focused strategy instruction students can be made aware of the value in strategies that are not necessarily within the limits of their cultural norms.

Gender-variation in learning strategy use. Gender differences regularly show up in studies on L2 learning and therefore they were expected to characterize the use of language learning strategies as well. Indeed, as Oxford (1996b) states, gender often influences strategy use, with females typically reporting more strategy use than males in many different cultures, and we can find several empirical studies in the literature arriving at the same conclusion (cf. Peacock & Ho, 2003). In one of the first systematic discussions of gender differences in learning strategy use, Oxford, Nyikos, and Ehrman (1988) started out by quoting the language learning folklore that 'women learn languages better than men,' and then formulated three questions:

1.   Why do the observed sex differences exist in strategy use?
2.   Can sex be viewed as a crucial and consistent variable in strategy use?
3.   If sex differences are crucial and consistent, how should they be interpreted?

These are indeed the key issues and more research will be needed before we can give a detailed answer to them. Based on the available data, Oxford et al. (1988) explained gender differences with a number of factors: (a) women's greater overall social orientation, (b) differences in men's and women's L2 speech, (c) women's greater desire for social approval, (d) women's greater willingness to accept existing norms, and (e) women's greater general verbal ability.

Kaylani's (1996) study in Jordan confirmed the existence of significant sex differences: Female students used significantly more memory, cognitive, compensation, and affective strategies than male students. At the same time, however, the differences in strategy use resulting from the influence of gender were not as great as differences resulting from proficiency: Successful female students' language learning strategy profiles resembled those of successful males more than they did those of unsuccessful females. Ehrman and Oxford's (1990) investigation also showed that the females-are-better-than-males generalization is simplistic and further research is needed to achieve a more subtle picture: In their study the number and kind of learning strategies reported by women were similar to those used by men who shared their psychological-type preferences. Thus, for example, with regard to the 'Thinkers/Feelers' distinction, female Thinkers had more in common with the male Thinkers than with female Feelers, and vice versa.

Discipline-based variation. In a recent study, Peacock and Ho (2003) compared learning strategy use among English for Academic Purposes students across eight disciplines in higher education: building, business, computing, engineering, English, math, primary education, and science. They found sharp disciplinary differences in strategy use, with English majors employing the most and computing students the fewest strategies.

Relating learning strategies to other ID factors. Some limited research has been conducted on relating language learning strategies to other ID factors, most notably to *motivation*. This, in theory makes sense: Learning strategies are, by definition, examples of motivated learning behavior and therefore meaningful links with motivation are expected to exist (cf. Cohen, 1998; Cohen & Dörnyei, 2002). The systematic study of the interrelationship between L2 motivation and language learning strategy use was initiated in the mid-1990s by Richard Schmidt, Peter MacIntyre, and their colleagues (e.g., MacIntyre, 1994; MacIntyre & Noels, 1996; Schmidt, Boraie, & Kassabgy, 1996). Building on these results, Schmidt and Watanabe (2001) further investigated the topic by obtaining data from over 2,000 university students in Hawaii. They found evidence that motivation affects strategy use but this impact showed considerable variation across the various motives and strategy types measured in their survey. In general, cognitive and metacognitive strategies were most affected by motivation and the least affected strategy type was social strategies, which were consistently associated only with the motivational component that the authors termed Cooperativeness, referring to an orientation toward relationships with classmates and the teacher.

Conscious strategy use is also logically linked to *learner beliefs*, since learners will obviously select the most appropriate strategies for themselves on the basis of what they believe is the most appropriate approach toward mastering and L2. This issue is further examined in the section on beliefs in chapter 7.

Strategy Training

Although the amount of research on language learning strategies has been on the decrease in general, there is one area which is a striking exception: language teaching methodology. When it comes to how to train learners the more effective use of strategic learning, there is a healthy supply of summaries, policy papers, and various sorts of training materials. Is this not a contradiction to the previous suggestion that learning strategies have contestable validity as a concept? I do not believe so. If we think about it, even if the notion *learning strategy* does not exist as a distinctive aspect of learning but only indicates creative and personalized learning behaviors, the training of these 'strategies' would be a highly desirable activity as it would amount, in effect, to the teaching of learners ways in which they can learn better. And no one would question the fact that most learners would benefit from an improvement of their study skills. Furthermore, as Pressley et al. (1992) argued convincingly over a decade ago, good strategy instruction is inherently motivating and interesting, which suggests that classrooms in which the instruction of effective cognitive strategies proliferates will produce students who will have "more skill and will" (p. 354).

The notion of *learning to learn* in L2 studies has a history of over two decades, starting with Ellis and Sinclair's (1989) famous coursebook, *Learning to Learn English: A Course in Learner Training,* and with more recent books highlighting the specific training of learner strategies (e.g., Chamot, Barnhardt, El-Dinary, & Robbins, 1999; Grenfell & Harris, 1999; Macaro, 2001). In educational psychology we can find the same type of publications, with titles highlighting either 'learning to learn' or 'learning strategies' (e.g., Dembo, 2000; VanderStoep & Pintrich, 2003). As Randi and Corno (2000) summarized,

> Encouraging students to take responsibility for their own learning is a loud refrain in current thinking on schooling. To help all students become "self-regulated," theory suggests the need for a better understanding of the strategies that successful students use to maintain effort and protect commitments in school. (p. 651)

Although the various strategy training frameworks differ in their details, they aim to achieve the same overall goals: to raise the learners' awareness about learning strategies and model strategies overtly along with the task; to encourage strategy use and give a rationale for it; to offer a wide menu of relevant strategies for learners to choose from; to offer controlled practice in the use of some strategies; and to provide some sort of a post-task analysis which allows students to reflect on their strategy use. Arguably the most inspiring and instructive parts of strategy training is the 'sharing session,' where students are asked to share their learning discoveries and self-generated learning strategies as a regular part of class. Students who are directly involved in the learning process often have fresh insights that they can share with fellow learners in simplified terms, and personal learning strategies are often quite amusing and therefore students usually enjoy discussing them.

In a recent special issue of *TESL-EJ* that has been entirely devoted to strategy research and training (Anderson, 2003), Harris (2003) provided a useful overview of various strategy instruction schemes. Table 6.1 presents Harris' comparative summary of the stages of four training models, by O'Malley and Chamot (1990), Oxford (1990), Chamot et al. (1999), and Grenfell and Harris (1999). It can be seen that the broad stages of the various schemes are similar. Figure 6.1 presents a further model of the "Learner strat-

Table 6.1. A comparison of the stages of four strategy instruction schemes (source: Harris, 2003, p. 7; cited with permission)

O'Malley and Chamot (1990)	Oxford (1990)	Chamot et al. (1999)	Grenfell and Harris (1999)
1. Students identify their current learning strategies	Learners do a task without any strategy training	*Preparation*	*Awareness raising.* Learners do a task "cold"

	They discuss how they did it and the teacher asks them to reflect on how their strategies may have facilitated their learning		They brainstorm the strategies used. Class shares strategies that work for them
2. Teacher explains additional strategies	Teacher demonstrates other helpful strategies, stressing the potential benefits	*Presentation*	*Modeling.* Teacher demonstrates new strategies, emphasizes their value and draws up a checklist of strategies for subsequent use
3. Teacher provides opportunities for practice	Learners are provided with opportunities to practice the new strategies	*Practice*	*General practice.* Learners are given a range of tasks to deploy new strategies
	Learners are shown how the strategies can be transferred to other tasks	*Expansion*	
	Learners are provided with further tasks and asked to make choices about which strategies they will use		*Action planning.* Learners are guided to select strategies that will help them address their particular difficulties *Further practice and fading out of reminders to use*
4. Teacher assists learners in evaluating their success with the new strategies	Teacher helps learners to understand the success of their strategy use and assess their progress toward more self-directed learning	*Evaluation*	*Evaluation.* Teacher guides learners to evaluate progress and strategy use and to set themselves new goals

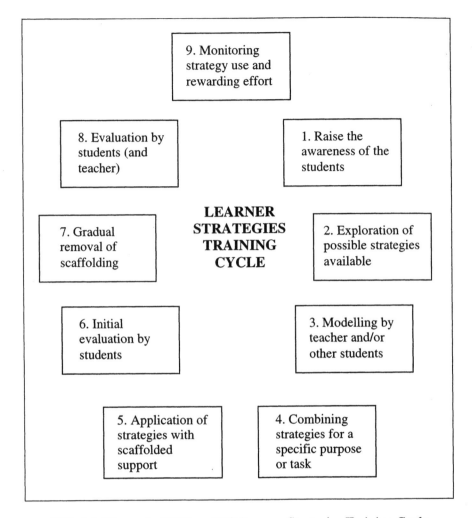

FIG. 6.1. Macaro's (2001, p. 176) Learner Strategies Training Cycle
(cited with permission).

egies training cycle" by Macaro (2001), and this again corresponds to the
other models in its overall structure.

Although the available strategy training materials and schemes are
generally creative and impressive, it is not clear whether the benefits of their
explicit employment warrant the time and effort spent on them in comparison to spending the same amount of creative energy designing 'ordinary'
learning activities. This is, in fact, exactly the same question as the one

asked about the teachability of communication strategies in the 1990s (for a review, see Dörnyei, 1995), but it is considerably more difficult to give a straightforward answer in the current case: Whereas communication strategies are related to speech production and therefore the impact of communication strategy interventions can be assessed by comparing post-treatment speech data to pre-treatment and control group data, learning strategies are related to the broad process of learning, and the effectiveness of learning also depends on a host of other variables, ranging from other ID factors such as aptitude to situational determinants such as peer influence. In a comprehensive review of learner strategies, McDonough (1999) arrived at the same conclusion: "The relationship between strategy use and proficiency is very complicated: Issues such as frequency and quality of strategy use do not bear a simple linear relationship to achievement in a second language" (p. 13).

After this caveat we must admit that the currently available evidence gives only moderate support, at best, for strategy training. Most of the empirical studies reported in the literature struggle with methodological problems related to assessment issues (see next) and the inherent difficulties of doing classroom research (cf. e.g., Rossiter, 2001). What we find is a mixed bag, with some cases when strategy instruction has resulted in improved performance and other cases when it has not. In a 1996 article surveying the effectiveness of strategy training in educational psychology, Hadwin and Winne (1996) also highlighted the lack of a sufficient empirical research base. As they summarized, of the 566 articles published about study skills and learning strategies in the literature, only 9% reported any sort of empirical test of the interventions' effects, and of these only 16 met rigorous research criteria. As the authors concluded, there was only a "*very* scant research base upon which to ground recommendations for study tactics that populate the many handbooks available or to justify mounting costly programs that promise to improve students' study skills" (p. 711).

Thus, the overall interpretation of the situation largely depends on the various scholars' personal disposition (for L2 reviews, see Chamot & Rubin, 1994; Chamot et al., 1999; Cohen, 1998; McDonough, 1995, 1999; Rees-Miller, 1993). Skeptics (e.g., Rees-Miller, 1993; Rossiter, 2003) caution teachers against investing too much effort into strategy training as this is not likely to be cost-effective. Proponents of strategy training claim that past research has accumulated enough positive evidence to justify further work in this area with an aim of fine-tuning both the methodology and the assessment procedures. I believe that McDonough's (1999) conclusion provides an accurate 'middle-of-the-road' summary: "teaching strategies is not universally successful, but the latest research is showing that, in certain circumstances and modes, particularly when incorporated into the teacher's normal classroom behavior, and thus involving teacher training as well as learner training, success is demonstrable" (p. 13). Indeed, studies such as Cohen,

Weaver, and Li (1995) and Nunan (1997) indicate the potentials of strategy interventions.

To conclude this section, let us have a look at the most ambitious recent initiative to integrate learning strategies into language instruction, Andrew Cohen's (2002; Cohen & Dörnyei, 2002) *Styles and strategies-based instruction* (SSBI), already mentioned briefly in the previous chapter. SSBI entails a learner-focused approach that combines strategy training with awareness raising whereby learners can become more cognizant of the fit between their style preferences and the strategies that they select for language learning and language use tasks. SSBI thus combines 'style stretching' and strategy instruction in a complementary manner in order to empower learners to be more effective L2 learners in partnership with the teacher. Cohen and Weaver (2004) developed a training manual for SSBI, and regular SSBI summer courses and workshops are run at the University of Minnesota to help to engage teachers in

> not just teaching the language but also in training learners to be more in touch with (a) their learning style preferences and language strategy choices on specific tasks, and (b) their motivational temperature. If language learners are more aware of how they learn best and take more responsibility for their learning, they may have lifelong-learning rather than having the more typical learned-but-forgotten language experience. (Cohen, 2002, p. 62)

The Assessment of Learning Strategies

Learning strategy use and, more generally, self-regulated learning, are typically measured by self-report questionnaires. These instruments are based on the assumption that strategy use and strategic learning are related to an underlying aptitude because items ask respondents to generalize their actions across situations rather than referencing singular and specific learning events (Winne & Perry, 2000). In the following I describe four questionnaires: (a) The Motivated Strategies for Learning Questionnaire (MSLQ), which is currently the best known instrument in this area in educational psychology, (b) Rebecca Oxford's Strategy Inventory for Language Learning (SILL), which is the most often used questionnaire in L2 studies, (c) Cohen and Chi's Language Strategy Use Inventory and Index, which reflects a new attempt to make the measurement of strategy use more practical, and (d) Tseng, Dörnyei, and Schmitt's Self-Regulat Capacity in Vocabulary Learning scale, which introduces a new approach to assessing strategic learning.

Motivated Strategies for Learning Questionnaire (MSLQ)

The Motivated Strategies for Learning Questionnaire (MSLQ) was developed at the University of Michigan by Paul Pintrich and his colleagues (Pintrich, Smith, Garcia, & McKeachie, 1991; reprinted in VanderStoep & Pintrich, 2003). The University of Michigan has traditionally been one of the leading international centers of educational psychological research, particularly in the areas of motivation and self-regulated learning, and therefore this battery represents the operationalization of cutting-edge theory. The development of the inventory took approximately three years, during which time items were tried and revised based on the results of factor analyses, reliability analyses, and correlations with achievement measures (Winne & Perry, 2000).

The MSLQ is aimed at college students and, as the name of the instrument indicates, the items cover two broad areas, *Motivation* and *Learning Strategies*; in this chapter only the latter part is discussed (for a description of the subscales and sample items, see Table 6.2). The complete questionnaire consists of 81 items, each using a 7-point scale anchored by 'not at all true of me' (1) and 'very true of me' (7). The Learning Strategies category includes 50 items and is divided into two sections: (a) Cognitive and Metacognitive Strategies, comprising subscales labeled *rehearsal, elaboration, organization, critical thinking*, and *metacognitive self-regulation*; (b) Resource Management Strategies, comprising the subscales of *time and study environment, effort regulation, peer learning*, and *help seeking*. These subscales are cumulative in the sense that subscale scores are formed by computing the means of the individual item scores in a subscale.

With regard to the psychometric properties of the instrument, Pintrich et al. (1991) stated in the MSLQ Manual that the goodness of fit indices of the test were not "stellar" but—as they argued—"reasonable" (pp. 78–80). In a more detailed analysis of the reliability and predictive validity of the MSLQ, Pintrich, Smith, Garcia, and McKeachie (1993) also gave a cautious 'go-ahead' by concluding that the questionnaire had "relatively good" reliability and the theoretical framework and the scales that measure it "seem to be valid" (p. 811).

Table 6.2. Description of the learning strategies part of Pintrich et al.'s (1991) Motivated Strategies for Learning Questionnaire (MSLQ)

I COGNITIVE AND METACOGNITIVE STRATEGIES (31 items)

Rehearsal	The cognitive activity of repeating facts or definitions. E.g., *"When studying for this class, I read my class notes and the course readings over and over."*
Elaboration	The process by which one can achieve sophisticated understanding of a topic by building connections to related topics. E.g., *"When I study for this class, I pull together information from different sources, such as lectures, readings, and discussions."*
Organization	The extent to which one's study behavior is organized. E.g., *"I make simple charts, diagrams, or tables to help me organize course material."*
Critical thinking	The ability to use the knowledge one has acquired in flexible and meaningful ways. E.g., *"I often find myself questioning things I hear or read in this course to decide if I find them convincing."*
Metacognitive self-regulation	The awareness and control one has over one's own cognition, involving planning, goal setting, and monitoring. E.g., *"When I study for this class, I set goals for myself in order to direct my activities in each study period."*

II. RESOURCE MANAGEMENT STRATEGIES (19 items)

Time and study environment	How well one manages one's time and chooses good places to study. E.g., *"I usually study in a place where I can concentrate on my course work."*
Effort regulation	Persistence in the face of difficulty or boredom. E.g., *"Even when course materials are dull and uninteresting, I manage to keep working until I finish."*
Peer (group) learning	How well one can work effectively in groups. E.g., *"When studying for this course, I often set aside time to discuss the course material with a group of students from the class."*
Help-seeking	How well one uses the resources of more competent people who are available. E.g., *"I ask the instructor to clarify concepts I don't understand well."*

Strategy Inventory for Language Learning (SILL)

The Strategy Inventory for Language Learning (SILL) is the most often employed instrument for assessing language learning strategy use. It was developed by Rebecca Oxford (1990) and is based on Oxford's strategy taxonomy described earlier. Thus, the questionnaire consists of six scales: (a) Remembering more effectively (memory strategies), (b) Using your mental processes (cognitive strategies), (c) Compensating for missing knowledge (compensation strategies), (d) Organizing and evaluating your learning (metacognitive strategies), (e) Managing your emotions (affective strategies), and (f) Learning with others (social strategies). Scale scores are obtained, similarly to the MSLQ, by computing the average of the item scores within a scale, and there is a very user-friendly worksheet attached to the battery for testtakers to be able to calculate their own score profile. The author has published two versions of the instrument, one for speakers of English learning other target languages (80 items) and one for learners of English as an L2 (50 items; see Table 6.3 for sample items).

The items on the SILL all involve 5-point rating scales ranging from 'never or almost never true of me' to 'always or almost always true of me.' At first sight, these scales are similar to the scales used in the MSLQ discussed above, but a closer look reveals two fundamental differences. First, although both scale types use the term "true of me," the MSLQ scales range from 'not at all' to 'very' whereas the SILL scales from 'never or almost never' to 'always or almost always.' Second, the items themselves are of a different nature. As Table 6.2 illustrates, the items in the MSLQ are general declarations or conditional relations focusing on general and prominent facets of the learning process (i.e., *when doing this... I try to...*). The SILL items, on the other hand, are more specific, each one more or less corresponding to a language learning strategy. These two changes result in a major difference in the psychometric character of the two inventories. The items in the MSLQ tap into some general trends and inclinations, and can therefore be assumed to be in a linear relationship with corresponding underlying learner traits. This is further enhanced by the rating scales asking about the extent of the correspondence between the item and the learner, answered by marking a point on a continuum between 'not at all' and 'very.' Thus, every attempt has been made to make the items *cumulative*, which is why scale scores can be computed by pooling all the scale items (i.e., calculating the mean scores of the items belonging to a scale). The SILL, on the other hand, focuses on specific strategic behaviors and the scale descriptors indicate *frequencies* of strategy use (ranging between 'never' to 'always'). These items are, therefore, *behavioral* items, which means that we cannot assume a linear relationship between the individual item scores and the total

Table 6.3. Sample items for Rebecca Oxford's (1990) Strategy Inventory for Language Learning (SILL)

Memory strategies	"I use a combination of sounds and images to remember the new word."
Cognitive strategies	"I look for patterns in the new language."
Compensation strategies	"I make up new words if I do not know the right one."
Metacognitive strategies	"I arrange my schedule to study and practice the new language consistently, not just when there is the pressure of a test."
Affective strategies	"I try to relax whenever I feel anxious about using the new language."
Social strategies	"I work with other language learners to practice, review, or share information."

scale scores; for example, one can be a generally good memory strategy user while scoring low on some of the items in the memory scale (e.g., "acting out a new word or using flashcards").

Thus, the scales in the SILL are not cumulative and computing mean scale scores is psychometrically not justifiable. A high score on the SILL is achieved by a learner using as many different strategies as possible and therefore it is largely the quantity that matters. This is in contradiction with strategy theory, which has indicated clearly that in strategy use it is not necessarily the quantity but the *quality* of the employed strategies that is important (cf. the discussion above about 'appropriateness' as a critical feature of learning strategies).[1] As an extreme, one can go a long way by using only one strategy that perfectly suits the particular learner's personality and learning style; and even if someone uses several strategies, it does not necessarily mean that the person is an able strategy user because, as Ehrman et al. (2003) also found, "less able learners often use strategies in a random, unconnected, and uncontrolled manner" (p. 315). It is interesting to read that

---

[1]This is a contestable claim because, as Rebecca Oxford (personal communication, July 29, 2004) pointed out, "More than 15 years of research—using varied instruments for strategy assessment—tell us that the quantity of strategies used, while not the only variable of note, has a significant association with many measures of learning success across many studies throughout the world." One reason for this, according to Oxford, is that more successful learners are known to use multiple strategies in coordinated sequences known as 'strategy chains.'

Oxford and her colleagues' recent reappraisal of this issue is in accordance with this argument:

> Low reported strategy use is not always a sign of ineffective learning. Also, reportedly high-frequency use of strategies does not guarantee that the learning is successful. In a casual class observation, one might see some learners working eagerly and using many strategies, but … do not employ those strategies effectively. Studies relying solely on frequency data may miss this point. Because frequency results alone do not explain everything about strategy use, it is necessary to include other indices of learners' behaviors that reflect their decision making. 'The more, the better' is not always the case in strategy use. (Yamamori et al., 2003, p. 384)

All this means that although the SILL may be a useful instrument for raising student awareness of L2 learning strategies and for initiating class discussions, its use for research purposes is questionable. This was well illustrated in a study by Gardner, Tremblay, and Masgoret (1997) using structural equation modeling, in which language learning strategy use (as measured by the SILL) related, quite unexpectedly, *negatively* to learning achievement, suggesting that "the use of language learning strategies is associated with low levels of achievement" (p. 353). As the authors pointed out, such an interpretation was not consistent with other studies of language learning strategies. They hypothesized that the contradictory finding in their sample—students who have had at least nine years of prior L2 training—was caused by the instrument: As they argued, successful language learners "may have adopted their own effective strategy and thus do not adopt the wide range of strategies" (p. 354).

Language Strategy Use Inventory and Index

Cohen and Chi's (2002) Language Strategy Use Inventory and Index (LSUII) offers an interesting development in devising learning strategy instruments. Although one of the main intended uses of the SILL was to serve practical purposes in raising language learners' awareness (hence the student-friendly worksheets attached to it that allow learners to calculate their own strategy use profile), the instrument also had research aspirations: The structure was based on a theoretical model and the six parts of the inventory were treated as cumulative scales in the psychometric sense— indeed, the SILL has been used in many research studies all over the world. However, as I argued above, the compromise that the SILL tried to achieve by combining practical and psychometric considerations was unsatisfactory and therefore the main question facing post-SILL researchers has been to decide which direction they wanted to move in: to develop a practical classroom tool or a research instrument? Cohen and Chi (2002) decided on the former, practical, route and they explicitly stated this in the introduction of the LSUII: "The purpose of this inventory is to find out more about yourself as a language learner and to help you discover strategies that can help you master a new language" (p. 16).

To the credit of the authors, once they have made this decision, they were willing to carry this practical purpose through the whole structure and format of the inventory: Thus, first, they structured the content according to a pragmatic, and to language teachers and learners familiar, system of the four basic language skill areas (listening, speaking, reading, and writing), to which they added vocabulary learning and translation skills. Second, they broke down these six categories into subscales to further orientate the learners. Third, instead of some sort of a continuous rating scale, they introduced a scale of four practical categories: "I use this strategy and like it," "I have tried this strategy and would use it again," "I've never used this strategy but am interested in it," and "This strategy doesn't fit for me." Thus, there is no attempt to have cumulative rating scales and the inventory is intended to serve as a checklist and index. Table 6.4 presents an outline of the structure and sample items.

Self-Regulating Capacity in Vocabulary Learning scale (SRCvoc)

Similarly to Cohen and Chi's LSUII described above, Tseng, Dörnyei, and Schmitt's (in press) Self-Regulating Capacity in Vocabulary Learning scale (SRCvoc) also offers a response to the practical vs. psychometric use dilemma, but unlike the LSUII, which pursued increased practical utility, the SRCvoc took the psychometric route. As described by Tseng et al., two main objectives guided the test construction process:

1. To devise items that tap into general learner traits rather than survey specific behavioral habits. We developed items that were similar to the MSLQ items in that they involved general declarations or conditional relations rather than descriptions of specific strategic behaviors. Accordingly, the SRCvoc does not measure strategy use but rather the learner's underlying self-regulatory capacity that will result in strategy use (for a detailed discussion of self-regulation, see later in this chapter).

Table 6.4. Structural outline and sample items of Cohen and Chi's (2002) Language Strategy Use Inventory and Index (LSUII)

LISTENING STRATEGY USE (26 items)

Strategies to increase my exposure to the target language	*"Listen to talk shows on the radio, watch TV shows, or see movies in the target language."*
Strategies to become more familiar with the sounds in the target language	*"Imitate the way native speakers talk."*
Strategies to prepare to listen to conversation in the target language	*"Pay special attention to specific aspects of the language; for example, the way the speaker pronounces certain sounds."*
Strategies to listen to conversation in the target language	*"Pay attention to when and how long people tend to pause."*
Strategies for when I do not understand some or most of what someone says in the target language	*"Ask speakers to slow down if they are speaking too fast."*

VOCABULARY STRATEGY USE (18 items)

Strategies to learn new words	*"Make a mental image of new words."*
Strategies to review vocabulary	*"Review words periodically so I don't forget them."*
Strategies to recall vocabulary	*"Visualize the spelling of new words in my mind."*
Strategies to make use of new vocabulary	*"Try using new words in a variety of ways."*

SPEAKING STRATEGY USE (18 items)

Strategies to practice speaking	*"Practice saying new expressions to myself."*
Strategies to engage in conversations	*"Regularly seek out opportunities to talk with native speakers."*
Strategies for when I can't think of a word or expression	*"Ask for help from my conversational partner."*

READING STRATEGY USE (11 items)

Strategies to improve my reading ability	*"Find reading material that is at or near my level."*
Strategies for when words and grammatical structures are not understood	*"Use a dictionary to get a detailed sense of what individual words mean."*

WRITING STRATEGY USE (10 items)

Strategies for basic writing	*"Take class notes in the target language as much as I'm able."*
Strategies for writing an essay or academic paper	*"Wait to edit my writing until all my ideas are down on paper."*
Strategies to use after writing a draft of an essay or paper	*"Revise my writing once or twice to improve the language and content."*

TRANSLATION STRATEGY USE (6 items)

Strategies for translation	*"Translate parts of a conversation into my own language to help me remember the conversation."*
Strategies for working directly in the target language as much as possible	*"Put my own language out of mind and think only in the target language as much as possible."*

2. To base the structure of the instrument on a theoretical construct. Because of the theoretical problems surrounding the existing learning strategy taxonomies, we decided to draw on Dörnyei's (2001) system of self-regulatory strategies, which in turn was based on Kuhl's (1987) and Corno and Kanfer's (1993) taxonomies of action control strategies (for more details, see chapt. 4). To further increase the validity of the construct, it was applied to one particular learning domain only, vocabulary learning—it is believed, however, that this situated construct can serve as a model for the assessment of other aspects of strategic learning as well, such as the other main language areas covered by the LSUII.

Thus, the SRCvoc focuses on five broad aspects of self-regulations in vocabulary learning (for the whole questionnaire, see Table 6.5; for the description of the scales, see the discussion of developing self-motivating strategies in chapt. 4): *Commitment control, Metacognitive control, Satiation control, Emotion control*, and *Environmental control*. Tseng et al (in press) report empirical data indicating that the instrument has good psychometric properties and that the five subscales load onto one higher-order factor that we have termed *Self-regulating capacity in vocabulary learning* (hence the name of the instrument).

Table 6.5. The 20 items of Tseng et al.'s (in press) Self-Regulating Capacity in Vocabulary Learning scale (SRCvoc)

Commitment Control

- When learning vocabulary, I have my special techniques to achieve my learning goals.
- When learning vocabulary, I believe I can achieve my goals more quickly than expected.
- When learning vocabulary, I persist until I reach the goals that I make for myself.
- I believe I can overcome all the difficulties related to achieving my vocabulary learning goals.

Metacognitive Control

- When learning vocabulary, I have my special techniques to keep my concentration focused.
- When learning vocabulary, I think my methods of controlling my concentration are effective.
- When it comes to learning vocabulary, I have my special techniques to prevent procrastination.
- When it comes to learning vocabulary, I think my methods of controlling procrastination are effective.

Satiation Control

- Once the novelty of learning vocabulary is gone, I easily become impatient with it. [Reversed score]
- During the process of learning vocabulary, I feel satisfied with the ways I eliminate boredom.
- During the process of learning vocabulary, I am confident that I can overcome any sense of boredom.
- When feeling bored with learning vocabulary, I know how to regulate my mood in order to invigorate the learning process.

Emotion Control

- When I feel stressed about vocabulary learning, I know how to reduce this stress.
- I feel satisfied with the methods I use to reduce the stress of vocabulary learning.
- When I feel stressed about vocabulary learning, I simply want to give up. [Reversed score]
- When I feel stressed about my vocabulary learning, I cope with this problem immediately.

Environment Control

- When I am studying vocabulary and the learning environment becomes unsuitable, I try to sort out the problem.
- When learning vocabulary, I know how to arrange the environment to make learning more efficient.
- When learning vocabulary, I am aware that the learning environment matters.
- When I study vocabulary, I look for a good learning environment.

LEARNING STRATEGIES AND STUDENT SELF-REGULATION IN EDUCATIONAL PSYCHOLOGY

So far the arguments presented in this chapter have pointed to the claim that although the concept of learning strategy has been influential in developments in language teaching methodology, the unresolved theoretical problems surrounding the concept and its measurement made it less appropriate for research purposes: In the absence of a tight definition, it is unclear what different researchers mean by the term *language learning strategy* and the actual language learning strategy measures presented in the various studies tend not to have sufficient psychometric properties. The logical question is, then, whether or not we need to abandon the concept altogether. In considering this question, let us turn to the field of educational psychology, which faced the same question in the 1990s.

As Weinstein et al. (2000) described, the origins of learning strategy research go back to the late 1960s when information processing theories were applied in the area of memory strategies to be used in educational settings. Various mnemonic strategies were developed to improve students' paired-associate learning and, as a result, the conception of the 'learner' shifted from a passive receptacle for knowledge to an active, self-determined individual who processes information in complex ways. This shift led to the broader conceptualization of planful and self-directed *cognitive strategies,* and subsequently, learning strategies became some of the 'hottest' issues in educational psychology in the 1980s, for the very reasons which also inspired L2 researchers to embrace the concept (described earlier): Learning strategies offered a unique insight into the mechanisms of the learning process in general and they also represented a significant mutable factor in promoting academic achievement for students.

Following the 'discovery' of learning strategies, several attempts were made in the 1980s to theorize the concept. Perhaps the most far-reaching of these theoretical discussions was Schmeck's (1988) and Kirby's (1988) analyses. As Schmeck outlined, the term *strategy* was originally a military term, referring to procedures for implementing the plan of a large-scale military operation, and in non-military use *strategy* had come to refer to the implementation of a set of procedures (tactics) for accomplishing something. Thus, a *learning strategy*, according to Schmeck, was in a more general sense a "sequence of procedures for accomplishing learning" (p. 5). Kirby took Schmeck's reasoning further by trying to specify the relationship between strategies, skills, and abilities. As he argued,

> *skills* are existing cognitive routines for performing specified tasks, and *strategies* are the means of selecting, combining, or redesigning those cognitive routines. Skills range from *knowledge skills*, the accessing by stimulus patterns of stored representations and associations (e.g., knowing that "7" says "seven") to *action skills*, the transforming of input information to obtain desired results... Skills are fundamentally related to *abilities*, to the extent that the latter sets some sort of upper limit to the development of the former. (p. 230)

Thus, skills according to Schmeck and Kirby are, broadly speaking, the things we can do (constrained by our ability), whereas strategies and tactics involve the conscious decisions to implement these skills. Although this distinction appears to make sense, it still leaves the exact level of analysis of strategies and skills open: At which conceptual level are the processes that are governed by strategies and skills best conceived? Are we talking about neurological, cognitive, or behavioral processes? Recall that according to Weinstein et al.'s (2000, p. 727) definition, learning strategies include "any thoughts, behaviors, beliefs, or emotions that facilitate the acquisition, understanding, or later transfer of new knowledge and skills." How can something be either a thought or a behavior or an emotion? These issues have been seen as distinct aspects of human functioning in psychology and it is difficult to accept the existence of an entity that simply cuts across them. And how do knowledge systems, emotional states/processes, cognitive operations, and motor skills interplay in producing action?

These are all valid questions that would need to be answered in order to use the term *learning strategy* in a scientifically rigorous sense. However, the currently available neurobiological information about the nature of concepts such as knowledge, skills, ability, and, more generally, learning appears to be insufficient to define precisely the class of learning behaviors that constitute learning strategy use. As a consequence, the amount of educational psychological research that targeted learning strategies dropped dramatically in the 1990s and researchers increasingly turned to a related concept, *self-regulation*. In the final part of this chapter we examine how this new concept is connected to learning strategies on the one hand and individual differences on the other hand.

Self-Regulation and Self-Regulatory Capacity

At the beginning of this chapter I mentioned the general observation that certain learners are more effective strategy users than others, which suggests that there is some sort of a trait-like strategic potential that enables some to excel in this area. As Macaro (2001) concluded about language learners, "One thing seems to be increasingly clear and that is that, across learning contexts, those learners who are proactive in their pursuit of language learning appear to learn best" (p. 264). After researchers started to accept that examining the strategies that these 'good' learners applied was not a fruitful direction, they set out to capture the secret of the strategic learners' 'proactiveness' by focusing on the self-regulatory process and the specific learner capacity underlying it. Thus, scholars increasingly recognized that the important thing about the proactive strategic learners is not necessarily the exact nature of the strategies, tactics, or techniques they apply, but rather the fact that they do apply them. That is, what makes strategic learners special is not so much what they do as the fact that they choose to put creative effort into improving their own learning and that they have the capacity to do so.

One may feel that this change has been a mere face-lift and research into self-regulation carried on doing the same kind of investigations as before by simply replacing the term *strategy* (which seemed to cause most of the confusion) with a trendy new metaphor. Although for some scholars this may have indeed been the case, and they merely jumped from one band wagon onto another at the beginning of the 1990s, there are at least two aspects of this orientational shift that turned out to be truly significant:

(a) The new perspective on self-regulation offered a far broader perspective than the previous focus on learning strategies, allowing scholars to make links with aspects of self-regulation that are not confined to the area of learning but concern other types of cognitive and behavioral processes (e.g., in clinical, health, and organizational psychology); an excellent summary of this cross-disciplinary effort is provided by Boekaerts, Pintrich, and Zeidner's (2000a) *Handbook of Self-Regulation.*

(b) By shifting the focus from the *product* (strategies) to the *process* (self-regulation), researchers have created more leeway for themselves: Although the so-called 'self-regulatory mechanisms' are very similar to 'learning strategies' and carry the same problems, these mechanisms— as we will see—are not the only important elements within the self-regulatory process and therefore their insufficient understanding does not necessarily prevent researchers from making headway in understanding other aspects of self-regulation.

As a result of this paradigm shift, by the beginning of the 1990s the study of self-regulation had come of age, causing a "virtual explosion of work in this area" (Zeidner, Boekaerts, & Pintrich, 2000, p. 750), and becoming a "natural and organic part of the landscape of psychology and education" (p. 749).

Let us now examine the concept of 'self-regulation' in more detail. As has already been mentioned, *self-regulation* refers to the degree to which individuals are active participants in their own learning; it is a more dynamic concept than learning strategy, highlighting the learners' own "strategic efforts to manage their own achievement through specific beliefs and processes" (Zimmerman & Risemberg, 1997, p. 105). The notion of *self-regulation of academic learning* is a multidimensional construct, including cognitive, metacognitive, motivational, behavioral, and environmental processes that learners can apply to enhance academic achievement. Thus, we face a rather blurry situation, not unlike we did in the study of learning strategies, namely that a particular concept overarches virtually all the main aspects of psychology. However, because in this case we have a process-oriented construct on our hand, it may be sufficient to identify the core dynamic energizer of the process, which is more manageable than to define the outcome. This new emphasis has been explicitly expressed by Zimmerman (2001): "Neither a mental ability nor an academic performance skill, self-regulation refers instead to the self-directive *process* through which learners transform their mental abilities into task-related academic skills" (p. 1).

According to Snow et al. (1996), self-regulation is centered around the volitional aspects of self- and task-management; that is, self-regulation involves "cognitive, affective, motivational, and behavioral components that provide the individual with the capacity to adjust his or her actions and goals to achieve desired results in light of changing environmental conditions" (Zeidner et al., 2000, p. 751). Although most scholars would agree with this general characterization, when we go beyond it we find a diverse and theoretically hard-to-define construct. As Boekaerts et al. (2000b) summarized in the introduction of their Handbook,

> It is clear from the diversity of the chapters in this handbook that self-regulation is a very difficult construct to define theoretically as well as to operationalize empirically. Nevertheless, the several years we worked together on the handbook have strengthened our conviction that self-regulation is an important topic that is highly relevant to the science of the mind and human behavior. At the same time, we are convinced that significant future progress is going to depend on our ability to clearly define the construct theoretically and to empirically distinguish it from other similar constructs. In this handbook many different definitions of self-regulation have been provided and a variety of explanations have been advanced to account for the observed effects of self-regulation on various outcome measures. (p. 4)

Indeed, self-regulation is often used synonymously with concepts such as self-management, self-control, action control, volition, self-change, self-directed behavior, coping behavior, and even metacognition and problem-solving. Yet, although there are many fuzzy boundaries and distinctions, as well as numerous unresolved issues ranging from the conceptual to the methodological, scholars appear to be keen to invest energy in researching the topic because the stakes have been raised considerably since the time when the target of research was learning strategies only: Self-regulation has become one of the important themes of scientific psychology in the 21st century (Zeidner et al., 2000).

Self-Regulation and Learning Strategies

As just discussed, the conceptualization of self-regulation has introduced a broad perspective involving a number of integrated and interrelated microprocesses, of which the use of learning strategies is only one. Other components, based on Kuhl and Goschke (1994), Winne and Perry (2000), and Zeidner et al. (2000), make up a long list: goal setting, strategic planning, action plans and action schemata, monitoring and metacognition, action control, volitional control mechanisms, strategic tactics and operations, effective time management, self-motivational beliefs (self-efficacy, outcome expectations, intrinsic interest, goal orientation, etc.), evaluation and self-reflection, receiving and processing feedback, experiencing pride and satisfaction with one's efforts, and establishing a congenial environment. This is where it becomes obvious what an important step it was to shift the attention from learning strategies to self-regulation. We are dealing here with a complex and far-reaching system, and learning strategies are not necessarily of primary importance among the battery of resources that are at the students' disposal.

By way of illustration, of the 23 studies that make up Boekaerts et al.'s (2000a) *Handbook of Self-Regulation* only three (by Randi & Corno, 2000; Weinstein et al., 2000; and Winne & Perry, 2000) mention 'learning/cognitive/self-regulatory strategies' at all, and even Winne and Perry's chapter tends to avoid the term most of the time by substituting it with 'cognitive operations' and 'cognitive tactics.' Kuhl and Goschke (1994) offered an explicit explanation of why they decided to use the term *volitional mechanisms* instead of strategies: Based on neurophysiological evidence, they believed that the traditional consciousness criterion of strategies—namely, that these are based on explicit metacognitive knowledge that people can use deliberately to improve volitional efficiency—was problematic because volitional functioning also involved a subconscious, implicit level.

In light of the above extensive list of self-regulatory components, we can also understand the nature of the shift from learning strategies to self-regulatory learning better: 'Learning strategies' were, in fact, never explicitly rejected (and, as mentioned earlier, the concept is still used in practical materials such as Dembo, 2000; VanderStoep & Pintrich, 2003) and, indeed, Boekaerts et al.'s (2000a) Handbook does contain a chapter by Weinstein et al. (2000) that specifically focuses on them. Instead, learning strategies were quietly sidelined: Because the use of the concept turned out to be unfruitful for broader research purposes, scholars specialized in this area simply turned their attention to other related concepts (of which, as we have seen, there are many). The long list of potential components of self-regulation also explains why specific operationalizations of the concept differ so widely—although the general thrust in every conceptualization is similar, researchers have defined and assessed the specific subprocesses and ingredients, and their interrelationships, differently.

Self-Regulatory Capacity as an Individual Difference Factor

In this final section of this chapter let us return to the question the chapter began with: Is self-regulation an individual difference factor at all? I indicated previously there that the answer is likely to be yes-and-no. Randi and Corno (2000), for example, argued that self-regulation was both an aptitude for (i.e., antecedent) and a potential outcome of schooling. Winne and Perry (2000) also highlighted the twofold nature of self-regulation when they stated that self-regulatory learning had properties of an aptitude or an event: The former dimension refers to a relatively enduring attribute of a person and is therefore an ID factor proper; the latter refers to a transient state embedded in a larger, longer series of states unfolding over time. This distinction bears a close resemblance to the trait–state distinction found in personality psychology (e.g., trait vs. state anxiety), and of particular importance for us here is the trait aspect.

According to Winne and Perry (2000), self-regulated learning as an aptitude comprises two main dimensions, *metacognitive knowledge* and *metacognitive monitoring*. Each are broken down to further components: Metacognitive knowledge is associated with the knowledge of cognitive tactics (defined as fine-grained cognitive operations), procedural knowledge to enact these, conditional knowledge about occasions to enact these, as well as knowledge of task parameters and self-parameters. Metacognitive monitoring concerns processes such as monitoring task difficulty and matching achievements to standards, as well as the confidence about one's accuracy of monitoring. Although these descriptors do not outline a conventional trait-like attribute, we should note that even with a more traditional ID factor such as motivation, recent definitions have adopted process-oriented features (cf. chapt. 4).

Kuhl (1994) used a different approach to trying to grasp what lies at the core of strategic behavior: He introduced the concept of 'volitional competence,' which is responsible for at least seven volitional mechanisms (Kuhl & Goschke, 1994): (1) *Intention control* in terms of maintenance of an active intention, (2) *attention control* in terms of selectively strengthening relevant input information, (3) *action control* in terms of inhibition of counter-intentional impulses, (4) *arousal control* in terms of readjusting the level of arousal, (5) *motivation* and *emotion control* facilitating the initiative, (6) *encoding control* concerning volitional selectivity during pre-attentional stages of information processing, and (7) *self-reflective thinking and planning*, which is a more sophisticated version of the maintenance function, involving a high degree of metacontrol over one's thought processes. Kuhl further proposed that the ability to use one's volitional competence was associated with an individual difference variable termed *action vs. state orientation*. This personality disposition is clearly a significant determinant of one's self-regulating capacity, concerning the individual's proactivity in acting out intentions. Action-oriented people are disposed to generate fully developed and realistic action plans upon which they act; in contrast, state-oriented people are prone to procrastinate, ruminate, hesitate, and in general display passivity. Unfortunately, when Kuhl starts explaining the interplay of these mechanisms, the theory becomes almost unmanageably complex; his conclusion about state vs. action orientation reflects this complexity well and applies to some extent to the whole area of self-regulation:

The attempt to relate the construct to this great number of antecedents and consequences is necessary because it relates to a core function affecting every goal-directed human action. However, the frustration that this complexity might produce in the reader as it sometimes does in us is not only a result of the complexity of the phenomenon under study, but it is also a sign of the many ambiguities, paradoxes, and unresolved problems that still remain. One of our motivation-control techniques for maintaining our intention to continue this difficult research is our attempt to disengage from the unrealistic goal of solving all these problems in this book and to focus instead on how rewarding it is to be able to describe the unresolved problems more clearly than before and help pave the way for future solutions. (p. 42)

CONCLUSION

I am in agreement with Hsiao and Oxford's (2002) belief that learning strategies constitute a useful tool kit for active and conscious learning, and that these strategies pave the way toward greater proficiency, learner autonomy, and self-regulation. However, the construct of learning strategies has been found to be less helpful for researchers when conducting in-depth analyses of the antecedents and ingredients of strategic learning, and as a consequence, the concept had been sidelined and marginalized in educational psychology by the 1990s. This does not mean that scholars have developed second thoughts about the virtues and benefits associated with learning strategies that made this line of research so popular in the 1980s. Far from it: the learners' proactive and informed contribution to increasing the effectiveness of their own learning is seen as more important than ever before. What has changed is the research perspective: It was realized that strategic learning is a far more complex issue than thought before and therefore simply focusing on the 'surface manifestations'—i.e., the tatics and techniques that strategic learners actually employ—does not do the topic justice. Therefore a new construct, 'self-regulation' or 'self-regulated learning,' was introduced in the educational psychological literature, and most of the research attention has turned toward examining variables that were more dynamic and process-oriented than learning/cognitive strategies. Furthermore, by linking self-regulation in learning to self-regulation in other disciplinary areas of cognitive and health sciences, the construct was extended into a grand theme in psychology. These are still early days in this line of research and our understanding of self-regulation is still rather sketchy, lacking real integration; given, however, the high status of this research area, we can expect major advances in the next decade.

7

Other Learner Characteristics

Having reviewed the five ID variables that have traditionally been seen as the main learner characteristics in L2 studies, this chapter provides a brief overview of another five variables—*anxiety, creativity, willingness to communicate* (WTC), *self-esteem*, and *learner beliefs*—whose discussion, for various reason, did not warrant a whole chapter. The first two of these variables, anxiety and creativity, cut across traditional ID categories: *Anxiety* is conceptualized as part of self-confidence in Clément's model and is therefore often seen as a component of motivation (cf. chapt. 4), but it is also a key constituent of the Neuroticism/Emotional Stability dimension of the Big Five personality model (cf. chapt. 2); what is more, it can also be conceived of as an emotion, a variant of fear (MacIntyre, 2002). *Creativity* is seen by many as a central component of intelligence (cf. chapt. 3) but it is, at the same time, a contributor to the Openness to Experience dimension of the Big Five model (cf. chapt. 2). *Willingness to communicate* (WTC) is a relatively new concept in L2 studies, but one that has a lot of potential and which has generated some interesting research during the past five years. *Self-esteem* is a well-known learner characteristics in educational psychology but little research has been conducted on it in the L2 field. Finally, *learner beliefs* were first highlighted in applied linguistics in the 1980s as a potentially important ID variable, but their exact role and nature is still open to debate.

Because the focus in this volume has been on the five primary ID dimensions described in chapters 2 through 6, the analysis of the additional variables in this chapter is not comprehensive. I believe that although all the five ID factors to be introduced have important theoretical and practical potential, further research is needed to do them full justice. To promote future research efforts, the summaries in this chapter outline what has already been done in the L2 field in each area and what the main current issues are. I also provide pointers, where relevant, to related work in psychology that can inform L2 research and strengthen the theoretical basis of the topics.

ANXIETY

There is no doubt that *anxiety* affects L2 performance—most of us will have had the experience that in an anxiety-provoking climate our L2 knowledge often deteriorates: We forget things that we otherwise know and also make silly mistakes. Indeed, most scholars would agree with Arnold and Brown's (1999, p. 8) conclusion that "Anxiety is quite possibly the affective factor that most pervasively obstructs the learning process." For this reason anxiety has been in the limelight of L2 research for decades (for reviews, see MacIntyre, 1999; Oxford, 1999a; Young, 1999) and there are several published research instruments available in the field which have been used extensively in research studies (e.g., Ely, 1986; Gardner, 1985; Horwitz, Horwitz, & Cope, 1986; MacIntyre & Gardner, 1991, 1994; Young, 1999).

Given the importance and the high profile of anxiety, it is surprising how ambiguous the conceptualization of the concept becomes when we go beyond the surface. As mentioned above, there is an overall uncertainty about the basic category: Is it a motivational component? A personality trait? Or an emotion? Furthermore, anxiety is usually not seen as a unitary factor but a complex made up of constituents that have different characteristics. Two important anxiety distinctions are usually mentioned:

- *Beneficial/facilitating* vs. *inhibitory/debilitating anxiety*: It has been observed that anxiety does not necessarily inhibit performance but in some cases can actually promote it. 'Worry,' which is considered the cognitive component of anxiety has been shown to have a negative impact on performance, whereas the affective component, emotionality, does not necessarily have detrimental effects.

- *Trait* vs. *state anxiety:* Trait anxiety refers to a stable predisposition to become anxious in a cross-section of situations; state anxiety is the transient, moment-to-moment experience of anxiety as an emotional reaction to the current situation.

Thus, anxiety is a complex construct with several different facets. However, as Scovel (2001) describes, in contrast to this multifaceted view, nonspecialists tend to equate anxiety simply with fear or phobia, and in language teaching methodological texts the variable is considered to be an arch enemy that needs to be eliminated at all cost. This perception, according to Scovel and many other researchers, is simply erroneous and confirms Scovel's belief that anxiety is the most misunderstood affective variable of all. As he argues, in sports psychology anxiety is not necessarily seen to inhibit performance; according to the 'Yerkes-Dodson law,' psychological arousal of this sort initially increases behavioral performance up to a certain point, after which there is a rapid decline. Furthermore, the degree of state anxiety interferes with the level of trait anxiety in a person, and Scovel cites a research study by Sonstroem and Bernardo, who found that during a basketball season the highest level of performance was achieved by high-trait anxiety players in moderate anxiety situations. Indeed, MacIntyre (2002) concluded that because to increase effort is a frequent response to anxiety, especially at milder levels, the overall consequence of being anxious may indeed be positive. Of course, we should note that personality type might also be a modifying variable in this respect because, as discussed in chapter 3, introverts and extraverts for example have different optimal arousal levels.

Discussing the impact of trait anxiety on academic performance in general, Chamorro-Premuzic and Furnham (2003a) assert that most of the studies in the literature that examined that relationship between primary personality traits and academic performance focused on the anxiety trait. It appears that even the harmful, 'worry' component of anxiety does not always result in general performance impairment but hinders only certain tasks, for example those that require intensive working memory involvement. Because L2 use depends on the effectiveness of the employment of attentional resources and of the working memory in particular (see chapt. 3), Dewaele (2002) concluded that high anxiety, especially when linked with high introversion, can lead to breakdowns in automatic processing and therefore can seriously hinder L2 fluency.

Language Anxiety

In a seminal paper in 1986, Horwitz et al. conceptualized a situation-specific anxiety construct that they called *foreign language anxiety,* stemming from the inherent linguistic deficit of L2 learners. In order to make this construct researchable, the authors also presented a 33-item, 5-point Likert-scale type instrument, the Foreign Language Classroom Anxiety Scale (FLCAS). As Horwitz (2001) summarized, language anxiety turned out to be a relatively independent factor, displaying only low correlations with general trait-anxiety. This indicates that this factor is not merely a transfer of anxiety from another domain such as test anxiety or communication apprehension but is a uniquely L2-related variable; as MacIntyre (1999) defines it, language anxiety involves the "worry and negative emotional reaction aroused when learning or using a second language" (p. 27). Horwitz provided a review of an impressive amount of literature that consistently evidenced the negative impact of language anxiety on language criterion measures. She acknowledged, however, that one particular line of research, by Sparks, Ganschow, and their colleagues on the 'Linguistic Coding Difference Hypothesis' (discussed in chapt. 3), regarded language anxiety merely as a consequence of the students' cognitive deficits, suggesting therefore that anxiety was not a core construct worthy of research but a mere byproduct. This view has been strongly contested by MacIntyre (1995a, 1995b, 1999) and Horwitz (2000).

MacIntyre and his colleagues' research (e.g., MacIntyre, 1999, 2001, 2002; MacIntyre & Gardner, 1991a, 1991b, 1994) offered further evidence that language anxiety is distinct from more general types of anxiety and that performance in the second language is negatively correlated with language anxiety but not with more general types of anxiety. MacIntyre (1999) therefore attributed the often conflicting or inconsistent findings of past research concerning the relationship between language anxiety and L2 achievement to the inconsistent conception of the type of anxiety measure employed.

In an important experimental study investigating the causal relationship between anxiety and academic performance, MacIntyre and Gardner (1994) intentionally aroused anxiety in language learners by introducing a video camera at various points in a vocabulary learning task. Seventy-one students of French were randomly assigned to one of four groups, the first three experiencing the 'camera condition' at different phases of task completion (input, processing, and output stages), while the fourth control group was not exposed to the camera. Significant increases in state anxiety were reported in all three groups when the video camera was introduced, and concomitant deficits in vocabulary acquisition were observed. This demonstrated conclusively that anxiety arousal can play a causal role and lead to performance deficit, which implies that language anxiety is not merely a function of poor performance due to insufficient cognitive skills and abilities.

It is clear from the reviews of relevant empirical studies on SLA (e.g., Horwitz, 2001; MacIntyre, 1999; MacIntyre & Gardner, 1993; MacIntyre, Noels, & Clément, 1997; Oxford, 1999a) that when anxiety is conceptualized as a situated L2-specific construct, it has a consistently negative bearing on L2 performance. As Gardner and MacIntyre (1993) concluded, "The results of these studies of language anxiety suggest that anxious students will have lower levels of verbal production ... and will be reluctant to express personally relevant information in a second-language conversation" (p. 6). However, the actual amount of impact the variable exerts also depends on the interplay between anxiety and other factors. Gregersen and Horwitz (2002), for example, established a link between language anxiety and perfectionism, and in a study already mentioned briefly, Dewaele (2002) discussed the combined effects of anxiety and introversion. Gardner and MacIntyre (1993) also argued that the effect of anxiety varies according to the social milieu, with multicultural settings possibly enhancing the correlates of language anxiety and generating a complex construct that combines language anxiety, self-perceptions of L2 proficiency, and attitudinal/motivational components. Clément's (1980) construct of self-confidence is in accordance with this conception.

In summary, the ID variable 'language anxiety' is undoubtedly an important learner characteristic with regard to L2 acquisition and use, consistently producing a significant impact on L2 criterion variables. We find, however, considerable variation in the literature in the way the anxiety factor has been integrated into research paradigms: It is sometimes used as a separate independent variable and some other times as a constituent of a larger construct. This, as we have seen, reflects a similar ambiguity found in the psychological literature concerning the exact position of the construct in the overall picture of ID variables. In any case, the measurement of language anxiety in one way or another is likely to remain an indispensable background variable component of L2 studies focusing on language performance.

Further research is needed to address several unresolved issues related to language anxiety. For example, Rodrígues and Abreu (2003) found language anxiety to be stable across different target languages, whereas Saito, Horwitz, and Garza (1999) reported a certain amount of variation in L2 reading anxiety depending on the L2 the students studied. Also, Oxford (1999) reminded us that we still have no clear theoretical understanding of the circumstances in which certain levels of language anxiety can be helpful and facilitating. One particularly promising research direction has been offered by Spielmann and Radnofsky (2001), who examined learner anxiety from an ethnographic perspective. Their data revealed that learners reported to experience a separate personality—or 'mask'—in the target language, and this inevitably created tension in them. However, this tension was found to cause either beneficial or inhibitory reactions in students, depending on how the students processed the personality-altering nature of the language learning experience in a given situation. The researchers, therefore, defined 'tension' as the "result of interaction between individual expectations and the perceived reality of a situation" (p. 273).

Because the vast majority of theoretical findings converge with language teachers' and learners' experience that language anxiety influences language behaviors negatively (and even in Spielmann & Radnofsky's, 2001, study tension was most frequently expressed as frustration), a great deal of effort has been made in the literature to develop methods to reduce anxiety. A relaxed, anxiety-free environment is for example a basic requirement for the teaching method 'suggestopedia' (Larsen-Freeman, 2000) and humanistic, student-centered methodologies in general also promote the elimination of learner anxiety and stress. An edited volume by Young (1999) contains several studies discussing the 'how to' aspects of this issue in accordance with the anthology's subtitle: *A Practical Guide to Creating a Low-Anxiety Classroom Atmosphere.* Although this is certainly an important goal, Spielmann and Radnofsky also emphasize the related need to foster a capacity in the learners to process tension in a facilitating manner.

CREATIVITY

Creativity is one of those grand psychological constructs that both professionals and laypeople seem to understand but no one can unambiguously define. The reason for this might be that, as mentioned earlier, creativity appears to overlap traditional ID categories. It is certainly a major constituent of intelligence (e.g., Eysenck, 1994)—in Sternberg's theory of successful intelligence it is one of the three basic aspects (for an L2-specific overview, see Sternberg, 2002). However, creativity also extends beyond the intellectual domain: "Sources of individual and developmental differences in creative performance include not only process aspects, but aspects of knowledge, thinking styles, personality, motivation, and the environmental context in which the individual operates" (Sternberg, 2002, p. 29). Indeed, recent personality theories usually include a prominent creativity component.

So what exactly is creativity? As Runco (2004) summarized in a recent review of the psychological literature, the scientific study of creativity was initiated by Guilford's 1950 presidential address to the American Psychological Association entitled 'Creativity.' The importance of the construct was soon embraced by many as it appeared to tap into a basic issue emerging in the zeitgeist of the time. Carl Rogers (1954) justified the significance of the concept as follows:

> In a time when knowledge, constructive and destructive, is advancing by the most incredible leaps and bounds into a fantastic atomic age, genuinely creative adaptation seems to represent the only possibility that man can keep abreast of the kaleidoscopic change in this world. ... Unless individuals, groups, and nations can imagine, construct, and creatively revise new ways of relating to these complex changes, the lights will go out. (p. 250)

Ever since those early days creativity has remained an important although somewhat underresearched subject in psychology, examined from diverse perspectives; in his comprehensive summary Runco (2004) reviewed relevant behavioral, biological, clinical, cognitive, developmental, economic, educational, historiometric, organizational, psychometric, and social research. In fact, Sternberg, Kaufman, and Pretz (2002) argued that part of the problem with the term had been that it did not fit into any single, traditional area of psychology—if a topic crosses so many subareas, each is likely to see it fitting into some other.

Interestingly, Runco's (2004) otherwise thorough overview of creativity research offers no explicit definition of the term, and this is not an exception but more like the rule in a considerable proportion of the creativity literature (according to a survey by Plucker, Beghetto, & Dow, 2004, only 34% of recent journal articles provide an explicit definition of creativity). It is somehow taken for granted that we know what human creativity is and if there is any systematic attempt to draw up the boundaries of the concept, it is usually restricted to defining the 'creative person,' 'creative thinking,' or the 'creative process/behavior/production/performance' rather than the actual construct. More generally, creativity is often associated with 'originality,' 'invention,' and 'discovery,' as well as divergent thinking about open-ended problems and flexible problem-solving in general.

A useful strategy to produce a definition of a concept that is hard to define is to turn to a dictionary. The *Longman Dictionary of Contemporary English* defines creativity as "the ability to produce new and original ideas and things; imagination and inventiveness." For a short definition this is probably as good as it gets: The first part of the definition is related to the verb 'create,' that is, to bring something new into existence, and the second to the concept of the 'creative mind' which is rich in ideas and is characterized by artistic or intellectual resourcefulness. A particularly detailed definition that encompasses these aspects has been offered by Feldhausen and Westby (2003):

> Creativity is the production of ideas, problem solutions, plans, works of art, musical compositions, sculptures, dance routines, poems, novels, essays, designs, theories, or devices that at the lowest level are new and of value to the creator and at the highest level are recognized, embraced, honored, or valued by all or large segments of society. Between the lowest and highest levels is a continuum of more or less recognized and useful creative productions, but always the production is new, novel, or unique relative to some definable context. (p. 95)

In a recent overview of creativity from an educational perspective, Plucker et al. (2004) emphasize that the construct of creativity has a great deal to offer to educational psychology, and yet the study of creativity, the authors conclude, is not nearly as robust as one would expect. This observation prompted the title of their summary: "Why isn't creativity more important to educational psychologists?" One reason, they argue, is that creativity is often seen as a 'fuzzy' or 'soft' construct:

> In courses and at professional conferences, we are always astonished at the degree to which people see the stereotypical creative person, if not as a dangerous loner, as a barefooted hippie running around a commune while rubbing crystals on his forehead. This stereotype leads many psychologists to think of creativity as "soft psychology," even though many of them study related constructs. (p. 86)

Plucker et al. (2004) point out that although this view is a false myth and research on creative cognition is strong and well-defined, the lack of a standard definition considerably weakens the reputation of the construct. As they explain, regardless of the surface appeal of higher-order cognitive constructs such as creativity, their utility is entirely dependent on the clarity and fidelity of their definitions and assessment procedures. Ironically, the authors observe, it is partly the great fascination the notion of creativity generates that has often obfuscated the path to a parsimonious, explicit, and empirically testable definition: Many researchers who have approached the study and practice of creativity with a great deal of fervor have unfortunately "followed the sequence of fire, aim, ready" (p. 87).

Several tests have been developed to operationalize creativity in specific measurable terms. These typically provide scores that assess both quantitative and qualitative aspects of performance. For example, as Sternberg et al. (2002) described, Torrance's famous creativity test, the Torrance Tests of Creative Thinking, can be scored for *originality* of the responses (how unique and unusual they are), *flexibility* (how varied they are), and *fluency* (how many unusual responses there are). Runco (2003) emphasized that none of the three indices are all-important in themselves but should be used in concert to describe the individual's ideational profile: "Some examinees are very fluent with ideas but relatively unoriginal or inflexible. Others are high in originality, flexibility, or both, but only moderately fluent" (p. 34). A version of the Torrance test, adapted for measuring creativity in L2 contexts by Ottó (1998), is described in more detail next, and the application of the same scoring dimensions within a standardized Hungarian creativity test, administered to L2 learners by Albert and Kormos (2004), is also presented.

Creativity in SLA

Is creativity a relevant concept from the point of view of educational research? There is a growing body of literature in educational psychology which provides evidence that it is (see e.g., the anthology edited by Houtz, 2003, or a recent special issue of the *Scandinavian Journal of Education Research*, 2003, Vol. 47/3). In the UK, for example, the Department for Education and Employment set up a special committee in 1998, the *National Advisory Committee on Creative and Cultural Education,* and in 2000 this committee produced a detailed report on "Creativity, Culture and Education" (NACCCE, 2000). This report stated that "Britain's economic prosperity and social cohesion" depended on developing a "national strategy for creative and cultural education " (p. 5). Although most of this educational interest looks at creativity as the dependent variable (i.e., examining how it can be promoted or trained rather than what its consequences are), there is some evidence that creativity is a positive correlate of academic performance (Chamorro-Premuzic & Furnham, 2003b).

How relevant is creativity to the attainment of a second language? Runco (2004) reported on studies that have found significant differences between classrooms within schools in terms of the level of creative thinking characterizing the students, highlighting the link between the immediate classroom environment and the emerging divergent thinking. The findings also indicate that student creativity is inhibited by certain common classroom conditions and tasks (e.g., test-like activities), whereas activities that are presented in a "permissive and gamelike fashion" (p. 671) appear to release creativity. This is an important result for L2 researchers because many of the language tasks favored by contemporary language teaching methodologies tend to be of the latter type, involving student-centered, interaction-based, and open-ended elements, and are therefore ideally suited to accommodate creative learner thinking and behavior.

The fact that typical communicative L2 learning activities can accommodate, and often even require, some creative thinking on the students' part also implies, however, that individual differences in learner creativity may considerably affect learner contribution to these tasks, a view that has also been supported by theoretical considerations. Sternberg (2002) argued that a good index of the creative intelligence component of his 'successful intelligence' construct was how well individuals could cope with relative novelty. Because an inherent feature of learning a new language is coping with relative novelty both in terms of the language code and the sociocultural and pragmatic conventions governing intercultural communication, Sternberg believed that creative intelligence was an important determiner of SLA. Although the assumption that creativity and language learning achievement are related is reasonable, so far only two L2 studies have been conducted to test this hypothesis, by Ottó (1998) and Albert and Kormos (2004). Both found a significant positive relationship between creativity and L2 learner performance. Let us look at these two pioneering studies in more detail.

In line with the above arguments, the starting point of Ottó's (1998) study was the observation that communicative language teaching emphasizes functional and situational language use and involves communicative tasks such as role play activities and simulations. Such tasks, the author argued, often require students to use their imagination, that is, to retrieve or construct their own ideas, and therefore it is reasonable to suggest that the outcomes may depend to a great extent on the students' creative abilities. To measure the learners' creativity, Ottó adapted five subtasks from the Torrance Tests of Creative Thinking:

(a) *Consequences*—presenting students with improbable situations and asking them to provide as many consequences as they could think of.

(b) *Unusual Uses*—asking students to list possible unusual uses for common objects such as a book or a pencil.

(c) *Common Problems*—asking students to list a number of problems that might occur in one of the following two everyday situations: Going to school in the morning or making a sandwich.

(d) *Categories*—asking students to list as many things as they could think of that belonged to a given category such as 'things that are red or more often red than not.'

(e) *Associations*—presenting participants with two words, for example, 'mirror' and 'rain,' and asking them to supply a third one that could be semantically associated with these.

Students were encouraged to provide as many responses as they could think of for each task in their L1. The scores of the five subtests were correlated separately and also as a composite with the students' English grades. All the correlations were significant, with the correlation with the total test score being the highest ($r=.63$), explaining roughly 40% of the variance in the students' grades.

Albert and Kormos's (2004) study followed a task-based approach. Their participants carried out an oral narrative task and then filled in s standardized creativity test developed for use in Hungary, examining how the three standard aspects of creativity—*originality, flexibility,* and *fluency*—influenced a variety of measures of task performance. Thus, the Albert and Kormos study differed from Ottó's in the criterion measures: Ottó used a holistic outcome measure, course grades, whereas Albert and Kormos looked at the impact of creativity on actual task-specific learner behaviors.

The findings of Albert and Kormos (2004) showed that two components of creativity, *originality* and *creative fluency*, were associated with some measures of task performance, but no significant correlations were found between task-related variables and *flexibility* or the *total creativity score*. Although even the significant correlations were moderate at best (with the highest being 0.39), explaining approximately 10%-16% of the variance in linguistic measures, and of the several correlations computed only six reached statistical significance, Albert and Kormos emphasized that except for complexity and accuracy, all the characteristics of task performance investigated in their study were influenced by certain components of creativity. Thus, on the basis of the results the authors argued that the ability to produce original, novel ideas in general does moderately affect how students perform in a particular language learning task.

In summary, creativity is certainly an ID variable to be aware of in future L2 studies for at least three reasons: First, its theoretical significance is indisputable although its exact categorization has shown considerable (and rather confusing) variation. Second, we can construct a strong argument to explain why the emergence and spread of communicative, student-centered methodologies have increased the relevance of creativity in instructed SLA. Third, the limited empirical L2 data that is available on the impact of creativity on language learning provides evidence that creativity does play a role in shaping L2 outcomes. What we need now is more research and theoretical clarification on which aspects of creativity affect which aspects of language learning and use, and how creativity interacts with other ID variables.

WILLINGNESS TO COMMUNICATE

Broadly speaking, the purpose of communicative language teaching approaches is to promote the learners' communicative competence in the target language. However, it is not uncommon to find people who tend to avoid entering L2 communication situations even if they possess a high level of communicative competence. This implies that there is a further layer of mediating factors between having the competence to communicate and putting this competence into practice. Because this substrate is the immediate antecedent of the actual initiation of L2 communication, it must be highly situated in nature and it is likely to be made up of a combination of a number of psychological, linguistic, and contextual variables.

The main push for pursuing the above speculation further in the L2 field was the realization in the early 1990s that L1 communication studies had developed a construct called *Willingness to Communicate* (WTC; e.g., McCroskey & Baer, 1985; McCroskey & Richmond, 1987, 1991), and this appeared to capture a great deal of the phenomenon just described. The principal proponent of the adaptation of this L1 construct for L2 studies has been Peter MacIntyre, but as MacIntyre, Baker, Clément, and Donovan (2003) pointed out, the need to conceptualize an ID variable that would explain the 'willingness' to talk, in contrast to the necessary aptitude, was actually expressed as early as 1989 by Skehan, when he wrote, "dealing with the willingness different learners have to talk in order to learn, ... a non-cognitive ID, may be altogether more elusive for researchers" (p. 48).

MacIntyre and his associates started out by examining WTC in first language use (MacIntyre, 1994; MacIntyre, Babin, & Clément, 1999) and then focused on the analysis of L2 WTC (Baker & MacIntyre, 2000; Clément, Baker, & MacIntyre, 2003; MacIntyre & Charos, 1996; MacIntyre, Baker, Clément, & Conrod, 2001; MacIntyre, Baker, Clément, & Donovan, 2002, 2003; MacIntyre, Clément, Dörnyei, & Noels, 1998; see also Wen & Clément, 2003). The challenge of further exploring WTC in an L2 was also taken up by Yashima and her colleagues in Japan (Yashima, 1998, 2002; Yashima et al., 2004), and WTC has also been used as an independent background variable by Dörnyei (2002), Dörnyei and Kormos (2000), and Kormos and Dörnyei (2004). All the studies mentioned so far have followed a primarily quantitative approach and therefore a recent study by Kang (in press) has been a welcome addition to the literature as it employed a qualitative methodology, offering fresh insights into the nature of WTC. Let us now examine the construct more closely.

As MacIntyre et al. (2002) explain, individuals display consistent tendencies in their predisposition toward or away from communicating, given the choice. In one's first language, WTC is a fairly stable personality trait, developed over the years and resulting in a "global, personality-based orientation toward talking" (MacIntyre et al., 2003, p. 591). However, the situation is more complex with regard to L2 use, because here the level of one's L2 proficiency, and particularly that of the individual's L2 communicative competence, is an additional powerful modifying variable. Thus, MacIntyre et al. (1998) argued that L2 WTC needs to be conceptualized as a situated construct that includes both state and trait characteristics, and have defined the concept as the individual's "readiness to enter into discourse at a particular time with a specific person or persons, using a L2" (p. 547). Accordingly, we proposed a multilayered 'pyramid' model, subsuming a range of linguistic and psychological variables, including linguistic self-confidence (both state and trait); the desire to affiliate with a person; interpersonal motivation; intergroup attitudes, motivation, and climate; parameters of the social situation; communicative competence and experience; and various personality traits (see Fig. 7.1).

Although the pyramid model in Figure 7.1 offers a clear representation of the multiple layers and variables feeding into the behavioral intention of WTC, it fails to describe the interrelationship and the weighting of the various components. MacIntyre and his colleagues have conducted several studies attempting to empirically validate some parts of the complex construct, and this research effort has shown that two of the strongest predictors of WTC are *communication anxiety* and *perceived communication competence* (cf. Clément et al., 2003). Thus, WTC is closely related to the concept of language anxiety reviewed at the beginning of this chapter.

MacIntyre et al. (2001) added a further important dimension to WTC by linking the concept to Ajzen's (1988) 'theory of planned behavior:' This theory suggests that in situations where people do not have complete control over their behavior, their behavioral intention—such as WTC—alone is insufficient to explain action and therefore we need to also consider a modifying component, *perceived behavioral control,* which concerns the perceived ease or difficulty of performing the behavior (e.g., perceptions of the presence of required resources or potential impediments and obstacles). Behavioral performance can then be predicted from the combination of people's intentions to perform the behavior in question and their perceptions of control over the behavior. Thus, MacIntyre et al. argue that beliefs concerning opportunities, such as the opportunity for L2 communication, influence

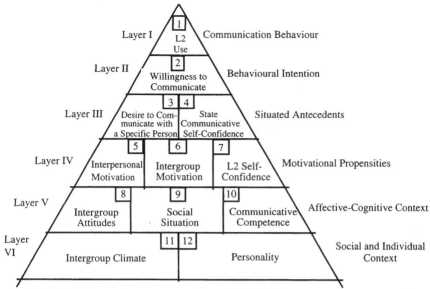

FIG. 7.1. Schematic representation of the WTC construct as proposed by MacIntyre et al. (1998).

perceived control over behavior and, consequently, behavioral outcomes. In this sense, 'learner beliefs,' which will be discussed in a separate section later, are inherently linked to WTC.

The emphasis on available opportunities also highlights the importance of the traditional distinction between foreign language learning (FLL) and second language acquisition, with the former referring to school learning with no or only limited contact with L2 speakers, and the latter to language attainment at least partly embedded in the host environment. In an attempt to tap into this distinction, Baker and MacIntyre (2000) examined immersion vs. non-immersion students, as the contrast in their learning situations offers a close approximation of the FLL–SLA environmental difference. The results did indeed reveal considerable situational variation: Immersion students displayed higher WTC and more frequent actual communication in the L2 than did their non-immersion counterparts.

Yashima and her colleagues' empirical research in Japan (Yashima, 1998, 2002; Yashima et al., 2004) confirmed that the WTC construct is also applicable to a markedly different social context. In Yashima's (1998) sample, perceived communicative competence was the most significant constituent of WTC, explaining over 30% of the variance in the WTC scores. Using structural equation modeling, Yashima (2002) replicated this finding in a larger sample, and here the latent variable L2 Communication Confidence, which was determined by Perceived Communication Competence and to a lesser degree Communication Anxiety, explained 46% of the variance of L2 WTC. Interestingly, there was one more variable that directly influenced WTC, International Posture (discussed in detail in chapt. 4), which is in line with the proposed pyramid model in Figure 7.1. Given that, as I argued in chapter 4, international posture is related to the learners' Ideal L2 Self, we may hypothesize that L2 WTC is the resultant of the interplay of linguistic self-confidence and the Ideal L2 Self. It is noteworthy that Yashima et al. (2004) also suggested that the self perspective described in Dörnyei (2003b; and in more detail in chapt. 4) offered a plausible theoretical framework to interpret their results.

Finally, Kang's (in press) recent study deserves special attention because the qualitative methodology employed allowed her to explore situational variables affecting WTC in detail. As described above, a unique feature of L2 WTC, in contrast to WTC in L1, is its situated nature, and therefore the study of variables related to the social and psychological context of communication is particularly relevant here. Investigating four male Korean students at an American university for a period of eight months, Kang found that the degree of their L2 WTC was determined by the interaction of the psychological conditions of *excitement*, *responsibility*, and *security*, as well as situational variables such as the *topic*, the *interlocutors*, and the *conversational context* of the communication.

In summary, WTC is a composite ID variable that draws together a host of learner variables that have been well established as influences on second language acquisition and use, resulting in a construct in which psychological and linguistic factors are integrated in an organic manner. Additional importance is lent to the concept by the fact that it can be seen as the ultimate goal of L2 instruction—thus, WTC is a means and an end at the same time. Although the construct has already been subject to considerable empirical research, there are still several open questions. For example, an important issue that MacIntyre et al. (2001) raised is how WTC correlates across various modalities of communication (speaking, listening, reading, or writing). A further question to be explored is whether WTC ends at the initiation of communication (MacIntyre et al., 1999) or whether, as Kang (in press) argues, it exerts its influence at the initiation of each conversational turn in an ongoing manner. This issue bears a close resemblance to the point made with regard to L2 motivation, namely that if the construct has been conceptualized in a situated manner, the effects of time and temporal fluctuation cannot be overlooked (cf. chapt. 4). Finally, MacIntyre et al. (2003) linked WTC to both L2 acquisition and use, which is not surprising with a learning process such as SLA that relies heavily on learning through participatory experience in communication. Yet, just like with language learning strategies (cf. chapt. 6), it can lead to conceptual confusion to mix up language acquisition and language use processes because they may be related to different types of antecedents and attributes. Only future research can tell whether this and the other concerns are valid issues.

SELF-ESTEEM

Although as Brown (2000, p. 145) stated, "Self esteem is probably the most pervasive aspect of any human behavior," and in educational psychology the concept is well established, this importance is not reflected in the amount of L2 research that has specifically targeted the variable. This is partly due to the fact that self-esteem is closely related to the notion of self-confidence, which has a vigorous research tradition in applied linguistics (cf. chapt. 4) and which, therefore, may have diverted scholars from the study of self-esteem. Indeed, both self-esteem and self-confidence (and also self-efficacy) share a common emphasis on the individual's beliefs about his or her attributes and abilities as a person, and various measures of self-esteem and self-confidence/efficacy have been found to correlate with each other highly (cf. Valentine, DuBois, & Cooper, 2004).

Like so many of the ID variables, self-esteem has been conceptualized both in a global (trait-like), and in a situational (state-like) manner. As Carver et al. (1994) summarized, self-esteem is the evaluative quality of the self-image or self-concept, and therefore global self-esteem refers to "individuals' overall evaluation or appraisal of themselves, whether they approve or disapprove of themselves, like or dislike themselves" (Higgins, 1996, p. 1073). Of course, as Higgins pointed out, if we differentiate between different types of selves (e.g., actual self, possible self, ought self, ideal self—see chapt. 4) the notion of self-esteem can become rather complex because it may vary depending on which self functions act as the reference point for evaluation. For example, feeling worthless in relation to an ought self guide may not result in a general low self-esteem if, say, a person tends to activate his or her ideal self instead (e.g., someone ignores the criticism about what he has not done and focuses single-mindedly on achieving a personal goal). Thus, the same individual can have high, low, and moderate levels of different kinds of self-esteem at the same time.

In any case, there is no question that the way people think about themselves is a crucial aspect of their general conduct, and this has been given due recognition in Covington's (1992) 'self-worth' theory of motivation. Covington argued that the "search for self-acceptance is the highest human priority" (p. 74) and therefore people are highly motivated to maintain a fundamental sense of personal value and worth, especially in the face of competition, failure, and negative feedback. Hogg and Vaughan (2002) also emphasize the human tendency to see ourselves through 'rose-tinted glasses,' thereby producing a widely favorable self-image. This shows, the authors conclude, that self-esteem is also closely associated with social identity: By identifying with a prestigious group, the group's high status attaches to one's self-concept.

Is self-esteem an ID variable? After all, one could argue that it is merely a reflection of one's performance—if you are an Olympic champion, your self-esteem will be understandably more positive than if you came in second. While this is partly true, we often find that some people hold themselves in a low regard despite their obvious qualities, whereas others seem to have a staggeringly positive impression of themselves, a sort of 'inflated ego.' It appears that these differences are related to an underlying deep-seated, trait-like disposition, and indeed, as Baumeister (1999) asserted, trait self-esteem has been one of the most studied individual differences in personality in the 1990s. The focal issue in this research effort was to examine how people with low self-esteem differed from others with high self-esteem and how this difference was reflected in their behavior and learning. According to Baumeister's summary, high self-esteem is generally associated with greater persistence in the face of failure, whereas people with low self-esteem are more vulnerable to the psychological impact of everyday events (e.g., experience wider mood swings) and are also more malleable and therefore more strongly affected by persuasion and influence. Although they want success and approval, they are often skeptical about their chances of achieving it.

Self-esteem has traditionally been seen as having important educational implications although empirical research has typically produced only moderate correlations at best between self-beliefs (broadly defined) and student achievement (Valentine et al., 2004). Along with many others, Raffini (1996) argued that students with high self-esteem are more likely to succeed in learning because they have a clearer sense of direction regarding their priorities and goals. Another argument is that students with positive views of themselves may strive to 'live up to' their self-image and thus be more likely to achieve highly in school on this basis, for example by applying various self-regulatory mechanisms (cf. chapt. 4). Positive self-esteem has also been conceptualized as a resource for coping with failure (Baumeister, 1999), and there is a further obvious link between self-esteem and 'possible/ideal selves' (discussed in chapt. 4), which constitute the 'doing' aspects of the self.

Although the exact mechanisms whereby self-esteem promotes learning have been subject to discussion, it is broadly accepted by scholars that consciously designed intervention can raise people's self-esteem, and self-esteem is also modifiable by means of the individual's self-regulation. No wonder therefore that a whole industry has developed, especially in the U.S., to find ways of promoting children's (and also adults' to a smaller extent) self-esteem, with numerous books written about practical strategies of achieving this. A quick search on the internet-based bookstore Amazon, for example, has yielded over 1,000 titles focusing explicitly on self-esteem, most of which fall into the *100-Ways-to-Build-Your-Self-Esteem* category.

How is self-esteem related to actual performance? As Covin, Donovan, and MacIntyre (2003) summarized, we can find both positive, negative, and null correlations in the literature, indicating that the issue is highly complex and is not associated with any straightforward and obvious trends. In their study, for example, they examined the self-esteem–performance relationship when students had received information about their peers' success or failure. Covin et al. found that self-esteem correlated positively with achievement in the failure information group and negatively in the success information group. This demonstrates that beliefs about the self can have complex relationships with behavior, and therefore self-esteem may be too general a measure to have a direct linear link with achievement. This conclusion coincides with the summary of a recent meta-analytic review of past research by Valentine et al. (2004, p. 128), in which the authors concluded, "constructs such as general self-concept and global self-esteem simply may be too broad and multifaceted to be of significant predictive utility with respect to adaptive outcomes occurring in a relatively specific realm of functioning such as school." More specific related measures with demonstrated motivational impact are *self-worth* and *self-efficacy*, the former already mentioned, the latter referring to one's beliefs in one's capabilities to carry out certain specific tasks (for a recent summary on how academic self-concept and self-efficacy are related, see Bong & Skaalvik, 2003).

Several measures have been developed to assess the degree of one's self-esteem. According to Farnham, Greenwald, and Banaji's (1999) summary, standard self-report measures of self-esteem ask respondents either to rate themselves on a variety of specific tasks or to indicate how they feel about themselves globally. The authors warned, however, that such instruments carry the danger of eliciting a positive self-enhancing bias, and therefore they recommended the use of more indirect measures of self-esteem. An example of such an approach is the procedure whereby individuals perform a task that they can complete more efficiently if they have high implicit self-esteem. For example, the Implicit Association Test that Farnham et al. described presents subjects with a series of words on a computer screen and asks them to categorize each word as quickly as possible—by pressing a left or a right key on the keyboard—into one of the categories displayed to the left and right of the word. A measure of self-esteem using this technique examines the extent to which people are faster at categorizing self words and pleasant words together than self words and unpleasant words together.

In conclusion, it is difficult to decide whether including self-esteem in research paradigms is advisable. My personal feeling is that other self-evaluative concepts that have more direct theoretical links with learning behavior might be more useful; therefore in my own research I have used 'self-confidence' and 'possible selves' as frameworks to capture self-based ID variation. On the other hand, from a pedagogical point of view, the emphasis on student self-esteem is certainly welcome because it provides a systematic framework for justifying and promoting student-centered, humanistic teaching practices (see, e.g., Canfield & Wells, 1994).

LEARNER BELIEFS

The final variable discussed in this chapter, *learner beliefs*, presents us with a real dilemma in that it does not seem to be a proper ID variable because it is difficult to conceive beliefs as an enduring, trait-like factor. There is no doubt that learner beliefs greatly affect behavior, for example when someone believes in a particular method of learning and therefore resists another, perhaps better, approach, but we can easily argue that this is simply an example of false cognition that can be changed by rational explanation. The main difference, in fact, between the conception of attitudes and beliefs is exactly that the latter have a stronger factual support whereas the former are more deeply embedded in our minds and can be rooted back in our past or in the influence of the modeling example of some significant person around us.

The other side of the coin, however, is that ever since their introduction into the L2 literature by Elaine Horwitz (1985, 1987, 1988), language learner beliefs have been recognized as learner characteristics to count with when explaining learning outcomes. Horwitz also presented empirical data obtained from American learners of German, French, and Spanish that confirmed that certain belief systems are quite common among learners and are consistent across different language groups. That is, there is a certain amount of stability about beliefs that would justify their classification as ID variables.

Learner beliefs have traditionally been measured by Horwitz's (1988) questionnaire, the Beliefs About Language Learning Inventory (BALLI), which consists of 34 self-report items and which assesses student beliefs in five major areas: (a) difficulty of language learning, (b) foreign language aptitude, (c) the nature of language learning, (d) learning and communication strategies, and (e) motivation and expectations. Although these areas are salient facets of student self-analysis and therefore any beliefs held with respect to them will obviously be consequential, we can easily add further important areas to this list (e.g., beliefs about the self), indicating that the taxonomy is an open one. This was confirmed by Horwitz (1999) when she stated that "the beliefs I reported were merely example of the kinds of beliefs that teachers might encounter in their own classrooms" (p. 558). In this sense, the term *belief* could in fact be replaced with the less scientific-sounding word *view*, which again questions the psychological validity of the concept as an ID facet.

As just mentioned, if we could identify consistent belief patterns in cross-cultural studies, it would constitute a strong argument in favor of keeping the notion of beliefs. Horwitz (1999) provides a comprehensive review of the cross-cultural belief literature but although she does highlight several salient intergroup differences, her conclusion is not positive:

> Unfortunately, this data did not point to any unambiguous differences in the groups examined. For that reason, in spite of a number of intriguing group differences, it seems premature to conclude that beliefs about language learning vary by cultural group. Rather, the results point to the possibility that within-group differences, whether related to individual characteristics or differences in instructional practices, likely account for as much variation as the cultural differences. (p. 575)

The year 1999 was a special one for research into learner beliefs because of the publication of a number of important studies. Horwitz's (1999) study just cited appeared as part of a special issue of the journal *System* (Vol. 27/4) on "Metacognitive Knowledge and Beliefs," edited by Anita Wenden. In the introduction of this thematic issue, Wenden (1999) established an important link between metacognitive knowledge and learner beliefs. She argued that *metacognitive knowledge* was the specialized portion of a learner's acquired knowledge base, consisting of what learners know about learning. The term *learner beliefs*, Wenden concluded, appears to be interchangeable with the term metacognitive knowledge, although beliefs are distinct in that they are value-related and are held more tenaciously. This latter claim clearly relates beliefs to attitudes. Wenden (2001) further elaborated on the importance of metacognitive knowledge in L2 learning, also linking it to the ability to self-regulate one's learning.

Wenden's (1999) attempt to broaden the theoretical basis of learner beliefs was an important move and one that future researchers of the topic will need to follow up. Unfortunately and surprisingly, while Wenden highlighted the relevance of metacognitive knowledge, she did not draw attention to a much more obvious link in educational psychology, the study of *'epistemological beliefs'* (i.e., beliefs about the nature of knowledge and learning), even though there was a growing body of literature on this topic in the 1990s (for recent reviews, see Chan & Elliott, 2002; Schommer-Aikins & Hutter, 2002). The 1999 special issue of *System* also contained a number of empirical studies by Cotterall (1999), Sakui and Gaies (1999), White (1999), and Yang (1999). These offer interesting insights into several aspects of L2 learner beliefs, ranging from their link to learning strategies to the cultural dimension of belief systems, but they do not address the theoretical basis of the concept. The only other theoretical analysis in the volume was provided by Benson and Lor (1999), who connected beliefs to the 'Student Approaches to Learning' paradigm, famous for the distinction between the 'deep learning' and 'surface learning' approaches (see, e.g., Ramsden, 1988).

Although the educational psychological research on epistemological beliefs was not analyzed in the 1999 special issue of *System*, an article by Mori (1999) from the same year explicitly addressed this link. The objective to integrate the two research traditions was reflected in Mori's research design because the questionnaire that the participants were asked to fill in contained a section on non-L2-specific epistemological beliefs and one on language learning beliefs. Separate factor analyses of the two sets of items produced somewhat different belief structures. With regard to beliefs about learning in general, Mori's results were compatible with Schommer's (1990) pioneering findings: He identified five relatively independent belief dimensions about the nature of knowledge and knowledge acquisition: (a) *the structure of knowledge*, (b) *the attainability of knowledge*, (c) *the source of knowledge*, (d) *the controllability of the ability to acquire knowledge*, and (e) *the speed of knowledge acquisition*.

Regarding language learning beliefs, Mori (1999) submitted an extensive number of belief dimensions to factor analysis and found that these could be reduced to three main dimensions, comprising six factors and accounting for three quarters of the variance: (a) *perception of the difficulty of language learning* (Kanji is difficult, Japanese is easy); (b) *the effectiveness of approaches to or strategies for language learning* (Risk taking, Analytic approach, Avoid ambiguity); and (c) *the source of linguistic knowledge* (Reliance on L1). It is apparent that the two taxonomies (i.e., focusing on general vs. L2-specific learner beliefs) are qualitatively different, which Mori explained by the different degree of abstractness of the beliefs in question.

In summary, I believe that past research in the area has produced some evidence that the beliefs language learners hold considerably affect the way they go about mastering the L2. Research findings in educational psychology also point to the fact that epistemological beliefs influence higher order thinking, particularly when learners encounter complex information, and therefore the study of epistemological beliefs provides insightful theoretical explanations of cognitions, such as comprehension and cognitive flexibility (Schommer-Aikins & Hutter, 2002). However, it also appears that the study of learner beliefs has reached a similar stage to that of learning strategies, namely that future developments will require thorough theoretical groundwork. Thus, Horwitz's original concept of language learning beliefs may need to be linked to metacognitive knowledge along the lines set out by

Wenden (1999), and learner belief research in L2 studies may need to be continuously informed by corresponding investigations in educational psychology, following Mori's (1999) example.

With regard to the question as to whether learner beliefs are ID variables proper, we cannot as yet provide a definite answer. Knowledge systems, no matter how important they are, are not necessarily enduring learner traits in themselves. However, if we succeed in identifying a closed system of basic beliefs about L2 attainment that are relevant to language learners across diverse learning contexts, and if we manage to keep the categories separate from related and well-established ID categories such as language attitudes or self-efficacy/confidence beliefs, then learner belief research can undoubtedly enrich our understanding of SLA. Furthermore, it is worth emphasizing that although the concept of language learning beliefs currently carries theoretical ambiguities, it is a highly useful notion for practical purposes. I argued elsewhere (Dörnyei, 2001a) that creating realistic learner beliefs is an important motivational strategy, and periodically administering the BALLI, or a similar instrument, to groups of learners is a valuable means of raising their awareness of the nature of language learning. The important point—similarly to learning strategy research—is to keep practical and theoretical aspects separate, a distinction that recent learning strategy inventories have successfully observed (cf. chapt. 6).

8

Conclusion

Although I have spent the past two decades conducting research on ID variables in SLA, the preparation of this book brought two real surprises. First, although I had been aware that ID research was a fertile area within SLA, it was only after summarizing the relevant work in the L2 field for this book that I fully realized the wealth of past research. Second, this overview made it clear to me that all the variables described in this book are either in the process of, or in desperate need of, theoretical 'restructuring.' I sincerely hope that my overview will contribute to this process.

By considering the existing research on the various ID variables together, I have discovered three intriguing parallels. The most striking aspect of nearly all the recent ID literature is the emerging theme of *context*: It appears that cutting-edge research in all these diverse areas has been addressing the same issue, that is, the situated nature of the ID factors in question. Scholars have come to reject the notion that the various traits are context-independent and absolute, and are now increasingly proposing new dynamic conceptualizations in which ID factors enter into some interaction with the situational parameters rather than cutting across tasks and environments. Ellis (2004) expressed this very clearly when he outlined the necessary features of a future overarching ID theory:

> The theory will need to acknowledge the *situated* nature of L2 learning. That is, it must reflect the fact that the role of individual learner factors is influenced by the specific setting in which learning takes place and the kinds of tasks learners are asked to perform in the L2. (pp. 546–547)

This recognition has important methodological implications as well, because the dynamic and situated nature of ID variables is likely to be investigated more effectively by means of qualitative rather than quantitative methods; we do find, indeed, a marked shift in some areas of ID research (e.g., motivation research) toward complementing traditional questionnaire and test-based research designs with qualitative components.

The second common aspect of much of the best research in the field is the suggestion that instead of trying to detect linear relationships between certain ID factors and corresponding outcome or performance variables in isolation, researchers should work with more complex theoretical paradigms. In these, the various ID factors are seen either to operate in concert or to interfere with each other in a clearly delineated manner. Because scholars have come to the assumption that combinations of traits have more predictive power than traits in isolation, I described in chapter 3 recent research initiatives that attempt to identify various *aptitude complexes*. In my view this integrating effort needs to be extended to the whole domain of ID research. As Alexander and Murphy (1999) concluded in their overview of learner profiles, "Research on individual differences that is multidimensional and acknowledges the influence of motivational factors, as well as cognitive forces, seems more in keeping with the complexity of formal learning" (p. 428). Although the range of ID variables that can affect L2 learning success is wide, the variety of possible optimal combinations may not be unlimited. Thus, the goal of identifying a few archetypal 'good-language-learner' profiles may not be unrealistic.

The third important theme that connects the various bodies of research is the recent attempt in the literature to try and relate ID variables to specific SLA processes. This, of course, has been made possible by the increasingly elaborate mapping of the mental mechanisms underlying SLA during the past decade and it seems that ID researchers have welcomed the opportunity to integrate their field into mainstream SLA research. As I stated in the Introduction, I am convinced that the future of L2 studies in general lies in the integration of linguistic and psychological approaches in a balanced and complementary manner, and it seems that the study of individual differences has taken this forward-pointing route. If this initiative is successful, this will mean that ID-based differences will no longer constitute a mere source of irritation to so many SLA scholars, but rather, their understanding will genuinely help to map the rugged terrain of L2 attainment.

Of course, the overall picture is not entirely rosy. The most important problem in my view is the almost irresistible temptation of applied linguists to adopt somewhat simplistic psychological models. Although from a personal point of view this is understandable, as it is difficult to acquire sufficient expertise in two such different fields as linguistics and psychology, the result, I believe, is extremely harmful. Whole generations of scholars can be misled by such theoretical shortcuts—one example that immediately comes to mind is the equation of language learning motivation with the sum of instrumental and integrative motivation. Thus, my primary intention with this book has been to show the complexity of the various issues, while providing at the same time useful and accessible organizing principles.

References

Ackerman, P. L. (2003). Aptitude complexes and trait complexes. *Educational Psychologist, 38*(2), 85–93.

Aiken, L. R. (1999). *Human differences.* Mahwah, NJ: Lawrence Erlbaum Associates.

Ajzen, I. (1988). *Attitudes, personality and behavior.* Chicago: Dorsey Press.

Albert, À., & Kormos, J. (2004). Creativity and narrative task performance: An exploratory study. *Language Learning, 54*(2), 277–310.

Alexander, P. A., & Murphy, P. K. (1999). Learner profiles: Valuing individual differences within classroom communities. In P. L. Ackerman, P. C. Kyllonen & R. D. Roberts (Eds.), *Learning and individual differences: Process, trait, and content determinants* (pp. 413–431). Washington, DC: American Psychological Association.

Anastasi, A. (1994). Differential psychology. In R. J. Corsini (Ed.), *Encyclopedia of psychology* (2nd ed., Vol. 1, pp. 419–423). New York: John Wiley.

Anderson, J. R. (1983). *The architecture of cognition.* Cambridge, MA: Cambridge University Press.

Anderson, J. R. (1985). *Cognitive psychology and its implications* (2nd ed.). New York: Freeman.

Anderson, N. J. (2003). Strategy research and training. Special issue. *TESL-EJ, 7*(2).

Arnett, J. J. (2002). The psychology of globalization. *American Psychologist, 57*(10), 774-783.

Arnold, J., & Brown, H. D. (1999). A map of the terrain. In J. Arnold (Ed.), *Affect in language learning* (pp. 1–24). Cambridge: Cambridge University Press.

Atkinson, J. W., & Birch, D. (1974). The dynamics of achievement-oriented activity. In J. W. Atkinson & J. O. Raynor (Eds.), *Motivation and achievement* (pp. 271–325). Washington, DC: Winston & Sons.

Bachman, L. F., & Palmer, A. S. (1996). *Language testing in practice.* Oxford: Oxford University Press.

Baddeley, A. D. (2003). Working memory and language: An overview. *Journal of Communication Disorders, 36*, 189–208.

Bailey, P., Onwuegbuzie, A. J., & Daley, C. E. (2000). Using learning style to predict foreign language achievement at the college level. *System, 28*, 115–133.

Baker, S. C., & MacIntyre, P. D. (2000). The role of gender and immersion in communication and second language orientations. *Language Learning, 50,* 311–341.

Bates, E., Dale, P. S., & Thal, D. (1995). Individual differences and their implications for theories of language development. In P. Fletcher & B. MacWhinney (Eds.), *The handbook of child language* (pp. 96–151). Oxford: Blackwell.

Baumeister, R. F. (1999). The nature and structure of the self: An overview. In R. F. Baumeister (Ed.), *The self in social psychology* (pp. 1–20). Philadelphia, PA: Psychology Press.

Bedell, D. A., & Oxford, R. L. (1996). Cross-cultural comparison of language learning strategies in the People's Republic of China and other countries. In R. L. Oxford (Ed.), *Language learning strategies around the world: Cross-cultural perspectives* (pp. 47–60). Honolulu: University of Hawaii Press.

Benson, P., & Lor, W. (1999). Conceptions of language and language learning. *System, 27,* 459–472.

Bialystok, E., & Fröhlich, M. (1978). Variables of classroom achievement in second language learning. *Modern Language Journal, 62,* 327–336.

Birch, A., & Hayward, S. (1994). *Individual differences.* Basingstoke: Macmillan.

Boekaerts, M. (1998). Boosting students' capacity to promote their own learning: A goal theory perspective. *Research Dialogue in Learning and Instruction, 1,* 13–22.

Boekaerts, M., Pintrich, P. R., & Zeidner, M. (2000a). *Handbook on self-regulation.* San Diego: Academic Press.

Boekaerts, M., Pintrich, P. R., & Zeidner, M. (2000b). Self-regulation: An introductory overview. In M. Boekaerts, P. R. Pintrich & M. Zeidner (Eds.), *Handbook of self-regulation* (pp. 1–9). San Diego: Academic Press.

Bong, M., & Skaalvik, E. M. (2003). Academic self-concept and self-efficacy: How different are they really? *Educational Psychology Review, 15*(1), 1–40.

Breen, M. P. (Ed.). (2001). *Learner contributions to language learning: New directions in research.* Harlow, England: Longman.

Breslin, F. D. (1994). Individual differences. In R. J. Corsini (Ed.), *Encyclopedia of psychology* (2nd ed., Vol. 2, pp. 224–226). New York: John Wiley.

Brown, H. D. (1990). M&Ms for language classrooms? Another look at motivation. In J. E. Alatis (Ed.), *Georgetown University round table on language and linguistics* (pp. 383–393). Washington, DC: Georgetown University Press.

Brown, H. D. (1994). *Teaching by principles.* Englewood Cliffs, NJ: Prentice Hall.

Brown, H. D. (2000). *Principles of language learning and teaching* (4th ed.). New York: Longman.

Brown, J. D. (1992). The biggest problems TESOL members see facing ESL/EFL teachers today. *TESOL Matters, 2*(2), 1–5.

Brown, J. D., Robson, G., & Rosenkjar, P. R. (2001). Personality, motivation, anxiety, strategies, and language proficiency of Japanese students. In R. Schmidt (Ed.), *Motivation and second language acquisition* (pp. 361–398). Honolulu: University of Hawaii Press.

Canfield, J., & Wells, H. C. (1994). *100 ways to enhance self-concept in the classroom: A handbook for teachers, counselors, and group leaders.* Needham Heights, MA: Allyn and Bacon.

Cantor, N. (1990). From thought to behavior: 'Having' and 'doing' in the study of personality and cognition. *American Psychologist, 45*(6), 735–750.

Carrell, P. L., Prince, M. S., & Astika, G. G. (1996). Personality types and language learning in an EFL context. *Language Learning, 46*(1), 75–99.

Carroll, J. B. (1973). Implications of aptitude test research and psycholinguistic theory for foreign language teaching. *International Journal of Psycholinguistics, 2*, 5–14.

Carroll, J. B. (1981). Twenty-five years of research in foreign language aptitude. In K. C. Diller (Ed.), *Individual differences and universals in language learning aptitude.* Rowley, MA.: Newbury House.

Carroll, J. B. (1990). Cognitive abilities in foreign language aptitude: Then and now. In T. Parry & C. Stansfield (Eds.), *Language Aptitude Reconsidered* (pp. 11–29). Englewood Cliffs, NJ: Prentice- Hall Regents.

Carroll, J. B. (1993). *Human cognitive abilities: A survey of factor-analytic studies.* Cambridge: Cambridge University Press.

Carroll, J. B., & Sapon, S. (1959). *The Modern Languages Aptitude Test.* San Antonio, TX: Psychological Corporation.

Carver, C. C., Reynolds, S. L., & Scheier, M. F. (1994). The possible selves of optimists and pessimists. *Journal of Research in Personality, 28*, 133–141.

Chambers, G. N. (1999). *Motivating language learners.* Clevedon, England: Multilingual Matters.

Chamorro-Premuzic, T., & Furnham, A. (2003a). Personality predicts academic performance: Evidence from two longitudinal university samples. *Journal of Research in Personality, 37*, 319–338.

Chamorro-Premuzic, T., & Furnham, A. (2003b). Personality traits and academic examination performance. *European Journal of Personality, 17*, 237–250.

Chamot, A. U. (2001). The role of learning strategies in second language acquisition. In M. P. Breen (Ed.), *Learner contributions to language learning: New directions in research* (pp. 25–43). Harlow, England: Longman.

Chamot, A. U., Barnhardt, S., El-Dinary, P. B., & Robbins, J. (1999). *The learning strategies handbook.* New York: Longman.

Chamot, A. U., & Rubin, J. (1994). Comments on Janie Rees-Miller's "A critical appraisal of learner training: Theoretical bases and teaching implications." *TESOL Quarterly, 28*, 771–776.

Chan, K.-W., & Elliott, R. G. (2002). Exploratory study of Hong Kong teacher education students' epistemological beliefs: Cultural perspectives and implications for beliefs research. *Contemporary Educational Psychology, 27,* 392–414.

Chapelle, C. A. (1992). Disembedding "Disembedded figures in the landscape...": An appraisal of Griffiths and Sheen's "Reappraisal of L2 research on field dependence/independence". *Applied Linguistics, 13,* 375–384.

Chapelle, C. A. (1995). Field-dependence/field-independence in the L2 classroom. In J. M. Reid (Ed.), *Learning styles In the ESL/EFL classroom* (pp. 158–168). Boston: Heinle and Heinle.

Child, J. R. (1998). Language aptitude testing. *Applied Language Learning, 9,* 1–10.

Clément, R. (1980). Ethnicity, contact and communicative competence in a second language. In H. Giles, W. P. Robinson & P. M. Smith (Eds.), *Language: Social psychological perspectives* (pp. 147–154). Oxford: Pergamon.

Clément, R., Baker, S. C., & MacIntyre, P. D. (2003). Willingness to communicate in a second language: The effects of context, norms, and vitality. *Journal of Language and Social Psychology, 22*(2), 190–209.

Clément, R., Dörnyei, Z., & Noels, K. (1994). Motivation, self-confidence and group cohesion in the foreign language classroom. *Language Learning, 44,* 417–448.

Clément, R., & Gardner, R. C. (2001). Second language mastery. In H. Giles & W. P. Robinson (Eds.), *The new handbook of language and social psychology* (2nd ed.). London: Wiley.

Clément, R., Gardner, R. C., & Smythe, P. C. (1977). Motivational variables in second language acquisition: A study of francophones learning English. *Canadian Journal of Behavioural Science, 9,* 123–133.

Clément, R., & Kruidenier, B. (1983). Orientations on second language acquisition: 1. The effects of ethnicity, milieu and their target language on their emergence. *Language Learning, 33,* 273–291.

Clément, R., & Kruidenier, B. G. (1985). Aptitude, attitude and motivation in second language proficiency: A test of Clément's model. *Journal of Language and Social Psychology, 4,* 21–37.

Cohen, A. D. (1998). *Strategies in learning and using a second language.* Harlow: Longman.

Cohen, A. D. (2002). Preparing teachers for styles- and strategies-based instruction. In V. Crew, C. Davison & B. Mak (Eds.), *Reflecting on language in education* (pp. 49–69). Hong Kong: The Hong Kong Institute of Education.

Cohen, A. D., & Chi, J. C. (2002). Language strategy use inventory and index. In R. M. Paige, A. D. Cohen, B. Kappler, J. C. Chi & J. P. Lassegard (Eds.), *Maximizing study abroad* (pp. 16–28). Minneapolis: Center for Advanced Research for Language Acquisition, University of Minnesota.

Cohen, A. D., & Dörnyei, Z. (2002). Focus on the language learner: Motivation, styles, and strategies. In N. Schmitt (Ed.), *An introduction to applied linguistics* (pp. 170–190). London: Arnold.

Cohen, A. D., & Oxford, R. L. (2001). *Learning Styles Survey for Young Learners.* Online: http://carla.acad.umn.edu/profiles/Cohen-profile.html.

Cohen, A. D., Oxford, R. L., & Chi, J. C. (2001). *Learning style survey.* Online: http://carla.acad.umn.edu/profiles/Cohen-profile.html.

Cohen, A. D., & Weaver, S. J. (2004). *A teachers' guide to styles- and strategies-based instruction. Revised version of CARLA (Working Paper Series #7).* Minneapolis, MN: Center for Advanced Research on Language Acquisition.

Cohen, A. D., Weaver, S. J., & Li, T. Y. (1995). *The impact of strategies-based instruction on speaking a foreign language.* Minneapolis: National Language Resource Center, University of Minnesota.

Cook, V. (2002). *Portrait of the L2 user.* Clevedon, England: Multilingual Matters.

Cooper, C. (2002). *Individual differences* (2nd ed.). London: Arnold.

Corno, L. (1993). The best-laid plans: Modern conceptions of volition and educational research. *Educational Researcher, 22,* 14–22.

Corno, L. (2000). Special double issue on conceptions of volition: Theoretical investigation and studies of practice. *International Journal of Educational Research, 33,* 659–663.

Corno, L., Cronbach, L. J., Kupermintz, H., Lohman, D. F., Mandinach, E. B., Porteus, A. W., et al. (2002). *Remaking the concept of aptitude: Extending the legacy of Richard E. Snow.* Mahwah, NJ: Lawrence Erlbaum.

Corno, L., & Kanfer, R. (1993). The role of volition in learning and performance. *Review of Research in Education, 19,* 301–341.

Cornwell, S., & Robinson, P. (Eds.). (2000). *Individual differences in foreign language learning: Effects of aptitude, intelligence, and motivation.* Tokyo: Aoyama Gakuin University.

Costa, P. T., & McCrae, R. R. (1992). *NEO-PI-R: Professional manual.* Odessa, FL: Psychological Assessment Resources.

Cotterrall, S. (1999). Key variables in language learning: What do learners believe about them? *System, 27,* 493–513.

Covin, R., Donovan, L. A., & MacIntyre, P. D. (2003). The relationship between self-esteem and performance when information regarding others' performance is available. *Journal of Social Psychology, 143*(4), 541–544.

Covington, M. (1992). *Making the grade: A Self-worth perspective on motivation and school reform.* Cambridge: Cambridge University Press.

Crookes, G., & Schmidt, R. (1991). Motivation: Reopening the research agenda. *Language Learning, 41,* 469–512.

Csikszentmihalyi, M. (1990). *Flow: The psychology of optimal experience.* New York: Harper & Row.

Csikszentmihalyi, M. (1997). Intrinsic motivation and effective teaching: A flow analysis. In J. L. Bess (Ed.), *Teaching well and liking it: Motivating faculty to teach effectively* (pp. 72 89). Baltimore: Johns Hopkins University Press.

Csizér, K., & Dörnyei, Z. (2005). The internal structure of language learning motivation: Results of structural equation modelling. *Modern Language Journal, 89*(1), 19–36.

Curral, S. C., & Kirk, R. E. (1986). Predicting success in intensive foreign language courses. *Modern Language Journal, 70,* 107–113.

Curtin, C., Avner, A., & Smith, L. A. (1983). The Pimsleur Battery as a predictor of student performance. *Modern Language Journal, 67*(1), 33–40.

Daneman, M., & Carpenter, P. A. (1980). Individual differences in working memory and reading. *Journal of Verbal Learning and Verbal Behavior, 19,* 450–466.

De Raad, B. (2000). Differential psychology. In A. E. Kazdin (Ed.), *Encyclopedia of psychology* (Vol. 3, pp. 41–44). Oxford: American Psychological Association and Oxford University Press.

Deary, J. I., Whalley, J. L., Lemmon, H., Crawford, J. R., & Starr, J. M. (2000). The stability of individual differences in mental ability from childhood to old age: Follow-up of the 1932 Scottish mental survey. *Intelligence, 28*(1), 49–55.

Deci, E. L., & Ryan, R. M. (1985). *Intrinsic motivation and self-determination in human behavior.* New York: Plenum.

Deci, E. L., & Ryan, R. M. (Eds.). (2002). *Handbook of self-determination.* Rochester: University of Rochester Press.

Dembo, M. H. (2000). *Motivation and learning strategies for college success: A self-management approach.* Mahwah, NJ: Lawrence Erlbaum Associates.

Dewaele, J.-M. (2002a). Individual differences in L2 fluency: The effect of neurobiological correlates. In V. Cook (Ed.), *Portraits of the L2 user* (pp. 221–249). Clevedon, England: Multilingual Matters.

Dewaele, J.-M. (2002b). Psychological and sociodemographic correlates of communicative anxiety in L2 and L3 production. *International Journal of Bilingualism, 6,* 23–39.

Dewaele, J.-M. (2004). Individual differences in the use of colloquial vocabulary: The effects of sociobiological and psychological factors. In P. Bogaards & B. Laufer (Eds.), *Vocabulary in a second language: Selection, acquisition, and testing* (pp. 127–153). Amsterdam: John Benjamins.

Dewaele, J.-M., & Furnham, A. (1999). Extraversion: The unloved variable in applied linguistic research. *Language Learning, 43*(3), 509–544.

Dewaele, J.-M., & Furnham, A. (2000). Personality and speech production: A pilot study of second language learners. *Personality and Individual Differences, 28,* 355–365.

Donitsa-Schmidt, S., Inbar, O., & Shohamy, E. (2004). The effect of teaching spoken Arabic on students' attitudes and motivation in Israel. *Modern Language Journal, 88*(2), 217–228.

Dörnyei, Z. (1990). Conceptualizing motivation in foreign language learning. *Language Learning, 40,* 46–78.

Dörnyei, Z. (1994a). Motivation and motivating in the foreign language classroom. *Modern Language Journal, 78,* 273–284.

Dörnyei, Z. (1994b). Understanding second language motivation: On with the challenge! *Modern Language Journal, 78*, 515–523.

Dörnyei, Z. (1995). On the teachability of communication strategies. *TESOL Quarterly, 29*, 55–85.

Dörnyei, Z. (1997). Psychological processes in cooperative language learning: Group dynamics and motivation. *Modern Language Journal, 81*, 482–493.

Dörnyei, Z. (1998). Motivation in second and foreign language learning. *Language Teaching, 78*, 117–135.

Dörnyei, Z. (1999a). Motivation. In J. Verschueren, J.-O. Östmann, J. Blommaert & C. Bulcaen (Eds.), *Handbook of pragmatics 1999* (pp. 1–22). Amsterdam: John Benjamins.

Dörnyei, Z. (1999b). Motivation. In B. Spolsky (Ed.), *Concise encyclopedia of educational linguistics* (pp. 525–532). Oxford: Pergamon.

Dörnyei, Z. (2000a). Motivation. In M. Byram (Ed.), *Routledge encyclopedia of language teaching and learning* (pp. 425–432). London: Routledge.

Dörnyei, Z. (2000b). Motivation in action: Towards a process-oriented conceptualisation of student motivation. *British Journal of Educational Psychology, 70*, 519–538.

Dörnyei, Z. (2001a). *Motivational strategies in the language classroom.* Cambridge: Cambridge University Press.

Dörnyei, Z. (2001b). New themes and approaches in second language motivation research. *Annual Review of Applied Linguistics, 21*, 43–59.

Dörnyei, Z. (2001c). *Teaching and researching motivation.* Harlow: Longman.

Dörnyei, Z. (2002). The motivational basis of language learning tasks. In P. Robinson (Ed.), *Individual differences in second language acquisition* (pp. 137–158). Amsterdam: John Benjamins.

Dörnyei, Z. (Ed.). (2003a). *Attitudes, orientations, and motivations in language learning.* Oxford: Blackwell.

Dörnyei, Z. (2003b). Attitudes, orientations, and motivations in language learning: Advances in theory, research, and applications. In Z. Dörnyei (Ed.), *Attitudes, orientations, and motivations in language learning* (pp. 3–32). Oxford: Blackwell.

Dörnyei, Z. (2003c). *Questionnaires in second language research: Construction, administration, and processing.* Mahwah, NJ: Lawrence Erlbaum Associates.

Dörnyei, Z. (in press). Creating a motivating classroom environment. In J. Cummins & C. Davison (Eds.), *The handbook of English language teaching.* Dordrecht: Kluwer.

Dörnyei, Z., & Clément, R. (2001). Motivational characteristics of learning different target languages: Results of a nationwide survey. In Z. Dörnyei & R. Schmidt (Eds.), *Motivation and second language acquisition* (pp. 399–432). Honolulu: University of Hawaii Press.

Dörnyei, Z., & Csizér, K. (2002). Some dynamics of language attitudes and motivation: Results of a longitudinal nationwide survey. *Applied Linguistics, 23*, 421–462.

Dörnyei, Z., & Kormos, J. (1998). Problem-solving mechanisms in L2 communication: A psycholinguistic perspective. *Studies in Second Language Acquisition, 20,* 349–385.

Dörnyei, Z., & Kormos, J. (2000). The role of individual and social variables in oral task performance. *Language Teaching Research, 4,* 275–300.

Dörnyei, Z., & Malderez, A. (1997). Group dynamics and foreign language teaching. *System, 25,* 65–81.

Dörnyei, Z., & Malderez, A. (1999). Group dynamics in foreign language learning and teaching. In J. Arnold (Ed.), *Affective language learning* (pp. 155–169). Cambridge: Cambridge University Press.

Dörnyei, Z., & Murphey, T. (2003). *Group dynamics in the language classroom.* Cambridge: Cambridge University Press.

Dörnyei, Z., & Ottó, I. (1998). Motivation in action: A process model of L2 motivation. *Working Papers in Applied Linguistics, (Thames Valley University, London), 4,* 43–69. Online: http://eprints.nottingham.ac.uk/archive/00000039/00/Motivation_in_action.pdf

Dörnyei, Z., & Skehan, P. (2003). Individual differences in second language learning. In C. J. Doughty & M. H. Long (Eds.), *The handbook of second language acquisition* (pp. 589–630). Oxford: Blackwell.

Doyle, T., & Kim, Y. M. (1999). Teacher motivation and satisfaction in the United States and Korea. *MEXTESOL Journal, 23,* 35–48.

Dufva, M., & Voeten, M. J. M. (1999). Native language literacy and phonological memory as prerequisites for learning English as a foreign language. *Applied Psycholinguistics, 20,* 329–348.

Edmondson, W. (2004). Individual motivation profiles: The interaction between external and internal factors. *Zeitschrift für Interkulturellen Fremdsprachenunterricht* [Online], *9*(2), 21.

Egbert, J. (2003). A study of flow theory in the foreign language classroom. *Modern Language Journal, 87*(4), 499–518.

Ehrman, M. E. (1990). The role of personality type in adult language learning: An ongoing investigation. In T. Parry & C. Stansfield (Eds.), *Language Aptitude Reconsidered* (pp. 126–178). Englewood Cliffs, NJ: Prentice-Hall Regents.

Ehrman, M. E. (1993). Ego boundaries revisited: Toward a model of personality and learning. In J. E. Alatis (Ed.), *Strategic interaction and language acquisition: Theory, practice, and research* (pp. 331–362). Washington, DC: Georgetown University.

Ehrman, M. E. (1994). The type differentiation indicator and adult foreign language learning success. *Journal of Psychological Type, 30,* 10–29.

Ehrman, M. E. (1996). *Understanding second language difficulties.* Thousand Oaks, CA: Sage.

Ehrman, M. E. (1998a). Field independence, field dependence, and field sensitivity in another light. In J. M. Reid (Ed.), *Understanding learning styles in the second language classroom* (pp. 62–70). Upper Saddle River, NJ: Prentice-Hall Regents.

Ehrman, M. E. (1998b). The Modern Language Aptitude Test for predicting learning success and advising students. *Applied Language Learning, 9*, 31–70.

Ehrman, M. E. (1999). Ego boundaries and tolerance of ambiguity in second language learning. In J. Arnold (Ed.), *Affect in language learning* (pp. 68–86). Cambridge: Cambridge University Press.

Ehrman, M. E. (2001). Bringing learning strategies to the learner: The FSI language learning consultation service. In J. E. Alatis & A. Tan (Eds.), *Language in our time: Bilingual education and official English, Ebonics and standard English, immigration and the Unz Initiative* (pp. 41–58). Washington, DC: Georgetown University.

Ehrman, M. E., & Dörnyei, Z. (1998). *Interpersonal dynamics in second language education: The visible and invisible classroom.* Thousand Oaks, CA: Sage.

Ehrman, M. E., & Leaver, B. L. (2003). Cognitive styles in the service of language learning. *System, 31*, 391–415.

Ehrman, M. E., Leaver, B. L., & Oxford, R. L. (2003). A brief overview of individual differences in second language learning. *System, 31*, 313–330.

Ehrman, M. E., & Oxford, R. L. (1990). Adult language learning styles and strategies in an intensive training setting. *Modern Language Journal, 54*(3), 311–327.

Ehrman, M. E., & Oxford, R. L. (1995). Cognition plus: Correlates of language learning success. *Modern Language Journal, 79*(1), 67–89.

Eisenstein, M. (1980). Childhood bilingualism and adult language learning aptitude. *International Review of Applied Psychology, 29*, 159–174.

Ellis, G., & Sinclair, B. (1989). *Learning to learn English: A course in learner training.* Cambridge: Cambridge University Press.

Ellis, N. (Ed.). (1994). *Implicit and explicit learning of languages.* New York: Academic Press.

Ellis, N. (2001). Memory for language. In P. Robinson (Ed.), *Cognition and second language instruction* (pp. 33–68). Cambridge: Cambridge University Press.

Ellis, R. (1994). *The study of second language acquisition.* Oxford: Oxford University Press.

Ellis, R. (2003). *Task-based language learning and teaching.* Oxford: Oxford University Press.

Ellis, R. (2004). Individual differences in second language learning. In A. Davies & C. Elder (Eds.), *The handbook of applied linguistics* (pp. 525–551). Oxford: Blackwell.

Ely, C. M. (1986). An analysis of discomfort, risktaking, sociability, and motivation in the L2 classroom. *Language Learning, 36*, 1–25.

Eysenck, H. J., & Eysenck, M. W. (1985). *Personality and individual differences.* New York: Plenum.

Eysenck, M. W. (1994). *Individual differences: Normal and abnormal.* Hove, England: Lawrence Erlbaum Associates.

Farnham, S. D., Greenwald, A. G., & Banaji, M. R. (1999). Implicit self-esteem. In D. Abrams & M. A. Hogg (Eds.), *Social identity and social cognition* (pp. 231–248). Oxford: Blackwell.

Farsides, T., & Woodfield, R. (2003). Individual differences and undergraduate academic success: The roles of personality, intelligence, and application. *Personality and Individual Differences, 34*, 1225–1243.

Feldhausen, J. F., & Westby, E. L. (2003). Creative and affective behavior: Cognition, personality, and motivation. In J. C. Houtz (Ed.), *The educational psychology of creativity* (pp. 95–105). Cresskill, NJ: Hampton Press.

Funder, D. C. (2001). Personality. *Annual Review of Psychology, 52*, 197–221.

Furnham, A. (1990). Language and personality. In H. Giles & W. P. Robinson (Eds.), *Handbook of Language and Social Psychology* (pp. 73–95). London: John Wiley.

Garcia, T. (1999). Maintaining the motivation to learn: An introduction to the special issue of 'Learning and Individual Differences.' *Learning and Individual Differences, 11*(3), 231–232.

Gardner, H. (1983). *Frames of mind: The theory of multiple intelligences.* New York: Basic Books.

Gardner, R. C. (1985). *Social psychology and second language learning: The role of attitudes and motivation.* London: Edward Arnold.

Gardner, R. C. (2000). Correlation, causation, motivation, and second language acquisition. *Canadian Psychology, 41*, 10–24.

Gardner, R. C. (2001a). Integrative motivation and second language acquisition. In Z. Dörnyei & R. Schmidt (Eds.), *Motivation and second language acquisition* (pp. 1–20). Honolulu: University of Hawaii Press.

Gardner, R. C. (2001b). *Psychological statistics using SPSS for Windows.* Upper Saddle River, NJ: Prentice Hall.

Gardner, R. C., & Lambert, W. E. (1972). *Attitudes and motivation in second language learning.* Rowley, MA: Newbury House.

Gardner, R. C., & MacIntyre, P. (1992). A student's contributions to second language learning. Part I: Cognitive variables. *Language Teaching, 25*, 211–220.

Gardner, R. C., & MacIntyre, P. D. (1993a). On the measurement of affective variables in second language learning. *Language Learning, 43*, 157–194.

Gardner, R. C., & MacIntyre, P. D. (1993b). A student's contributions to second-language learning. Part II: Affective variables. *Language Teaching, 26*, 1–11.

Gardner, R. C., Masgoret, A.-M., Tennant, J., & Mihic, L. (2004). Integrative motivation: Changes during a year-long intermediate-level language course. *Language Learning, 54*(1), 1–34.

Gardner, R. C., Tremblay, P. F., & Masgoret, A.-M. (1997). Towards a full model of second language learning: An empirical investigation. *Modern Language Journal, 81*, 344–362.

Gathercole, S. E., & Thorn, A. S. C. (1998). Phonological short-term memory and foreign language learning. In A. F. Healy & L. E. Bourne (Eds.), *For-*

eign language learning: Psycholinguistic studies on training and retention (pp. 141–158). Mahwah, NJ: Lawrence Erlbaum Associates.

Gheralis-Roussos, E. (2003). *The motivation of English language teachers in Greek secondary schools.* Unpublished PhD dissertation, University of Nottingham.

Goldberg, L. R. (1992). The development of markers for the Big-Five factor structure. *Psychological Assessment, 4*(1), 26–42.

Goldberg, L. R. (1993). The structure of phenotypic personality traits. *American Psychologist, 48,* 26–34.

Green, P. (1975). *The language laboratory in school: The York study.* London: Oliver and Boyd.

Gregersen, T., & Horwitz, E. K. (2002). Language learning and perfectionism: Anxious and non-anxious language learners' reactions to their own oral performance. *Modern Language Journal, 86*(4), 562–570.

Grenfell, M., & Harris, V. (1999). *Modern languages and learning strategies: In theory and practice.* London: Routledge.

Griffiths, C. (2003). Patterns of language learning strategy use. *System, 31,* 367–383.

Griffiths, R. (1991). Language learning and the Japanese personality: Hypotheses from the psychological literature. In T. Hayes & K. Yoshioka (Eds.), *Proceedings of the conference on second language acquisition research in Japan* (pp. 61–122). Nigata: International University of Japan.

Griffiths, R., & Sheen, R. (1992). Disembedded figures in the landscape: A reappraisal of L2 research on field dependence/independence. *Applied Linguistics, 13,* 133–148.

Grigorenko, E., Sternberg, R., & Ehrman, M. E. (2000). A theory based approach to the measurement of foreign language learning ability: The Canal-F theory and test. *Modern Language Journal, 84*(3), 390–405.

GTCfE. (2002). *Teachers on teaching: A survey of the teaching profession.* London: General Teaching Council for England.

Hadwin, A. F., & Winne, P. H. (1996). Study strategies have meager support: A review with recommendations for implementation. *Journal of Higher Education, 67*(6), 692–715.

Hampson, S. E., & Colman, A. M. (1994). Introduction. In S. E. Hampson & A. M. Colman (Eds.), *Individual differences and personality* (pp. ix–xiv). Harlow, England: Longman.

Hansen, J. Q., & Stansfield, C. W. (1981). The relationship of field dependent-independent cognitive styles to foreign language achievement. *Language Learning, 31,* 349–367.

Harley, B., & Hart, D. (1997). Language aptitude and second language proficiency in classroom learners of different starting ages. *Studies in Second Language Acquisition, 19*(3), 379–400.

Harley, B., & Hart, D. (2002). Age, aptitude and second language learning on a bilingual exchange. In P. Robinson (Ed.), *Individual differences and instructed language learning* (pp. 301–330). Amsterdam: John Benjamins.

Harris, V. (2003). Adapting classroom-based strategy instruction to a distance learning context. *TESL-EJ, 7*(2), 1–19.

Heckhausen, H. (1991). *Motivation and action.* New York: Springer.

Heckhausen, H., & Kuhl, J. (1985). From wishes to action: The dead ends and short cuts on the long way to action. In M. Frese & J. Sabini (Eds.), *Goal-directed behavior: The concept of action in psychology* (pp. 134–160). Hillsdale, NJ: Lawrence Erlbaum Associates.

Higgins, E. T. (1987). Self-discrepancy: A theory relating self and affect. *Psychological Review, 94,* 319–340.

Higgins, E. T. (1996). The 'self-digest': Self-knowledge serving self-regulatory functions. *Journal of Personality and Social Psychology, 71*(6), 1062–1083.

Higgins, E. T. (1998). Promotion and prevention: Regulatory focus as a motivational principle. *Advances in Experimental Social Psychology, 30,* 1–46.

Hoffman, S. Q. (1997). Field dependence/independence in second language acquisition and implications for educators and instructional designers. *Foreign Language Annals, 30,* 221–234.

Hogan, R., Harkness, A. R., & Lubinski, D. (2000). Personality and individual differences. In K. Pawlik & M. R. Rosenzweig (Eds.), *International handbook of psychology* (pp. 283–304). London: Sage.

Hogg, M. A., & Vaughan, G. M. (2002). *Social Psychology* (3rd ed.). Harlow, England: Prentice Hall.

Horwitz, E. K. (1985). Using student beliefs about language learning and teaching in the foreign language methods course. *Foreign Language Annals, 18,* 333–340.

Horwitz, E. K. (1987). Surveying student beliefs about language learning. In A. L. Wenden & J. Rubin (Eds.), *Learner strategies in language learning* (pp. 119–129). Hemel Hempstead: Prentice Hall.

Horwitz, E. K. (1988). The beliefs about language learning of beginning university foreign language students. *Modern Language Journal, 72,* 283–294.

Horwitz, E. K. (1999). Cultural and situational influences on foreign language learners' beliefs about language learning: A review of BALLI studies. *System, 27*(4), 557–576.

Horwitz, E. K. (2000). It ain't over till it's over: On foreign language anxiety, first language deficits, and the confounding of variables. *Modern Language Journal, 84*(2), 256–259.

Horwitz, E. K. (2001). Language anxiety and achievement. *Annual Review of Applied Linguistics, 21,* 112–126.

Horwitz, E. K., Horwitz, M. B., & Cope, J. (1986). Foreign language classroom anxiety. *Modern Language Journal, 70,* 125–132.

Houtz, J. C. (Ed.). (2003). *The educational psychology of creativity.* Cresskill, NJ: Hampton Press.

Hsiao, T.-Y., & Oxford, R. L. (2002). Comparing theories of language learning strategies: A confirmatory factor analysis. *Modern Language Journal, 86*(3), 368–383.

Inbar, O., Donitsa-Schmidt, S., & Shohamy, E. (2001). Students' motivation as a function of language learning: The teaching of Arabic in Israel. In Z. Dörnyei & R. Schmidt (Eds.), *Motivation and second language acquisition* (pp. 297–311). Honolulu: University of Hawaii Press.

Irie, K. (2003). What do we know about the language learning motivation of university students in Japan? Some patterns in survey studies. *JALT Journal, 25*(1), 86–100.

Irvine, S. H. (2001). Self-concept and status as determinants of cognitive style. In J. M. Collis & S. Messick (Eds.), *Intelligence and personality: Bridging the gap in theory and measurement* (pp. 273–288). Mahwah, NJ: Lawrence Erlbaum Associates.

Jacques, S. R. (2001). Preferences for instructional activities and motivation: A comparison of student and teacher perspectives. In Z. Dörnyei & R. Schmidt (Eds.), *Motivation and second language acquisition* (pp. 187–214). Honolulu: University of Hawaii Press.

Johnson, J., Prior, S., & Artuso, M. (2000). Field dependence as a factor in second language communicative production. *Language Learning, 50*(3), 529–567.

Julkunen, K. (1989). *Situation-and task-specific motivation in foreign-language learning and teaching.* Joensuu: University of Joensuu.

Julkunen, K. (2001). Situation- and task-specific motivation in foreign language learning. In Z. Dörnyei & R. Schmidt (Eds.), *Motivation and second language acquisition* (pp. 29–42). Honolulu: University of Hawaii Press.

Juvonen, J., & Nishina, A. (1997). Social motivation in the classroom: Attributional accounts and developmental analysis. *Advances in Motivation and Achievement, 10*, 181–211.

Kang, S.-J. (in press). Dynamic emergence of situational willingness to communicate and its effects on second language communication. *System.*

Kassabgy, O., Boraie, D., & Schmidt, R. (2001). Values, rewards, and job satisfaction in ESL/EFL. In Z. Dörnyei & R. Schmidt (Eds.), *Motivation and second language acquisition* (pp. 213–237). Honolulu: University of Hawaii Press.

Kaylani, C. (1996). The influence of gender and motivation on EFL learning strategy use in Jordan. In R. L. Oxford (Ed.), *Language learning strategies around the world: Cross-cultural perspectives* (pp. 75–88). Honolulu: University of Hawaii Press.

Kiany, G. R. (1997). Personality and language learning: The contradiction between psychologists and applied linguists. *I. T. L. Review of Applied Linguistics, 115/116*, 111–136.

Kimura, Y. (2003). English language learning motivation: Interpreting qualitative data situated in a classroom task. *Annual Review of English Language Education in Japan, 14*, 71–80.

Kimura, Y., Nakata, Y., & Okumura, T. (2001). Language learning motivation of EFL learners in Japan: A cross-sectional analysis of various learning milieus. *JALT Journal, 23*, 47–68.

Kinsella, K. (1995). Understanding and empowering diverse learners in ESL classrooms. In J. Reid (Ed.), *Learning styles in the ESL/EFL classroom* (pp. 170–194). Boston: Heinle & Heinle.

Kirby, J. R. (1988). Style, strategy, and skill in reading. In R. R. Schmeck (Ed.), *Learning strategies and learning styles* (pp. 3–19). New York: Plenum.

Kiss, C., & Nikolov, M. (in press). Developing, piloting, and validating an instrument to measure young learners' aptitude. *Language Learning.*

Koizumi, R., & Matsuo, K. (1993). A longitudinal study of attitudes and motivation in learning English among Japanese seventh-grade students. *Japanese Psychological Research, 35*, 1–11.

Kolb, D. A. (1984). *Experiential learning: Experience as the source of learning and development.* Englewood Cliffs, NJ: Prentice Hall.

Kolb, D. A. (1999). *Learning Style Inventory, Version 3.* Boston: TRG Hay/McBer.

Kolb, D. A., Boyatzis, R. E., & Mainemelis, C. (2001). Experiential learning theory: Previous research and new directions. In R. J. Sternberg & L.-F. Zhang (Eds.), *Perspectives on thinking, learning, and cognitive styles* (pp. 227–247). Mahwah, NJ: Lawrence Erlbaum Associates.

Kormos, J. (1999). The effect of speaker variables on the self-correction behavior of L2 learners. *System, 27,* 207–221.

Kormos, J., & Dörnyei, Z. (2004). The interaction of linguistic and motivational variables in second language task performance. *Zeitschrift für Interkulturellen Fremdsprachenunterricht [Online], 9*(2), 19. http://www.ualberta.ca/~german/ejournal/kormos2.htm

Krashen, S. (1978). Individual variation in the use of the monitor. In W. Ritchie (Ed.), *Second language acquisition research* (pp. 175–183). New York: Academic Press.

Krashen, S. (1981). Aptitude and attitude in relation to second language acquisition and learning. In K. C. Diller (Ed.), *Individual differences and universals in language learning aptitude.* Rowley, MA.: Newbury House.

Kuhl, J. (1985). Volitional mediators of cognition-behavior consistency: Self-regulatory processes and action versus state orientation. In J. Kuhl & J. Beckmann (Eds.), *Action control: From cognition to behavior.* New York: Springer.

Kuhl, J. (1987). Action control: The maintenance of motivational states. In F. Halish & J. Kuhl (Eds.), *Motivation, intention and volition* (pp. 279–291). Berlin: Springer.

Kuhl, J. (1994). A theory of action and state orientations. In J. Kuhl & J. Beckmann (Eds.), *Volition and personality: Action versus state orientation* (pp. 9–45). Seattle, WA: Hogrefe & Huber.

Kuhl, J., & Beckmann, J. (Eds.). (1994). *Volition and personality: Action versus state orientation.* Seattle, WA: Hogrefe and Huber.

Kuhl, J., & Goschke, T. (1994). A theory of action control: Mental subsystems, modes of control, and volitional conflict-resolution strategies. In J. Kuhl &

J. Beckmann (Eds.), *Volition and personality: Action versus state orientation* (pp. 93–124). Seattle, WA: Hogrefe & Huber.

Kurahachi, J. (1994). Individual differences in learning a second language. *Japanese Journal of Educational Psychology, 42*(2), 227–239.

Kyriacou, C., & Benmansour, N. (1997). Motivation and learning preferences of high school students learning English as a foreign language in Morocco. *Mediterranean Journal of Educational Studies, 2*(1), 79–86.

Lalonde, R. N., & Gardner, R. C. (1984). Investigating a causal model of second language acquisition: Where does personality fit. *Canadian Journal of Behavioural Science, 15*, 224–237.

Lalonde, R. N., Lee, P. A., & Gardner, R. C. (1987). The common view of the good language learner: An investigation of teachers' beliefs. *Canadian Modern Language Review, 44*, 16–34.

Lamb, M. (2004). Integrative motivation in a globalizing world. *System, 32*, 3–19.

Lan, R., & Oxford, R. L. (2003). Language learning strategy profiles of elementary school students in Taiwan. *IRAL, 41*(4), 339–379.

Larsen-Freeman, D. (2000). *Techniques and principles in language teaching* (2nd ed.). Oxford: Oxford University Press.

Lawrence, G. D. (1997). *Looking at type and learning styles.* Gainesville, FL: Center for Applications of Psychological Type.

Leaver, B. L., Ehrman, M. E., & Shekhtman, B. (in press). *Achieving success in second language acquisition.* Cambridge: Cambridge University Press.

Lett, J. A. J., & O'Mara, F. E. (1990). Predictors of success in an intensive foreign language learning context: Correlates of language learning at the Defense Language Institute Foreign Language Center. In T. S. Parry & C. W. Stansfield (Eds.), *Language aptitude reconsidered* (pp. 222–260). Englewood Cliffs, NJ: Prentice-Hall Regents.

Levine, A., Reves, T., & Leaver, B. L. (1996). Relationship between language learning strategies and Israeli versus Russian cultural-educational factors. In R. L. Oxford (Ed.), *Language learning strategies around the world: Cross-cultural perspectives* (pp. 35–45). Honolulu: University of Hawaii Press.

Lim, H. Y. (2002). The interaction of motivation, perception, and environment: One EFL learner's experience. *Hong Kong Journal of Applied Linguistics, 7*(2), 91–106.

Lounsbury, J. W., Sundstrom, E., Loveland, J. M., & Gibson, L. W. (2003). Intelligence, "Big Five" personality traits, and work drive as predictors of course grade. *Personality and Individual Differences, 35*, 1231–1239.

Macaro, E. (2001). *Learning strategies in foreign and second language classrooms.* London: Continuum.

MacIntyre, P. D. (1994a). Toward a social psychological model of strategy use. *Foreign Language Annals, 27*, 185–195.

MacIntyre, P. D. (1994b). Variables underlying willingness top communicate: A causal analysis. *Communication Research Reports, 11*, 135–142.

MacIntyre, P. D. (1995a). How does anxiety affect second language learning? A reply to Sparks and Ganschow. *Modern Language Journal, 79,* 90–99.

MacIntyre, P. D. (1995b). On seeing the forest and the trees: A rejoinder to Sparks and Ganschow. *Modern Language Journal, 79,* 245–248.

MacIntyre, P. D. (1999). Language anxiety: A review of the research for language teachers. In D. J. Young (Ed.), *Affect in foreign language and second language learning* (pp. 24–45). Boston: McGraw-Hill.

MacIntyre, P. D. (2002). Motivation, anxiety and emotion in second language acquisition. In P. Robinson (Ed.), *Individual differences in second language acquisition* (pp. 45–68). Amsterdam: John Benjamins.

MacIntyre, P. D., Babin, P. A., & Clément, R. (1999). Willingness to communicate: Antecedents and consequences. *Communication Quarterly, 47,* 215–229.

MacIntyre, P. D., Baker, S. C., Clément, R., & Conrod, S. (2001). Willingness to communicate, social support, and language learning orientations of immersion students. *Studies in Second Language Acquisition, 23,* 369–388.

MacIntyre, P. D., Baker, S. C., Clément, R., & Donovan, L. A. (2002). Sex and age effects on willingness to communicate, anxiety, perceived competence, and L2 motivation among junior high school French immersion students. *Language Learning, 52,* 537–564.

MacIntyre, P. D., Baker, S. C., Clément, R., & Donovan, L. A. (2003). Talking in order to learn: Willingness to communicate and intensive language programs. *Canadian Modern Language Review, 59*(4), 589–607.

MacIntyre, P. D., & Charos, C. (1996). Personality, attitudes, and affect as predictors of second language communication. *Journal of Language and Social Psychology, 15,* 3–26.

MacIntyre, P. D., Clément, R., Dörnyei, Z., & Noels, K. A. (1998). Conceptualizing willingness to communicate in a L2: A situated model of confidence and affiliation. *Modern Language Journal, 82,* 545–562.

MacIntyre, P. D., & Gardner, R. C. (1991a). Language anxiety: Its relation to other anxieties and to processing in native and second languages. *Language Learning, 41,* 513–534.

MacIntyre, P. D., & Gardner, R. C. (1991b). Methods and results in the study of anxiety in language learning: A review of the literature. *Language Learning, 41,* 85–117.

MacIntyre, P. D., & Gardner, R. C. (1994). The subtle effects of language anxiety on cognitive processing in the second language. *Language Learning, 44,* 283–305.

MacIntyre, P. D., & Noels, K. (1994). The good language learner: A retrospective review. *System, 22,* 269–280.

MacIntyre, P. D., & Noels, K. A. (1996). Using social-psychological variables to predict the use of language learning strategies. *Foreign Language Annals, 29,* 373–386.

MacIntyre, P. D., Noels, K. A., & Clément, R. (1997). Biases in self-ratings of second language proficiency: The role of language anxiety. *Language Learning, 47*(2), 265–287.

Manolopoulou-Sergi, E. (in press). Motivation within the information processing model of foreign language learning. *System.*

Markee, N. (2001, March). *Reopening the research agenda: Respecifying motivation as a locally-occasioned phenomenon.* Paper presented at the annual conference of the American Association of Applied Linguistics (AAAL), St. Louis, MI, USA.

Markus, H., & Nurius, P. (1986). Possible selves. *American Psychologist, 41*, 954–969.

Markus, H., & Ruvolo, A. (1989). Possible selves: Personalized representations of goals. In L. A. Pervin (Ed.), *Goal concepts in personality and social psychology* (pp. 211–241). Hillsdale, NJ: Lawrence Erlbaum Associates.

Masgoret, A.-M., & Gardner, R. C. (2003). Attitudes, motivation, and second language learning: A meta-analysis of studies conducted by Gardner and associates. *Language Learning, 53*, 123–163.

Matthews, G. (1999). Personality and skill: A cognitive-adaptive framework. In P. L. Ackerman, P. C. Kyllonen & R. D. Roberts (Eds.), *Learning and individual differences: Process, trait, and content determinants* (pp. 251–271). Washington, DC: American Psychological Association.

Matthews, G., Davies, D. R., Westerman, S. J., & Stammers, R. B. (2000). *Human performance: Cognition, stress and individual differences.* Hove, England: Psychology Press.

McClelland, N. (2000). Goal orientations in Japanese college students learning EFL. In S. Cornwell & P. Robinson (Eds.), *Individual differences in foreign language learning: Effects of aptitude, intelligence, and motivation* (pp. 99–115). Tokyo: Japanese Association for Language Teaching.

McCrae, R. R., & Costa, P. T. (2003). *Personality in adulthood : A five-factor theory perspective* (2nd ed.). New York: Guilford Press.

McCroskey, J. C., & Baer, J. E. (1985, November). *Willingness to communicate: The construct and it's measurement.* Paper presented at the annual convention of the Speech Communication Association, Denver.

McCroskey, J. C., & Richmond, V. P. (1987). Willingness to communicate. In J. C. McCroskey & J. A. Daly (Eds.), *Personality and interpersonal communication* (pp. 129–156). Newbury Park, CA: Sage.

McCroskey, J. C., & Richmond, V. P. (1991). Willingness to communicate: A cognitive view. In M. Booth-Butterfield (Ed.), *Communication, cognition and anxiety* (pp. 19–37). Newbury Park, CA: Sage.

McDonough, S. (1995). *Strategy and skill in learning a foreign language.* London: Edward Arnold.

McDonough, S. (1999). Learner strategies. *Language Teaching Research, 32*, 1–18.

McGroarty, M. (1998). Constructive and constructivist challenges for applied linguistics. *Language Learning Journal, 48*, 591–622.

McGroarty, M. (2001). Situating second language motivation. In Z. Dörnyei & R. Schmidt (Eds.), *Motivation and second language acquisition* (pp. 69–90). Honolulu, H: University of Hawaii Press.

McIntosh, C. N., & Noels, K. (2004). Self-determined motivation for language learning: The role of need for cognition and language learning strategies. *Zeitschrift für Interkulturellen Fremdsprachenunterricht* [Online], *9*(2), 19.

McLaughlin, B. (1995). Aptitude from an information-processing perspective. *Language Testing, 12*(3), 370–387.

Messick, S. (1994). Cognitive styles and learning. In T. Husén & T. N. Postlethwaite (Eds.), *The international encyclopedia of education* (2nd ed., Vol. 2, pp. 868–872). Oxford: Pergamon.

Miller, A., & Phillips, D. (1982). Towards a new language aptitude test. *British Journal of Language Teaching, 20*, 97–100.

Mischel, W. (1999). Personality coherence and dispositions in a cognitive-affective personality system (CAPS) approach. In D. Cervone & Y. Shoda (Eds.), *The coherence of personality* (pp. 37–60). New York: Guilford.

Miyake, A., & Friedman, D. (1998). Individual differences in second language proficiency: Working memory as language aptitude. In A. F. Healy & L. E. Bourne (Eds.), *Foreign Language Learning: Psycholinguistic studies on training and retention* (pp. 339–364). Mahwah, NJ: Lawrence Erlbaum Associates.

Moody, R. (1988). Personality preferences and foreign language learning. *Modern Language Journal, 72*(4), 389–401.

Mori, Y. (1999). Epistemological beliefs and language learning beliefs: What do language learners believe about their learning? *Language Learning, 49*(3), 377–415.

Murphey, T. (1998). *Language hungry: An introduction to language learning, fun and self-esteem.* Tokyo: Macmillan Languagehouse.

Myers, I. B., & Briggs, K. (1976). *The Myers-Briggs Type Indicator, Farm G.* Paolo Alto, CA: Consulting Psychologists Press.

NACCCE (2000). *All our futures: Creativity, culture and education.* London: DfEE.

Naiman, N., Fröhlich, M., Stern, H., & Todesco, A. (1978). *The good language learner.* Toronto: Ontario Institute for Studies in Education.

Nakata, Y. (1995a). New attitudes among Japanese learners of English. In K. Kitao, S. K. Kitao, J. H. Miller, J. W. Carpenter & C. C. Rinnert (Eds.), *Culture and Communication* (pp. 173–184).

Nakata, Y. (1995b). New goals for Japanese learners of English. *The Language Teacher, 19*(5), 17–20.

Nasby, W. (1997). Self-consciousness and cognitive prototypes of the ideal self. *Journal of Research in Personality, 31*, 543–563.

Neufeld, G. G. (1978). A theoretical perspective on the nature of linguistic aptitude. *International Review of Applied Linguistics, 16*(1), 15–26.

Neufeld, G. G. (1979). Towards a theory of language learning ability. *Language Learning, 29*(2), 227–241.

Nikolov, M. (1999). 'Why do you learn English?' 'Because the teacher is short.' A study of Hungarian children's foreign language learning motivation. *Language Teaching Research, 3,* 33–56.

Nikolov, M. (2001). A study of unsuccessful language learners. In Z. Dörnyei & R. Schmidt (Eds.), *Motivation and second language acquisition* (pp. 147–172). Honolulu: University of Hawaii Press.

Nizegorodcew, A. (1980). The role of aptitude in foreign language learning in secondary grammar school pupils. *Glottodidactica, 13,* 37–48.

Noels, K. A. (2001a). Learning Spanish as a second language: Learners' orientations and perceptions of their teachers' communication style. *Language Learning, 51,* 107–144.

Noels, K. A. (2001b). New orientations in language learning motivation: Toward a contextual model of intrinsic, extrinsic, and integrative orientations and motivation. In Z. Dörnyei & R. Schmidt (Eds.), *Motivation and second language acquisition* (pp. 43–68). Honolulu: University of Hawaii, Second Language Teaching & Curriculum Center.

Noels, K. A. (2003). Learning Spanish as a second language: Learners' orientations and perceptions of their teachers' communication style. In Z. Dörnyei (Ed.), *Attitudes, orientations, and motivations in language learning* (pp. 97–136). Oxford: Blackwell.

Noels, K. A., Clément, R., & Pelletier, L. G. (1999). Perceptions of teachers' communicative style and students' intrinsic and extrinsic motivation. *Modern Language Journal, 83,* 23–34.

Noels, K. A., Clément, R., & Pelletier, L. G. (2001). Intrinsic, extrinsic, and integrative orientations of French Canadian learners of English. *Canadian Modern Language Review, 57,* 424–444.

Noels, K. A., Pelletier, L. G., Clément, R., & Vallerand, R. J. (2000). Why are you learning a second language? Motivational orientations and self-determination theory. *Language Learning, 50,* 57–85.

Norton, B. (2001). Non-participation, imagined communities and the language classroom. In M. P. Breen (Ed.), *Learner contributions to language learning: New directions in research* (pp. 159–171). Harlow, England: Longman.

Norton, B., & Toohey, K. (2001). Changing perspectives on good language learners. *TESOL Quarterly, 35*(2), 307–322.

Nunan, D. (1997). Strategy training in the classroom: An empirical investigation. *RELC Journal, 28*(2), 56–81.

O'Malley, J. M., & Chamot, A. U. (1990). *Learning strategies in second language acquisition.* New York: Cambridge University Press.

O'Malley, J. M., & Chamot, A. U. (1994). Learning strategies in second language learning. In *The international encyclopedia of education* (Vol. 6, pp. 3329–3335). Oxford: Oxford: Pergamon Press.

Ottó, I. (1998). The relationship between individual differences in learner creativity and language learning success. *TESOL Quarterly, 32*(4), 763–773.

Oxford, R. L. (1989). Use of language learning strategies: A synthesis of studies with implications for strategy training. *System, 17*, 235–247.

Oxford, R. L. (1990). *Language learning strategies: What every teacher should know*. New York: Newbury House.

Oxford, R. L. (1993a). Research on second language learning strategies. *Annual Review of Applied Linguistics, 13*, 175–187.

Oxford, R. L. (1993b). *Style Analysis Survey (SAS)*. Tuscaloosa: University of Alabama. [Reprinted in Oxford, 1999d; Reid, 1995.]

Oxford, R. L. (1995). Gender differences in language learning styles: What do they mean? In J. M. Reid (Ed.), *Learning styles In the ESL/EFL classroom* (pp. 34–46). Boston: Heinle and Heinle.

Oxford, R. L. (1996a). Afterword: What have we learned about language learning strategies around the world? In R. L. Oxford (Ed.), *Language learning strategies around the world: Cross-cultural perspectives* (pp. 247–249). Honolulu: University of Hawaii Press.

Oxford, R. L. (1996b). Preface: Why is culture important for language learning strategies? In R. L. Oxford (Ed.), *Language learning strategies around the world: Cross-cultural perspectives* (pp. ix–xv). Honolulu: University of Hawaii Press.

Oxford, R. L. (Ed.). (1996c). *Language learning motivation: Pathways to the new century*. Honolulu: University of Hawaii Press.

Oxford, R. L. (1999a). Anxiety and the language learner: New insights. In J. Arnold (Ed.), *Affect in language learning* (pp. 58–67). Cambridge: Cambridge University Press.

Oxford, R. L. (1999b). Learning strategies. In B. Spolsky (Ed.), *Concise encyclopedia of educational linguistics* (pp. 518–522). Oxford: Elsevier.

Oxford, R. L. (1999c). Second language learning: Individual differences. In B. Spolsky (Ed.), *Concise encyclopedia of educational linguistics* (pp. 552–560). Oxford: Elsevier.

Oxford, R. L. (1999d). 'Style wars' as a source of anxiety in language classrooms. In D. J. Young (Ed.), *Affect in foreign language and second language learning* (pp. 216–237). Boston: McGraw-Hill.

Oxford, R. L. (2001). 'The bleached bones of a story': Learners constructions of language teachers. In M. P. Breen (Ed.), *Learner contributions to language learning: New directions in research* (pp. 86–111). Harlow, England: Longman.

Oxford, R. L., & Anderson, N. J. (1995). A crosscultural view of learning styles. *Language Teaching, 28*, 201–215.

Oxford, R. L., & Ehrman, M. E. (1993). Second language research on individual differences. *Annual Review of Applied Linguistics, 13*, 188–205.

Oxford, R. L., Ehrman, M. E., & Lavine, R. Z. (1991). "Style wars": Teacher-student style conflicts in the language classroom. In S. Magnan (Ed.), *Challenges in the 1990s for college foreign language programs* (pp. 1–25). Boston MA: Heinle & Heinle.

Oxford, R. L., & Massey, R. (in press). Transforming teacher-student style relationships: Toward a more welcoming and diverse classroom discourse. In J. Frodesen & C. Holten (Eds.), *The power of context in language teaching and learning*. Boston: Thomson/Heinle.

Oxford, R. L., Nyikos, M., & Ehrman, M. E. (1988). Vive la différence? Reflections on sex differences in use of language learning strategies. *Foreign Language Annals, 21*(4), 321–329.

Oyserman, D., Bybee, D., Terry, K., & Hart-Johnson, T. (2004). Possible selves as roadmaps. *Journal of Research in Personality, 38*, 130–149.

Oyserman, D., & Markus, H. R. (1990). Possible selves and delinquency. *Journal of Personality and Social Psychology, 59*, 112–125.

Oyserman, D., Terry, K., & Bybee, D. (2002). A possible selves intervention to enhance school involvement. *Journal of Adolescence, 25*, 313–326.

Pardee, L. J. (1998). Zero-based language aptitude test design: Where's the focus for the test? *Applied Language Learning, 9*, 11–30.

Parry, T. S., & Child, J. R. (1990). Preliminary investigation of the relationship between VORD, MLAT, and language proficiency. In T. S. Parry & C. W. Stansfield (Eds.), *Language Aptitude Reconsidered* (pp. 30–66). Englewood Cliffs, NJ: Prentice-Hall Regents.

Parry, T. S, & Stansfield, C. (1990). *Language aptitude reconsidered*. Englewood Cliffs, NJ: Prentice-Hall Regents.

Peacock, M. (2001). Match or mismatch? Learning styles and teaching styles in EFL. *International Journal of Applied Linguistics, 11*(1), 1–20.

Peacock, M., & Ho, M. (2003). Student language learning strategies across eight disciplines. *International Journal of Applied Linguistics, 13*(2), 179–200.

Pennington, M. C. (1992). Motivating English language teachers through job enrichment. *Language, Culture and Curriculum, 5*, 199–218.

Pennington, M. C. (1995). *Work satisfaction, motivation and commitment in teaching English as a second language. ERIC Document ED 404850.*

Pennington, M. C., & Ho, B. (1995). Do ESL educators suffer from burnout? *Prospect, 10*, 41–53.

Pervin, L. A., & John, O. P. (2001). *Personality: Theory and research* (8th ed.). New York: John Wiley & Sons.

Petersen, C., & Al-Haik, A. (1976). The development of the Defense Language Aptitude Battery. *Educational and Psychological Measurement, 36*, 369–380.

Peterson, E. R., Deary, J. I., & Austin, E. J. (2003a). The reliability of Riding's Cognitive Style Analysis test. *Personality and Individual Differences, 34*, 881–891.

Peterson, E. R., Deary, J. I., & Austin, E. J. (2003b). On the assessment of cognitive style: Four red herrings. *Personality and Individual Differences, 34*, 899–904.

Pimsleur, P. (1966). *The Pimsleur Language Aptitude Battery*. New York: Harcourt, Brace, Jovanovic.

Pintrich, P. R. (1999). Taking control of research on volitional control: Challenges for future theory and research. *Learning and Individual Differences, 11*(3), 335–354.

Pintrich, P. R., Smith, D. A. F., Garcia, T., & McKeachie, W. J. (1991). *A manual for the use of the Motivated Strategies for Learning Questionnaire (MSLQ).* Ann Arbor: NCRIPTAL, School of Education, University of Michigan.

Pintrich, P. R., Smith, D. A. F., Garcia, T., & McKeachie, W. J. (1993). Reliability and predictive validity of the Motivated Strategies for Learning Questionnaire (MSLQ). *Educational and Psychological Measurement, 53,* 801–813.

Pittaway, D. S. (2004). Investment and second language acquisition. *Critical Inquiry in Language Studies: An International Journal, 1*(4), 203–218.

Plucker, J. A., Beghetto, R. A., & Dow, G. T. (2004). Why isn't creativity more important to educational psychologists? Potentials, pitfalls, and future directions in creativity research. *Educational Psychologist, 39*(2), 83–96.

Pressley, M., El-Dinary, P. B., Marks, M. B., Brown, R., & Stein, S. (1992). Good strategy instruction is motivating and interesting. In K. A. Renninger, S. Hidi & A. Krapp (Eds.), *The role of interest in learning and development* (pp. 333–358). Mahwah, NJ: Lawrence Erlbaum Associates.

Purdie, N., & Oliver, R. (1999). Language learning strategies used by bilingual school-aged children. *System, 27,* 375–388.

Purpura, J. E. (1997). An analysis of the relationships between the test takers' cognitive and metacognitive strategy use and second language test performance. *Language Learning, 47,* 289–325.

Purpura, J. E. (1999). *Learner strategy use and performance on language tests: A structural equation modeling approach.* Cambridge: Cambridge University Press.

Raffini, J. P. (1996). *150 ways to increase intrinsic motivation in the classroom.* Needham Heights, MA: Allyn and Bacon.

Ramsden, P. (Ed.). (1988). *Improving learning: New perspectives.* London: Kogan Page.

Randi, J., & Corno, L. (2000). Teacher innovations in self-regulated learning. In M. Boekaerts, P. R. Pintrich & M. Zeidner (Eds.), *Handbook of self-regulation* (pp. 651–685). San Diego: Academic press.

Ranta, L. (2002). The role of learners' language analytic ability in the communicative classroom. In P. Robinson (Ed.), *Individual differences and instructed language learning* (pp. 159–180). Amsterdam: John Benjamins.

Rayner, S. G. (2000). Reconstructing style differences in thinking and learning: Profiling learning performance. In R. J. Riding & S. G. Rayner (Eds.), *Interpersonal perspectives on individual differences* (Vol. 1: Cognitive styles, pp. 115–177). Stamford, CI: Ablex.

Rees, J. (2000). Predicting the future of foreign language aptitude. In S. Cornwell & P. Robinson (Eds.), *Individual differences in foreign language learning: Effects of aptitude, intelligence, and motivation* (pp. 187–197). Tokyo: Aoyama Gakuin University.

Rees-Miller, J. (1993). A critical appraisal of learner training: Theoretical bases and teaching implications. *TESOL Quarterly, 27,* 679–689.

Reid, J. M. (1995a). Preface. In J. M. Reid (Ed.), *Learning styles In the ESL/EFL classroom* (pp. viii–xvii). Boston: Heinle and Heinle.

Reid, J. M. (Ed.). (1995b). *Learning styles In the ESL/EFL classroom.* Boston: Heinle and Heinle.

Reid, J. M. (Ed.). (1998). *Understanding learning styles in the second language classroom.* Upper Saddle River, NJ: Prentice-Hall Regents.

Reid, J. M., Vicioso, M. V. M., Gedeon, È., Takàcs, K., & Korotkikh, Z. (1998). Teachers as perceptual learning styles researchers. In J. M. Reid (Ed.), *Understanding learning styles in the second language classroom* (pp. 15–25). Upper Saddle River, NJ: Prentice-Hall Regents.

Revelle, W. (2000). Individual differences. In A. E. Kazdin (Ed.), *Encyclopedia of psychology* (Vol. 4, pp. 249–252). Oxford: American Psychological Association and Oxford University Press.

Riding, R. (1991). *Cognitive Styles Analysis.* Birmingham: Learning and Training Technology.

Riding, R. (2000a). Cognitive style: A review. In R. Riding & S. G. Rayner (Eds.), *Interpersonal perspectives on individual differences* (Vol. 1, Cognitive styles, pp. 315–344). Stamford, CT: Ablex.

Riding, R. (2000b). Cognitive style: A strategic approach for advancement. In R. J. Riding & S. G. Rayner (Eds.), *Interpersonal perspectives on individual differences* (Vol. 1: Cognitive styles, pp. 365–377). Stamford, CI: Ablex.

Riding, R. (2001). The nature and effects of cognitive style. In R. J. Sternberg & L.-F. Zhang (Eds.), *Perspectives on thinking, learning, and cognitive styles* (pp. 47–72). Mahwah, NJ: Lawrence Erlbaum Associates.

Riding, R. (2002). *School learning and cognitive style.* London: David Fulton.

Riding, R. (2003). On the assessment of cognitive style: A commentary on Peterson, Deary, and Austin. *Personality and Individual Differences, 34,* 893–897.

Riding, R., & Rayner, S. G. (1998). *Cognitive styles and learning strategies: Understanding style differences in learning and behavior.* London: David Fulton.

Robinson, P. (1995). Learning simple and complex rules under implicit, incidental, rule-search, and instructed conditions. *Studies in Second Language Acquisition, 8,* 27–67.

Robinson, P. (1997). Individual differences and the similarity of implicit and explicit adult second language learning. *Language Learning, 47,* 45–99.

Robinson, P. (2001). Individual differences, cognitive abilities, aptitude complexes and learning conditions in second language acquisition. *Second Language Research, 17*(4), 368–392.

Robinson, P. (2002a). Effects of individual differences in intelligence, aptitude and working memory on adult incidental SLA: A replication and extension of Reber, Walkenfield and Hernstadt (1991). In P. Robinson (Ed.), *Individual differences and instructed language learning* (pp. 211–266). Amsterdam: John Benjamins.

Robinson, P. (Ed.). (2002b). *Individual differences and instructed language learning.* Amsterdam: John Benjamins.

Robinson, P. (2002c). Introduction: Researching individual differences and instructed learning. In P. Robinson (Ed.), *Individual differences and instructed language learning* (pp. 1–10). Amsterdam: John Benjamins.

Robinson, P. (2002d). Learning conditions, aptitude complexes and SLA: A framework for research and pedagogy. In P. Robinson (Ed.), *Individual differences and instructed language learning* (pp. 113–133). Amsterdam: John Benjamins.

Robinson, P. (2003). Attention and memory during SLA. In C. J. Doughty & M. H. Long (Eds.), *The handbook of second language acquisition* (pp. 631–678). Oxford: Blackwell.

Robinson, P. (in press). Aptitudes, abilities, contexts and practice. In R. DeKeyser (Ed.), *Practice in second language learning: Perspectives from linguistics and psychology.* Cambridge: Cambridge University Press.

Rodrìguez, M., & Abreu, O. (2003). The stability of general foreign language classroom anxiety across English and French. *Modern Language Journal, 87*(3), 365–374.

Rogers, C. R. (1954). Towards a theory of creativity. *ETC: A Review of General Semantics, 11,* 249–260.

Ross, S., Yoshinaga, N., & Sasaki, M. (2002). Aptitude-exposure interaction effects on Wh-movement violation detection by pre-and-post-critical period Japanese bilinguals. In P. Robinson (Ed.), *Individual differences and instructed language learning* (pp. 267–299). Amsterdam: John Benjamins.

Rossiter, M. J. (2001). The challenges of classroom-based SLA research. *Applied Language Learning, 12*(1), 31–44.

Rossiter, M. J. (2003). The effects of affective strategy training in the ESL classroom. *TESL-EJ, 7*(2).

Rubin, J. (1975). What the 'Good Language Learner' can teach us. *TESOL Quarterly, 9,* 41–51.

Runco, M. A. (2003). Creativity, cognition, and their educational implications. In J. C. Houtz (Ed.), *The educational psychology of creativity* (pp. 25–56). Cresskill, NJ: Hampton Press.

Runco, M. A. (2004). Creativity. *Annual Review of Psychology, 55,* 657–687.

Ruvolo, A. P., & Markus, H. R. (1992). Possible selves and performance: The power of self-relevant imagery. *Social Cognition, 10*(1), 95–124.

Saito, Y., Horwitz, E. K., & Garza, T. J. (1999). Foreign language reading anxiety. *Modern Language Journal, 83,* 202–218.

Sakui, K., & Gaies, S. J. (1999). Investigating Japanese learners' beliefs about language learning. *System, 27,* 473–492.

Sasaki, M. (1993a). Relationships among second language proficiency, foreign language aptitude, and intelligence: A protocol analysis. *Language Learning, 43*(4), 469–505.

Sasaki, M. (1993b). Relationships among second language proficiency, foreign language aptitude, and intelligence: A structural equation modeling approach. *Language Learning, 43*(3), 313–344.

Sasaki, M. (1996). *Second language proficiency, foreign language aptitude, and Intelligence: Quantitative and qualitative analyses.* New York: Peter Lang.

Sawyer, M., & Ranta, L. (2001). Aptitude, individual differences, and instructional design. In P. Robinson (Ed.), *Cognition and second language acquisition* (pp. 319–353). New York: Cambridge University Press.

Schmeck, R. R. (1988). An introduction to strategies and styles of learning. In R. R. Schmeck (Ed.), *Learning strategies and learning styles* (pp. 3–19). New York: Plenum.

Schmidt, R., Boraie, D., & Kassabgy, O. (1996). Foreign language motivation: Internal structure and external connections. In R. Oxford (Ed.), *Language learning motivation: Pathways to the new century* (pp. 9–70). Honolulu: University of Hawaii Press.

Schmidt, R., & Watanabe, Y. (2001). Motivation, strategy use, and pedagogical preferences in foreign language learning. In Z. Dörnyei & R. Schmidt (Eds.), *Motivation and second language acquisition* (pp. 313–359). Honolulu: University of Hawaii Press.

Schneiderman, E. I., & Wesche, M. B. (1986). Right hemisphere processing and foreign language aptitude. *I. T. L. Review of Applied Linguistics, 71*, 43–64.

Schommer, M. (1990). Effects of beliefs about the nature of knowledge on comprehension. *Journal of Educational Psychology, 82*, 498–504.

Schommer-Aikins, M., & Hutter, R. (2002). Epistemological beliefs and thinking about everyday controversial issues. *Journal of Psychology, 136*(1), 5–20.

Schumann, J. H. (1998). *The neurobiology of affect in language.* Oxford: Blackwell.

Schumann, J. H. (1999). A neurobiological perspective on affect and methodology in second language learning. In J. Arnold (Ed.), *Affect in language learning* (pp. 28–42). Cambridge: Cambridge University Press.

Schumann, J. H. (2001a). Appraisal psychology, neurobiology, and language. *Annual Review of Applied Linguistics, 21*, 23–42.

Schumann, J. H. (2001b). Learning as foraging. In Z. Dörnyei & R. Schmidt (Eds.), *Motivation and second language acquisition* (pp. 21–28). Honolulu: University of Hawaii.

Schumann, J. H., Crowell, S. E., Jones, N. E., Lee, N., Schuchert, S. A., & Wood, L. A. (2004). *The neurobiology of learning: Perspectives from second language acquisition.* Mahwah, NJ: Lawrence Erlbaum Associates.

Scovel, T. (2001). *Learning new languages: A guide to second language acquisition.* Boston: Heinle and Heinle.

Segalowitz, N. (1997). Individual differences in second language acquisition. In A. de Groot, M. B. & J. F. Kroll (Eds.), *Tutorials in bilingualism: Psycholinguistic perspectives* (pp. 85–112). Mahwah, NJ: Lawrence Erlbaum Associates.

Seliger, H. W. (1980). Utterance planning and correction behavior: Its function in the grammar construction process for second language learners. In H. W. Dechert & M. Raupach (Eds.), *Towards a crosslinguistic assessment of speech production* (pp. 87–99). Frankfurt: Peter Lang.

Selinker, L. (1972). Interlanguage. *International Review of Applied Linguistics, 10*, 209–231.

Senior, R. (1997). Transforming language classes into bonded groups. *ELT Journal, 51*, 3–11.

Senior, R. (2002). A class-centred approach to language teaching. *ELT Journal, 56*, 397–403.

Shedivy, S. L. (2004). Factors that lead some students to continue the study of foreign language past the usual 2 years in high school. *System, 32*, 103–119.

Shoaib, A. (2004). *The motivation of teachers of English as a foreign language.* Unpublished PhD dissertation, University of Nottingham, Nottingham.

Shoaib, A., & Dörnyei, Z. (in press). Affect in life-long learning: Exploring L2 motivation as a dynamic process. In P. Benson & D. Nunan (Eds.), *Learners' stories: Difference and diversity in language learning.* Cambridge: Cambridge University Press.

Shore, C. M. (1995). *Individual differences in language development.* Thousand Oaks, CA: Sage.

Sick, J., & Irie, K. (2000). The Lunic Language Marathon: A new language aptitude instrument for Japanese foreign language learners. In S. Cornwell & P. Robinson (Eds.), *Individual differences in foreign language learning: Effects of aptitude, intelligence, and motivation* (pp. 173–185). Tokyo: Aoyama Gakuin University.

Skehan, P. (1986). Cluster analysis and the identification of learner types. In V. Cook (Ed.), *Experimental approaches to second language acquisition.* Oxford: Pergamon.

Skehan, P. (1989). *Individual differences in second language learning.* London: Edward Arnold.

Skehan, P. (1990). History of motivational research in education. *Journal of Educational Psychology, 82*, 616–622.

Skehan, P. (1991). Individual differences in second language learning. *Studies in Second Language Acquisition, 13*(2), 275–298.

Skehan, P. (1998). *A cognitive approach to language learning.* Oxford: Oxford University Press.

Skehan, P. (2002). Theorising and updating aptitude. In P. Robinson (Ed.), *Individual differences and instructed language learning* (pp. 69–93). Amsterdam: John Benjamins.

Skehan, P. (2003). Task-based instruction. *Language Teaching, 36*(1), 1–14.

Snow, R. E., Corno, L., & Jackson, D. N. (1996). Individual differences in affective and conative functions. In D. C. Berliner & R. C. Calfee (Eds.), *Handbook of educational psychology* (pp. 243–310). New York: Macmillan.

Sparks, R. L. (1995). Examining the Linguistic Coding Differences Hypothesis to explain individual differences in foreign language learning. *Annals of Dyslexia, 45*, 187–214.

Sparks, R. L., Artzer, M., Ganschow, L., Siebenhar, D., Plageman, M., & Patton, J. (1998). Differences in native-language skills, foreign-language aptitude and foreign-language grades among high-, average- and low-proficiency foreign-language learners: Two studies. *Language Testing, 15*(2), 181–216.

Sparks, R. L., & Ganschow, L. (1991). Foreign language learning differences: Affective or native language aptitude differences? *Modern Language Journal, 75*, 3–16.

Sparks, R. L., & Ganschow, L. (1999). Native language skills, foreign language aptitude and anxiety about foreign language learning. In D. J. Young (Ed.), *Affect in foreign language and second language learning* (pp. 169–190). Boston: McGraw-Hill.

Sparks, R. L., & Ganschow, L. (2001). Aptitude for learning a foreign language. *Annual Review of Applied Linguistics, 21*, 90–111.

Sparks, R. L., Ganschow, L., & Javorsky, J. (2000). Déjà vu all over again: A response to Saito, Horwitz, and Garza. *Modern Language Journal, 84*, 251–259.

Sparks, R. L., Ganschow, L., & Patton, J. (1995). Prediction of performance in first-year foreign language courses: Connections between native and foreign language learning. *Journal of Educational Psychology, 87*, 638–655.

Spielmann, G., & Radnofsky, M. L. (2001). Learning language under tension: New directions from a qualitative study. *Modern Language Journal, 85*(2), 259–278.

Spolsky, B. (1995). Prognostication and language aptitude testing, 1925-1962. *Language Testing, 12*(3), 321–340.

Stern, H. H. (1975). What can we learn from the good language learner? *Canadian Modern Language Review, 31*, 304–318.

Sternberg, R. J. (2001). Epilogue: Another mysterious affair at styles. In R. J. Sternberg & L.-F. Zhang (Eds.), *Perspectives on thinking, learning, and cognitive styles* (pp. 249-252). Mahwah, NJ: Lawrence Erlbaum Associates.

Sternberg, R. J. (2002). The theory of successful intelligence and its implications for language-aptitude testing. In P. Robinson (Ed.), *Individual differences and instructed language learning* (pp. 13–43). Amsterdam: John Benjamins.

Sternberg, R. J., & Grigorenko, E. L. (2001). A capsule history of theory and research on styles. In R. J. Sternberg & L.-F. Zhang (Eds.), *Perspectives on thinking, learning, and cognitive styles* (pp. 1–21). Mahwah, NJ: Lawrence Erlbaum Associates.

Sternberg, R. J., Kaufman, J. C., & Pretz, J. E. (2002). *The creativity conundrum: A propulsion model of creative contributions.* Philadelphia: Psychology Press.

Swain, M., & Burnaby, B. (1976). Personality characteristics and second language learning in young children: A pilot study. *Working Papers on Bilingualism, 11*, 116–128.

Tachibana, Y., Matsukawa, R., & Zhong, Q. X. (1996). Attitudes and motivation for learning English: A cross-national comparison of Japanese and Chinese high school students. *Psychological reports, 79*, 691–700.

Tarone, E. (1981). Some thoughts on the notion of 'communication strategy.' *TESOL Quarterly, 15*, 285–295.

Tremblay, P., & Gardner, R. C. (1995). Expanding the motivation construct in language learning. *Modern Language Journal, 79*, 505–518.

Trost, G., & Bickel, H. (1981). An aptitude test for studies in modern languages as part of a test battery for counseling applicants for higher education. In C. Klein-Braley & D. K. Stevenson (Eds.), *Practice and problems in language testing* (pp. 127–140). Frankfurt, Germany: Peter Lang.

Tseng, W.-T., Dörnyei, Z., & Schmitt, N. (in press). A new approach to assessing strategic learning: The case of self-regulation in vocabulary acquisition. *Applied Linguistics.*

Tucker, A. (2000). Relationships among FL aptitude, music aptitude, and L2 proficiency. In S. Cornwell & P. Robinson (Eds.), *Individual differences in foreign language learning: Effects of aptitude, intelligence, and motivation* (pp. 49–67). Tokyo: Aoyama Gakuin University.

Ushioda, E. (1996). Developing a dynamic concept of motivation. In T. J. Hickey (Ed.), *Language, education and society in a changing world* (pp. 239–245). Clevedon, England: Multilingual Matters.

Ushioda, E. (1998). Effective motivational thinking: A cognitive theoretical approach to the study of language learning motivation. In E. A. Soler & V. C. Espurz (Eds.), *Current issues in English language methodology* (pp. 77–89). Castelló de la Plana, Spain: Universitat Jaume.

Ushioda, E. (2001). Language learning at university: Exploring the role of motivational thinking. In Z. Dörnyei & R. Schmidt (Eds.), *Motivation and second language acquisition* (pp. 91-124). Honolulu, HI: University of Hawaii Press.

Ushioda, E. (2003). Motivation as a socially mediated process. In D. Little, J. Ridley & E. Ushioda (Eds.), *Learner autonomy in the foreign language classroom: Teacher, learner, curriculum, assessment* (pp. 90–102). Dublin: Authentik.

Valentine, J. C., DuBois, D. L., & Cooper, H. (2004). The relation between self-beliefs and academic achievement: A meta-analytic review. *Educational Psychologist, 39*(2), 111–133.

VanderStoep, S. W., & Pintrich, P. R. (2003). *Learning to learn: The skill and will of college success.* Upper Saddle River, NJ: Prentice Hall.

Verhoeven, L., & Vermeer, A. (2002). Communicative competence and personality dimensions in first and second language learners. *Applied Psycholinguistics, 23*, 361–374.

Wakamoto, N. (2000). Language learning strategy and personality variables: Focusing on extroversion and introversion. *IRAL, 38*(1), 71–81.

Warden, C., & Lin, H. J. (2000). Existence of integrative motivation in Asian EFL setting. *Foreign Language Annals, 33*, 535–547.

Weiner, B. (1992). *Human motivation: Metaphors, theories and research.* Newbury Park, CA: Sage.

Weinstein, C. E., Husman, J., & Dierking, D. R. (2000). Self-regulation interventions with a focus on learning strategies. In M. Boekaerts, P. R. Pintrich & M. Zeidner (Eds.), *Handbook of self-regulation* (pp. 727–747). San Diego: Academic Press.

Wen, W. P., & Clément, R. (2003). A Chinese conceptualisation of willingness to communicate in ESL. *Language, Culture and Curriculum, 16*(1), 18–38.

Wenden, A. (1991). *Learner strategies for learner autonomy.* Hemel Hempstead: Prentice Hall.

Wenden, A. (1999). An introduction to *Metacognitive knowledge and beliefs in language learning. System, 27*, 435–441.

Wenden, A. (2001). Metacognitive knowledge in SLA: The neglected variable. In M. P. Breen (Ed.), *Learner contributions to language learning: New directions in research* (pp. 44–64). Harlow, England: Longman.

Wenden, A., & Rubin, J. (Eds.). (1987). *Learner strategies in language learning.* Hemel Hempstead: Prentice Hall.

Wenger, E. (1998). *Communities of practice: Learning, meaning, and identity.* Cambridge: Cambridge University Press.

Wentzel, K. R. (1999). Social-motivational processes and interpersonal relationships: Implications for understanding motivation at school. *Journal of Educational Psychology, 91*, 76–97.

Wesche, M. B. (1981). Language aptitude measures in streaming, matching students with methods, and diagnosis of learning problems. In K. C. Diller (Ed.), *Individual differences and universals in language learning aptitude.* Rowley, MA: Newbury House.

Wesche, M. B., Edwards, H., & Wells, W. (1982). Foreign language aptitude and intelligence. *Applied Psycholinguistics, 3*, 127–140.

White, C. (1999). Expectations and emergent beliefs of self-instructed language learners. *System, 27*, 443–457.

Williams, M. (1994). Motivation in foreign and second language learning: An interactive perspective. *Educational and Child Psychology, 11*, 77–84.

Williams, M., & Burden, R. (1997). *Psychology for language teachers.* Cambridge: Cambridge University Press.

Williams, M., & Burden, R. (1999). Students' developing conceptions of themselves as language learners. *Modern Language Journal, 83*, 193–201.

Williams, M., Burden, R., & Al-Baharna, S. (2001). Making sense of success and failure: The role of the individual in motivation theory. In Z. Dörnyei & R. Schmidt (Eds.), *Motivation and second language acquisition* (pp. 173–186). Honolulu: University of Hawaii Press.

Williams, M., Burden, R., & Lanvers, U. (2002). 'French is the language of love and stuff': Student perceptions of issues related to motivation in learning a foreign language. *British Educational Research Journal, 28*, 503–528.

Winne, P. H. (1995). Inherent details in self-regulated learning. *Educational Psychologist, 30*, 173–187.

Winne, P. H. (2001). Self-regulated learning viewed from models of information processing. In B. J. Zimmerman & D. H. Schunk (Eds.), *Self-regulated learning and academic achievement: Theoretical perspectives* (2nd ed., pp. 153–189). Mahwah, NJ: Lawrence Erlbaum Associates.

Winne, P. H., & Perry, N. E. (2000). Measuring self-regulated learning. In M. Boekaerts, P. R. Pintrich & M. Zeidner (Eds.), *Handbook of self-regulation* (pp. 531–566). San Diego, CA: Academic Press.

Wintergerst, A. C., DeCapua, A., & Itzen, R. C. (2001). The construct validity of one learning styles instrument. *System, 29*, 385–403.

Wintergerst, A. C., DeCapua, A., & Verna, M. A. (2003). Conceptualizing learning style modalities for ESL/EFL students. *System, 31*, 85–106.

Wolters, C. A. (1999). The relation between high school students' motivational regulation and their use of learning strategies, effort, and classroom performance. *Learning and Individual Differences, 11*(3), 281–299.

Wolters, C. A. (2003). Regulation of motivation: Evaluating an underemphasized aspect of self-regulated learning. *Educational Psychologist, 38*(4), 189–205.

Wong-Fillmore, L. (1979). Individual differences in second language acquisition. In C. J. Fillmore, W.-S. Y. Wang & D. Kempler (Eds.), *Individual differences in language ability and language behavior.*

Wu, X. (2003). Intrinsic motivation and young language learners: The impact of the classroom environment. *System, 31*, 501–517.

Yamamori, K., Isoda, T., Hiromori, T., & Oxford, R. L. (2003). Using cluster analysis to uncover L2 learner differences in strategy use, will to learn, and achievement over time. *IRAL, 41*, 381–409.

Yang, N.-D. (1999). The relationship between EFL learners' beliefs and learning strategy use. *System, 27*, 515–535.

Yashima, T. (1998). Willingness to communicate in a foreign language: A preliminary study. *Kansai University Journal of Informatics, 9*, 121–134.

Yashima, T. (2000). Orientations and motivations in foreign language learning: A study of Japanese college students. *JACET Bulletin, 31*, 121–133.

Yashima, T. (2002). Willingness to communicate in a second language: The Japanese EFL context. *Modern Language Journal, 86*, 54–66.

Yashima, T., Zenuk-Nishide, L., & Shimizu, K. (2004). The influence of attitudes and affect on willingness to communicate and second language communication. *Language Learning, 54*(1), 119–152.

Yates, G. C. R. (2000). Applying learning style research in the classroom: Some cautions and the way ahead. In R. J. Riding & S. G. Rayner (Eds.), *Interpersonal perspectives on individual differences* (Vol. 1: Cognitive styles, pp. 347–364). Stamford, CI: Ablex.

Young, D. J. (Ed.). (1999). *Affect in foreign language and second language learning*. Boston: McGraw-Hill.

Yowell, C. M. (2002). Dreams of the future: The pursuit of education and career possible selves among ninth grade Latino youth. *Applied Developmental Science, 6*(2), 62–72.

Zeidner, M. (1986). Are English language aptitude tests biased towards culturally different minority groups? Some findings. *Language Testing, 3*, 80–98.

Zeidner, M., Boekaerts, M., & Pintrich, P. R. (2000). Self-regulation: Directions and challenges for future research. In M. Boekaerts, P. R. Pintrich & M. Zeidner (Eds.), *Handbook of self-regulation* (pp. 749–768). San Diego: Academic Press.

Zimmerman, B. J. (2001). Theories of self-regulated learning and academic achievement: An overview and analysis. In B. J. Zimmerman & D. H. Schunk (Eds.), *Self-regulated learning and academic achievement: Theoretical perspectives* (2nd ed., pp. 1–37). Mahwah, NJ: Lawrence Erlbaum Associates.

Zimmerman, B. J., & Risemberg, R. (1997). Self-regulatory dimensions of academic learning and motivation. In G. D. Phye (Ed.), *Handbook of academic learning* (pp. 105–125). San Diego: Academic Press.

Definition Index (Glossary)

A book of this comprehensive nature requires a Glossary to summarize and briefly explain the great number of technical terms introduced in the different chapters. However, I have always had a problem with the usefulness of Glossaries because to offer succinct definitions, they inevitably simplify complex meanings. For some concepts this may work well, whereas with some others we may lose the essence of the term or metaphor. This section intends to fulfill the function of a Glossary in a new way: I list all the important technical terms introduced in the book, but instead of providing a definition for them I include the exact page number(s) where the concept in question is introduced and explained. Further references to the concepts can be found in the Subject Index.

Author Index

Subject Index

A

Ability, 7, 24, 31, 32, 79, 80, 122, 125, 153
Abstract sequential/random style, 128, 133
Abstract style, 149, 151, 152
Abstract thinking style, 128, 130
Accommodators, 131
Action control, Action Control Theory, 81, 82, 85, 91, 112-116, 186, 192, 194
Action orientation, 195
Active information processing style, 130, 131, 133
Adaptor style, 128
Affective strategies, 168, 169, 181
Age, 8, 44-45
Agreeableness, 13, 15, 17, 22, 29
Alignment, 108
Altruism, 17
Amotivation, 78
AMTB, *see* Attitude/Motivation Test Battery
Analogue style, 148, 149, 151, 152
Analysis-oriented type, 152-153, 155
Analytics, 129, 135
Analytic style, 127, 134, 135, 137, 143, 144, 145, 149, 151, 152, 155, 159
Analytical intelligence, 50-51
Anxiety, 8, 16, 21, 22, 55, 77, 197, 198-202

B

Aptitude, 7, 32-34, 163, 194, 207
Aptitude complexes, 59, 60, 63, 219
Aptitude Test for Studies in Modern Languages, 41
Aptitude–treatment interaction, 22, 59, 75
Assimilator style, 128
Assimilators, 130
Attention, 56, 194
Attitude/Motivation Test Battery (AMTB), 70, 71, 72-73
Attitudes, *see* language attitudes
Attributions, attribution theory, 76, 79-80, 85, 113, 115
Auditory ability, 40
Auditory style, 140, 141, 155, 158
Autonomy, 77, 79, 85, 113

B

Bauhaus, 160
Beliefs About Language Learning Inventory (BALLI), 215, 217
Beneficial anxiety, 198
Big Five personality model, 13-18, 23, 25, 29, 30, 119, 123, 197

C

CANAL-FT, 50, 51, 52-53
Central executive, 56

Choice motivation, 84, 85
Choleric temperament, 11